FAMILY THERAPY

FAMILY THERAPY
A Practical Manual

By

J. BAILEY MOLINEUX, Ph.D.

Family Teaching Center
Helena, Montana

CHARLES C THOMAS • PUBLISHER
Springfield • Illinois • U.S.A.

Published and Distributed Throughout the World by

CHARLES C THOMAS • PUBLISHER
2600 South First Street
Springfield, Illinois 62717

© 1985 by CHARLES C THOMAS • PUBLISHER

ISBN 0-398-05069-4

Library of Congress Catalog Card Number: 84-16398

With THOMAS BOOKS *careful attention is given to all details of manufacturing and
design. It is the Publisher's desire to present books that are satisfactory as to their physical
qualities and artistic possibilities and appropriate for their particular use.* THOMAS
BOOKS *will be true to those laws of quality that assure a good name and good will.*

Library of Congress Cataloging in Publication Data

Molineux, J. Bailey.
  Family therapy.

  Bibliography: p.
  Includes index.
  1. Family psychotherapy. I. Title.
RC488.5.M64   1985   616.89'156   84-16398
ISBN 0-398-05069-4

Printed in the United States of America

PS-R-3

PREFACE

If it is true, as I believe it is, that for the most part people become psychologically disturbed because of the pathogenic influence of other people, then it follows that the way they can regain health is through other people. This is an assumption which underlies all psychotherapies but the manner in which it is actualized depends upon the therapeutic modality which is employed by the therapist. In individual therapy, the therapist attempts to provide those curative elements which will enable the client to regain health. In group therapy, health is gained by the caring, support and insight provided by the other group members, while in family therapy, all family members should become healthier as a result of their changed interactions with each other.

If it is also true, again as I believe it is, that the family is the single most important influence in the psychological, social and emotional development of the individual, then it follows that the most effective and quickest way to treat many psychological problems is to treat families. This is the assumption which underlies the practice of family therapy. It states that family members can have a far more powerful influence on each other— for good or ill—than can most individual therapists or therapy group members. By changing their interactions, the goal of family therapy is to replace pathogenic family influences with influences which promote mental health. Rather than being sources of emotional pain, family members in family therapy should ideally become more viable sources of strength, support, and self-esteem enhancement for each other.

There is another assumption which underlies this book, an assumption which has been taught by many spiritual leaders in different cultures throughout the ages. And it is this: love is the most powerful and curative psychological force in the world. It is an answer to many of our interpersonal problems.

This book is based on a specific, practical, step-by-step description of marital and family therapy as practiced by staff at the Family Teaching Center of Helena, Montana. Since many of the problems we treat involve conflicts between parents and their offspring, we define parental love as consisting of three abilities:

—the ability to express love for children through hugs, kisses, praise, appreciation, I love you's and time spent together,

—the ability to discipline children effectively using more rewards than punishments and

—the ability to grant children more autonomy as they grow older and prove through responsible behavior they can handle it.

Obviously, most of our therapeutic efforts are designed to strengthen these abilities in parents.

At the Family Teaching Center, we assume that most parents are loving parents who want to do the best job they can raising their children. If they make mistakes, if they don't express as much love as is ideal, it is because they are suffering from some problems of their own—depression, alcoholism, marital problems, family of origin problems or custody disputes—which interfere with the full expression of their love for their offspring. Our therapeutic efforts then become directed toward alleviating those problems so as to free up more love for children and adolescents.

A private, non-profit agency, the Family Teaching Center is a training institute for the Montana Department of Social and Rehabilitation Services. Under contract with the department, we have been training statewide for the past several years. This book is simply a natural extension of our training.

Although we do not neglect theory in our workshops, our major training goal has been to give trainees specific, practical ideas and techniques to diagnose and treat families with behavior disordered children. Hence this book, written primarily for the beginning family therapist, contains the same specific concepts and tools we have taught to over 270 helping professionals throughout Montana.

My thanks to the staff of the Family Teaching Center with whom I have shared many hours of stimulating and exciting discussions about family therapy. My thanks also to Sandy Ashley and my wife, Mary Anne, for their editorial and proofreading comments, and to Jo Schmitz for her superb typing.

CONTENTS

FAMILY THERAPY

Chapter 1

INTRODUCTION TO THE WORLD
OF FAMILY THERAPY

A CASE EXAMPLE

John's family is in an uproar since he's just been arrested for shoplifting. His mother calls your office, asking that he be seen as soon as possible. If you're a therapist who does individual therapy, you might grant her request. But if you're a family therapist, you or your secretary would ask that all the members of John's family who are living at home come in for an appointment.

It is at this point that family therapy begins.

John's mother may balk at your request. She can't understand why you want to see the whole family when it's John's problem, not their's. Besides, she exclaims, it's not easy to get everyone to your office at the same time. She and her husband will have to take time off from work while the other children will have to miss school.

But you hold your ground. You have to if you are going to diagnose John's behavior from a family systems perspective. You explain to the mother that you can best understand and treat John by gathering as much information about him from those who know him best: the members of his family.

Regrettably, you're only being half-truthful. Although you do want to find out as much about the boy as you can by talking to the members of his immediate family, you also want to meet with them because you assume John's behavior plays some yet undiscovered part in their functioning as a family unit.

When you meet the members of John's family, you will most likely find a family under considerable stress. Rather than diagnosing his behavior as a function of internal states or dynamics, you can probably better understand it in light of several possible problems in the family:

—His may be a chaotic, poorly organized family in which parental authority is weak or diffuse and in which family members feel isolated and misunderstood by one another. Several of the children may have been in frequent trouble because they have not been consistently disciplined.

—There may be overwhelming parental problems in John's family. Father may be an alcoholic or mother may be depressed. Or father and mother may have been unhappily married for years. Or John may not have had contact with his father since he divorced his mother and left five years ago.

—John may have been a compliant boy and good student, never having been in trouble until recently. But now his parents are in the midst of a bitter divorce and custody battle with each asking John to side with him or her.

—More subtly, John's parents may say everything in the family has been fine except for his misbehavior. At first, they complain of no marital problems, praise their other offspring for being model children but claim John has been a constant source of worry for them. Only after several sessions with the family do you begin to gain a glimpse of the marital difficulties, Mom's depression or Dad's deep dissatisfaction with his job.

Assuming you succeed in persuading John's mother to have everyone in the family come into your office, you may find yourself confronted by a somewhat large and unruly mob. If you're a beginning family therapist, you may ask yourself, with some trepidation, "What do I do now?" You've read about the theory of family systems and how the masters do family therapy, but you're not sure exactly what you're supposed to do with the family members now that they're in your office.

By describing in detail the work of one family counseling agency—the Family Teaching Center of Helena, Montana—this book is designed to answer this question for you.

OUTLINE OF THE BOOK

Established to develop, test and disseminate a model of family counseling throughout Montana, staff from the Family Teaching

Center have been treating families since 1976 and training statewide since 1978. This book describes the therapeutic approaches we employ to treat a variety of family problems. Although theory is not neglected, the major emphasis in this book is on a clearly delineated, practical, step-by-step approach to marital and family therapy. It is my hope that as a result of reading this book, you will be able to use many elements of our approach to treat several different types of family problems using ·several different techniques in your own practice.

After a brief descriptive overview of our program in this chapter, Chapter 2 is devoted to theory. It presents some theoretical assumptions which underlie the practice of family therapy.

Chapter 3 is devoted to a discussion of family functioning. It describes an ideally healthy family, the developmental stages all families must pass through and the functioning of disturbed families whose members become locked into self-perpetuating patterns of behavior from which they usually cannot escape by themselves. Your function as a family therapist is to help family members break free of these patterns.

Chapter 4 discusses the functioning of family therapists. After describing three skills required for effective therapy and discussing the differences between individual and family therapy, it concludes with a list and description of ten guidelines to guide you in your therapeutic work with families.

Chapter 5 begins the presentation of the specifics of family therapy as practiced by staff at the Family Teaching Center. It describes in detail our intake process while Chapter 6 presents our counseling program designed to treat families with young children. Chapters 7 and 8 describe the ways we teach family members communication, negotiating and contracting skills, while Chapter 9 is devoted to a discussion of specific family problems: stealing, lying, fighting, vandalism, temper tantrums, poor academic performance, eating problems, elimination control problems, bedtime problems, school phobias, chemical dependency and sexual abuse.

In family therapy, working directly on the family's presenting problems may not be enough to bring relief. Since the behavioral problems of youth are often a reflection of other family problems, you need the knowledge and skills to treat these problems which are presented in Chapters 10 through 12.

Chapter 10 is devoted to marital counseling. It describes specific ways to help a couple look more objectively at their marriage, determine what changes they need to implement to improve their relationship and, with that information, decide what to do about it.

Since many of the families you will see in your practice will be either divorced, single parent or stepfamilies, Chapter 11 describes the usual patterns of behavior and problems found in these families. It suggests ways for you to help restructure them so as to provide the best possible home atmosphere for growing children who are undergoing the stress of divorce and remarriage.

Chapter 12 describes the processes and problems involved in custody counseling. Even though you may not do this type of counseling, you should still be aware of custody issues to be able to deal with the custody problems which may be presented by divorced or stepfamilies. However, since custody counseling primarily involves negotiating and contracting, you may feel comfortable doing it once you've gained experience teaching negotiating and contracting skills to family members struggling with adolescent behavior problems.

If other family therapy techniques are not working, you may have to resort to paradoxical techniques to induce changes in the family. However, these techniques should be used only with families with chronic, unresolved problems which have not first responded to non-paradoxical techniques. After discussing the theoretical assumptions which underlie paradoxical techniques, Chapter 13 describes several of these techniques: relabeling, predicting the symptom, prescribing the symptom, discouraging change, declared therapist helplessness and positioning.

Finally, since family therapy is more complex than individual therapy, since it involves more people, more interactions and more information, it should help you as a family therapist to keep certain goals in mind as you are confronted with the many issues and problems presented by the family. Chapter 14 summarizes this book by discussing the goals of family therapy as practiced at the Family Teaching Center.

SCHOOLS OF FAMILY THERAPY

Beginning in earnest in the 1950's, family therapy is a relatively new approach to psychological problems. As a result, there is not yet a unified, generally accepted theory of family functioning and a universally employed method of family treatment. The field is simply too new. There is so much research to be done before we can say with certainty exactly what types of therapies should be employed to treat what types of problems.

One family therapist operates one way while another, with a different theoretical orientation, operates another way. One does one thing while another seemingly does the opposite. One works with all members of the family while another sees whomever comes in for treatment. One takes a family history while another does not. One is concerned only with observable behaviors while another is interested in unconscious projective mechanisms. One believes family therapy must be long term while another is convinced it should be short term. One is interested in fostering insight while another is not. One works directly on the symptom while another aims towards other goals.

To you as a beginning family therapist, this state of affairs may be confusing and discouraging. "If the masters don't agree on ways to treat families," you may ask yourself, "how can I expect to know what to do? What is the best way to treat families?"

But this lack of agreement about causes of family pathology and treatment can also be a source of comfort and excitement. It may be comforting to know we're all learning and exciting to realize there is a need for more innovation and research in the field.

Because there are so many approaches to family therapy— Levant (1984) claims there are twenty-two—there have been several attempts to classify the types of family therapies, none of which are in complete agreement. Goldenberg and Goldenberg (1980) distinguish between four general classes of family therapies: psychodynamic, communications, structural and behavior. Walsh (1980) lists six general classes: communications, systems, structural, social learning, integrative and psychodynamic. Gurman and Kniskern (1981) divide their edited handbook into four approaches: psychoanalytic and object-relations, intergenerational, systems theory and behavioral. Levant (1984) classifies family therapies into three general models: the historical, structure/process and experiential. He then describes three schools within each model. The historical model includes psychodynamic, multigenerational and intergenerational-contextual schools; the structure/process model includes communicational, structural and behavioral schools; and the experiential model includes gestalt, client-centered and experiential schools.

Levant (1984) distinguishes each of his models according to several characteristics: the time perspective, focus of therapeutic change, role of the therapist, duration of therapy and principal theoretical background. Not surprisingly, the time perspective of the historical model is the past. Working with individuals in a family context, its goal is to provide insight and to free clients from behavior patterns which are the result of past relationships. Influenced by psychoanalysis, the historical model of family therapy is usually long term with a therapist who is the least active of the three models of family therapy.

The time perspective of the structure/process model is the present but it includes a history of the presenting problem and an emphasis on behavior change in the near future. Of the three models, the structure/process model approaches the presenting problem most directly, either by working on it or changing the structure or processes of the family. In contrast to the other two models, the focus of the structure/process model is primarily on the family as an interacting, interdependent system and not on the individuals in that system. Influenced by systems theory and learning theory, it involves short term therapy by an active, directive expert who diagnoses the family's problems and gives specific behavioral prescriptions for change.

The time perspective of the experiential model is also on the present but in a phenomenological sense rather than an explanatory sense. Influenced by existentialism and phenomonology, it is interested in the here-and-now experiences of each individual in the family. Like the historical model, it too focuses on the individual in the family. But unlike the historical model which perceives the individual as an object caught in lawful patterns, the experiential models treats the individual as an emoting, suffering subject. Its goal is to improve the quality of life for all family members by intensifying their emotional experiences. It achieves this goal through an intermediate-term therapy with a therapist who actively participates with the family members as they explore their affective lives.

THE FAMILY TEACHING CENTER

One founding purpose at the Family Teaching Center was, and still is, to reduce the incidence of child abuse and juvenile delinquency in the Helena, Montana area. Most of the therapeutic work we do is with families with behavior disordered children. The problems we see in young children are usually not minding, sibling rivalry and temper tantrums. In adolescents, we treat many problems: poor academic performance, stealing, vandalism, fighting with siblings or peers, violation of parental rules and running away. Occasionally, we treat school phobic children or children with other probias. We also see some children with elimination control problems, bedtime problems and eating problems.

Although we do not treat psychotic children, many of the youths we see are struggling with depression which is acted out in misbehavior. Since we're convinced that chemical dependency in a family member must be treated before any treatment can be effective, we refer all chemically dependent family members elsewhere for treatment, although we may prepare the other family members for an intervention with the chemically dependent member. In fact, when our program doesn't work, we usually suspect chemical dependency as the reason for its failure, and may then recommend an inpatient or outpatient chemical dependency evaluation of the young person.

Some of the families referred to us are abusive or potentially abusive. What we typically do with these families is work to reduce the current stresses in their lives—and there are usually many—and to give them ways to discipline their children other than physical punishment.

Most of the families we see are what we call changing families: divorced, step, single parent (never married) or widowed. In a recent study of 146 of our families, we found only 26% were intact, while 41% were divorced, 28% were stepfamilies, 2% were single parent families, 2% were widowed and 1% were foster families.

We offer five types of therapeutic services: our child program, our adolescent program, marital counseling, custody counseling and individual counseling. Except for individual counseling, each of these services are described in separate chapters.

Our child program consists of teaching parents of behavior disordered children specific behavior management skills: clear commands, the use of rewards to strengthen acceptable behaviors and the use of time-out to weaken unacceptable behaviors. Our adolescent program consists of teaching family members communications, negotiating and contracting skills. We sometimes offer marital counseling independently of our work with families, but more often we provide this counseling service as part of our treatment for behavior disordered youths. When our child or adolescent programs are not working, we often find there are serious marital problems which interfere with their effectiveness. Occasionally, we offer individual counseling to a parent or child, again as part of our treatment of behavior problems when our other approaches are not working. Custody counseling is a service we offer to any divorcing parents whether or not their children are displaying behavior or emotional problems, although often they do have such problems when their parents are bitterly fighting over custody issues.

We usually don't use co-therapists at the Family Teaching Center because of the time and expense involved. When we do, it is usually with more difficult cases such as large, multi-problem families, smaller, enmeshed families or unorganized, chaotic families. All of these families may require more vigilance and effort than can be provided by a lone therapist.

Although Gurman and Kniskern (1981) claim there is no evidence that co-therapy is superior to single therapist therapy, there are some advantages to using co-therapists to treat difficult families. It provides an extra set of eyes and ears to observe the family members and takes some of the pressure off a lone therapist to treat the family. While one therapist is involved with the family, the other can sit back and observe. When one therapist confronts a family member, the other can be supportive. If one becomes stuck in an interaction with the family, the other can come to his rescue.

But there are also disadvantages to co-therapy. It is essential that co-therapists work well together. They must be in agreement about therapeutic goals and treatment methods and be able to work out any differences which may arise between them. Any unresolved conflicts may hamper their work with a family and set a poor example for the family members.

At the Family Teaching Center, ours is a structured, systematic, step-by-step type of family therapy. We first try one approach, but if it doesn't work, we try another. If that doesn't work, we try another, and if the third approach doesn't work, we try a fourth.

The key to our therapy is to be adaptive and flexible. If we had a motto which sums up our therapeutic philosophy, it would be, "If it's not working, try something else."

Influenced by Epstein and Bishop (1981), we take two to four sessions to do a thorough, systematic intake in which we explore many areas of family functioning. Then we present our impressions and recommendations for treatment to the parents or the family members.

Before we proceed with our child or adolescent programs, we attempt to provide as much family emotional support for the target child—the child or adolescent whose misbehavior brought the family into therapy—as we can. If our child or adolescent programs do not work to bring symptom relief, we assume there are underlying emotional issues which the family members have not yet faced or resolved. If we believe they are strong enough, it then becomes our function to help them do so. We do this by identifying the emotional pain of all the family members and encouraging them to express it. Failing this, we may take a history of the parents' upbringing to uncover any family of origin problems and to work directly on them. If we think it would be helpful, as it often is, and if the grandparents live nearby, we may invite them in for a few sessions with the family.

If our efforts still do not bring symptomatic relief, we may then resort to paradoxical techniques to induce family change. Rather than encourage the family members to change, we may reverse ourselves and encourage them not to change by explaining, for example, that their lack of progress may be a message from their unconscious minds that change would be too disruptive. With families with chronic, unresolved problems who come to us after they have been to many other therapists, we may begin to use paradoxical techniques from the very beginning of our treatment efforts.

We may next offer individual or marital counseling if our therapy is still not successful. After gently but firmly confronting them, we may offer marital counseling to those parents whose unresolved marital problems are affecting the children in adverse ways. Or if we perceive her to be stuck in a pathogenic family which is not going to change, we may offer individual, supportive counseling to the target child in an attempt to insulate her from the family pathology. We may also offer individual therapy to a parent struggling with other psychological problems—depression, for example, or family of origin problems.

If our therapeutic efforts still don't prove effective, we would then consider an out-of-home placement of the target child for more intensive treatment. However, except in the case of a chemically dependent youth who needs immediate treatment, we would not consider this radical and expensive course of action until after all other therapeutic approaches have been tried. Although it must be considered in certain cases, one of our primary goals at the Family Teaching Center is to prevent the breakdown in families through out-of-home placements of youths.

Finally, if a family has dropped out of treatment with us, we may send the members a letter in which we confront them directly with a description of what we believe they will have to do to bring symptomatic relief. We conceive of this letter as our last chance to influence a system in need of change.

In terms of Levant's (1984) tripartite classification of family therapies, we first operate according to a structure/process model. The heart of our therapy at the Family Teaching Center is behavioral. By teaching the family members new skills, our goal with every family we see is to bring about behavior change. In working with families with young children, we teach the parents specific disciplinary techniques to control their children's behaviors, and in working with families with adolescents, we teach the family members negotiating and contracting skills so they can clearly delineate the family rules and back them up with rewards for acceptable behavior and punishments for unacceptable behaviors.

But we are also interested in communication patterns in families. Before we can have the family members solve their problems in precise behavioral terms, we have to insure they can communicate effectively with each other and support each other in caring ways.

If our behavioral and communications approaches don't work, we then usually switch to an experiential model as we attempt to identify the emotional pain each member of the family is experiencing and encourage each to express it. If this approach doesn't work, we may then switch to a historical model as we take a history of the marriage or of each parent's upbringing to uncover any marital or family of origin problems.

Although behavioral and communications orientations constitute the bulk of our work at the Family Teaching Center, we have also been influenced by other schools of family therapy, although to a lesser degree. From systems theory, we have taken our belief that we must consider the family as a total, interdependent, interacting entity in which a change in one part of the system influences all other parts of the system. From structural theory, we have learned to look at the family as a structure which needs modification.

The functional school of Barton and Alexander (1981) has also influenced our thinking about behavior. From their writings, we have learned that most behavioral interactions between family members either create distance, intimacy or control. In our marriage counseling, we look for differences between the spouses in their needs for distance or intimacy as the root cause of many marital conflicts.

Finally, from the strategic school of active family therapy, we have adopted a number of paradoxical techniques to bring about family change by encouraging the family members not to change. Paradoxical psychotherapy has also influenced our thinking about family dynamics as we observe the resistance to change manifested by some families.

Thus, we are truly an eclectic type of family therapy. Although behaviorism forms the core of our approach, that core is surrounded and supported by other treatment philosophies and methodologies. Purists may accuse us of being theoretically loose and disjointed, but we believe there is strength in eclecticism. The field of family therapy is simply too new for anyone to have all the answers. We believe we can learn from all family therapists no matter what their theoretical backgrounds. Until research provides us with more definitive answers, we are not going to bet exclusively on any one school but borrow ideas and techniques from all schools.

OUTCOME RESEARCH

During the period, November, 1983 to February, 1984, we called 146 families six to twelve months after we last saw the family members to ask how they were doing. In a structured interview with one member of the family, always a parent and usually the mother, our researcher determined the status of the family: whether the family members interviewed described the family as improved, the same or deteriorated. Both the presenting problem

Family Therapy

and other areas of family functioning were used to determine improvement or deterioration. For example, if the respondent described only the presenting problem as improved, claimed the presenting problem remained the same but the family members were doing better in other areas of family functioning or said there was improvement in both the presenting problem and other areas, the researcher rated the family as reporting improvement.

Of the 146 families, 44, or 30% of the total, had dropped out of treatment after they had completed the intake process while 14 families, or 10%, were what we called no go's—i.e., they did not even complete the intake process. Interestingly, in a study of 35 families, Patterson (1974) found the same dropout percentage—40%—as we found.

The overall results and results by program completion status are reported below in Table I.

The results in percentages by program type are presented below in Table II.

Frankly, we were surprised but pleased by these results. We had not expected so many respondents to report improvement six to twelve months after our last session with the family members.

Certainly, there were methodological weaknesses in our study. Our researcher was not a trained clinician and only talked with one member of each family. We did not do an extensive assessment of each family or contact any independent observers. Nor did we

TABLE I

OVERALL RESULTS AND RESULTS IN PERCENTAGES
BY COMPLETION STATUS

	Improved	No Change	Deteriorated
All Families (N = 146)	80%	19%	1%
Families Who Completed Therapy (N = 88)	91%	9%	
Drop Outs (N = 44)	66%	32%	2%
No Go's (N = 14)	57%	43%	

A chi square analysis revealed a significant relationship between completion status and reported improvement. ($\bar{X}^2 = 15.72$, df = 2, p < .01)

TABLE II

RESULTS IN PERCENTAGES BY PROGRAM TYPE

	Improved	No Change	Deteriorated
Child			
(N = 58)	84%	16%	
Adolescent			
(N = 61)	77%	21%	2%
Marital Counseling			
(N = 12)	67%	33%	
Custody Counseling			
(N = 15)	87%	13%	

A chi square analysis revealed a significant relationship between program type and reported improvement. ($X^2 = 6.72$, df = 3, p < .05)

have a matched control group with which to compare our families.

We also suspect the reported improvement rates are inflated for several possible reasons:

—We used a liberal criteria for improvement—i.e., both improvement in the presenting problem and/or improvement in other areas of family functioning.

—Because the researcher identified herself as an employee of the Family Teaching Center, some of the respondents may have been reluctant to say things had not changed or had deteriorated because they did not want to disappoint us, further discourage themselves or admit they should not have discontinued treatment.

—A few of the respondents who said things had improved later contacted us because problems had arisen again in the family despite their reports of initial improvement. It may be that in some families, improvement can be a fickle thing, here one moment and gone the next.

But for the most part, these shortcomings were constant across all groups and so may have cancelled each other out. Although we had no formal control group, we could consider the drop outs and no go's as comprising a crude control group. A comparison of these families with those who completed therapy does reveal a significantly greater reported improvement rate with the completion of therapy than without it.

In short, we believe this study demonstrates the effectiveness of our program. In support of this belief, Fleischman and Szykula (1981), in a study of 50 families in our child program, using both naturalistic observations and parents' reports, found a significant decrease in aversive behaviors four, eight and twelve months after termination.

ABOUT THE AUTHOR

Just a few words about myself: having undergone two years of psychoanalytically oriented psychotherapy as a young man, I became attracted to the study of psychology after college. My post master's degree experience was in analytically oriented individual psychotherapy, play therapy and marital therapy but my doctoral work exposed me more fully to behavioral approaches. My first post doctoral position found me working with colleagues who had been humanistically trained, so my early personal and professional experiences exposed me to the three major schools in clinical psychology at that time.

Later, I became interested in family therapy as my work in a mental health center made me realize I needed skills in that type of therapy if I was to function effectively in a general practice. Since then, I have become convinced that marital and family therapies are not only more effective techniques for many psychological problems but also much more interesting, exciting and challenging than individual therapy.

Obviously, my life has been strongly influenced by my own upbringing. Although love for me and pride in my accomplishments were present in my family, they were not fully expressed by my parents. This was the case with many parents who were made to feel economically insecure by the Great Depression and who pushed their children to succeed by exhorting them to do better. I am sure this is one reason why I emphasize so strongly the expression of love and the use of praise with many of the families I see.

Another recent but strong influence in my life has been spiritual in nature. I like to think I have worked through most of the neurotic problems of my childhood but now having reached middle age, my struggles and search are more spiritual than psychological. I have come to appreciate the spiritual emphasis on the unity of all creation and the promotion of love and reconciliation as a marvelous, yet practical guideline for everyday living and family life. For despite the limited practice of love in history and current affairs, potentially it still remains the greatest, most curative force in the world.

It is this ancient wisdom that I hope to teach many of the families I treat.

Chapter 2

SOME THEORETICAL ASSUMPTIONS

W hether conscious or not, all of us have a set of assumptions about the nature of the world which shape our cognitions, perceptions and behaviors. Those of us in the business of treating people for emotional and behavioral problems should be aware of our own idiosyncratic assumptions because of the profound influence they have on our diagnostic and treatment techniques. What follows is a list and description of the theoretical assumptions which underlie this book. Some are subject to experimental verification but others are not. Each is listed under one of five categories.

EPISTEMOLOGY

1. A theory is simply a way to organize and explain our perceptions of the universe. As such, it determines what we'll look for and what we'll miss. In other words, a theory forces us to focus in more sharply on what we perceive and so may give us more explanatory and predictive power. At the same time, however, a theory constricts our view of the world and so forces us to overlook certain aspects of what we are studying.

A family therapist, for example, examines closely the interactions between family members but pays less attention to individual psychodynamics. She assumes an examination of these interactions will give her more information and more power to change the family but in concentrating on them she may miss important psychodynamic information.

2. All theories are subject to constant modification and possible revision or rejection. None can be said to be true or false but are more or less useful in giving us explanatory and predictive power. None can ever give us a complete, accurate and unified view of the universe as there are limits to scientific knowledge. We can come closer and closer to an exact, unified model of the universe but can never arrive at a point at which we have completely explained or understood all the complex phenomena of the cosmos. Newton's theory was replaced by Einstein's because the latter gave us a more accurate model of the universe, but someday it, in turn, will be replaced by another theory which will give us even greater explanatory and predictive power. That theory, however, will in time be replaced by another theory and so on, ad infinitum.

3. There is no such thing as Reality with a capital R or Truth with a capital T which we can discover out there in the external world. Instead, since there are four billion of us on the planet, there are four billion realities with a small r, each of which is legitimate and authentic for the individual who lives in it.

There is an ancient Hindu tale of four blind men touching an elephant. One has the elephant by its trunk and describes it as long and narrow. One holds it by its ear and describes it as flappy. The third has embraced the leg and insists the elephant is round and thick. The fourth has grabbed the tail and claims the elephant is like a snake. Each of these blind men is right but only partially so. Each has accurately described a part of the elephant but none has a complete description of what it is like.

Like the four blind men and the elephant, each of us has a bit of the whole but none of us has the complete picture. What we perceive is accurate and legitimate for us but none of us has the whole truth nor will we ever have it.

This is another way of saying that perception is not the act of an isolated, independent subject observing a separate, external reality. Rather, perception is an interaction between subject and object which forms an interdependent perceptual system. What we experience is not the world directly as it is but as it interacts with our theories about it. Information comes to us directly from the world but we take that raw data and rearrange it to fit our theories. If the information disagrees with our theories, we either

reject or distort it or—something which is less likely to happen—
revise or reject our theories.

One clinical implication of this assumption involves communication between people. Spouses who fight frequently, for
example, especially in a bitter attempt to prove each is right and
the other wrong, do not subscribe to this assumption. They
assume there is an objective reality out there which each perceives
accurately but which their spouse is too stupid, blind or pigheaded
to see.

One type of marital argument which can be especially bitter
involves two spouses attempting to decide exactly what happened
in the past. Each is convinced he or she is right and the other is
wrong, when only an audio or video recording, which usually
doesn't exist, could settle the dispute.

What you can do in such a situation is simply point out that the
argument can't be decided without a recording. The only thing
the spouses can do is agree each remembers the past event
differently and let it go at that. And if it's important, the next time
a similar argument arises they should write down what each said
or agreed to do.

4. The relationship between cognitive theory building and
emotional, perceptual and behavioral processes is reciprocal.
Each process influences the others and is influenced by the others.
A change in one can result in a change in one or more of the
others.

The clinical implications of this assumption are many and
profound. Cognitive therapy is based upon it. By changing the
cognitions of a client, the cognitive therapist can help that client
change her perceptual, emotional and behavioral reactions to the
world. If the client believes she is unattractive or of little worth,
she will probably expect rejection from others and may behave in
such a way that she receives it, thereby confirming her beliefs
about herself. If through therapy, she can change her view of
herself, she will probably perceive others as less threatening or
rejecting, develop more positive feelings towards them and herself
and so behave in a friendlier way. This should bring a friendlier
reaction from others and confirm her new belief about herself.

5. Human behavior can be studied from four different levels,
each unique but each giving us useful information. Each
examines a part of the elephant but none perceives the whole.
These levels, from the least inclusive to the most inclusive, are:

—biological
—intrapsychic
—interpersonal
—socio-cultural

The biological level refers to those biochemical and physiological processes which influence behavior. Although they may be of interest to the non-medical therapist, they are not on her level of diagnosis and treatment. When a medical problem is suspected by the clinician, a referral to a physician is obviously indicated.

The intrapsychic level is the domain of the individually oriented therapist. It includes the psychological processes—cognitions, perceptions and emotions—which occur within an individual and which influence behavior. In working at the intrapsychic level, the therapist usually attempts to change these processes rather than what occurs in the client's external world.

The interpersonal level is the domain of the marital and family therapist. Although not ignoring what occurs within an individual intrapsychically, the family therapist is more interested in what occurs between individuals. Her concern is with interpersonal processes occurring within a social system.

Although the socio-cultural level is usually not the domain of practicing therapists, nevertheless it should be of interest to the on-line clinician. It refers to the larger social, cultural and historical forces which influence an individual and the family system within which he lives out his emotional and psychological life.

To illustrate how these four levels can be applied to the study of a particular clinical problem, consider depression as an example. Depression can be caused or exacerbated by biochemical factors; intrapsychic factors such as guilt, depressing thoughts or a negative self-concept; marital or family problems or socio-cultural factors such as discrimination or unemployment.

All four levels from which to examine human behavior are legitimate and should be employed as you conduct a diagnostic assessment. You can intervene effectively on the first three levels but obviously not as effectively on the fourth. However, this is not to say that you should not attempt to change the larger society. Most therapists are, or perhaps should be, social critics for we are daily witnesses to the harmful results of some of society's mores and practices.

FAMILY SYSTEM THEORY

Having examined some assumptions about human knowledge, we are now ready to examine one specific theory about human behavior. The level from which we study human behavior at the Family Teaching Center is obviously the third level. We believe diagnosing and intervening at the interpersonal level gives us the greatest predictive, explanatory and treatment power in changing dysfunctional behavior.

1. We do not live in social isolation. We are social creatures who are almost entirely dependent upon other people for the satisfaction of our needs, whether it be the unknown farmer who grows our food or the spouse we have known intimately for much of our adult lives.

2. The family is the system best suited to meet many of the physical, emotional, social and sexual needs of the individual. The infant depends upon his family for his very survival. As he grows older, it is the family which provides him—or fails to provide him—with the psychological support necessary for his growth into a mentally healthy, independent adult. For the adults in the family, the marriage is a convenient arrangement to meet their social, emotional, financial and sexual needs.

3. Since the family meets so many of our needs and has such a significant influence on us, the best way to understand the behavior of an individual is to understand the family system of which she is a part by interviewing as many members as possible. And the most effective way to treat many of a client's psychological problems is to treat her family so it will be better able to meet her needs.

If a young girl's acting out behavior, for example, is the result of depression and a poor self-concept because she is a blamed scapegoat in the family, individual therapy for her will probably do little to mitigate the negative influence of the family on her. In fact, it may make things worse for her at home because the family members will continue to assume she has the problem since the therapist has agreed to see her alone. But no matter how many sessions of individual therapy she has, it is doubtful her therapist could ever become as important to her psychological development as her family. Therefore, before doing individual therapy, every effort should be made to change her interaction with her family through family therapy to better provide for her psychological needs.

At the Family Teaching Center, we usually prefer to meet with everyone living at home for the first interview, along with any adult siblings living nearby. If there is a biological parent living outside the home, we attempt to contact him, either for a separate appointment or for a telephone interview if he lives too far away to come in for an appointment. Similarly, we attempt to see or interview by telephone any grandparents or other extended family members who are described as having a significant impact on the family.

Then we make our treatment recommendation based upon a family diagnosis. Whether our recommendation is for individual treatment—a rare event for us—marital treatment or family treatment, we are convinced that having met with as many members of the family as possible or relevant, we have much more information with which to provide effective treatment.

4. If not quite lawful, the behavior of individuals in a family is predictable. Family members often display certain recurrent patterns of behavior. Our function as family therapists is to discover and modify those patterns which prevent the family members from finding more effective ways to relate to each other.

This assumption addresses the problem of blame which many families in therapy face. Often the parents with a troubled child will either blame the child for the family's problems or will blame themselves. Although very common, the search for blame is usually a fruitless, futile exercise, but it is something which must be handled skillfully by you as a family therapist.

Since we assume the behavior in families is patterned, if not quite lawful, we take either one of two positions with regard to the question of blame: either no one is to blame because the behavior of family members is almost lawful or everyone is to blame because everyone contributes to the maintenance of the problem behavior. In either case, we do not take the position that one particular person is responsible for the family's problems or that some members are more responsible than others.

The common types of patterns we look for in families are cycles, rules, roles, triangles and relationships. We will discuss these in detail in the next chapter.

NEEDS AND EMOTIONS

1. As family therapists, we are dealing primarily with people's emotional pain. Just as the medical professional's primary

function is to discover the causes of physical pain and treat to remove or reduce them, so the primary function of the mental health professional is to diagnose the causes of emotional pain and treat to remove or reduce them.

2. People will seek the services of a mental health professional primarily when they are in emotional pain or causing other people pain. In the first case, they will probably come to therapy voluntarily; in the second case, they may have to be pressured to seek the services of a therapist.

3. The primary cause of emotional pain is unmet psychological needs. People are emotionally pained when their social, emotional and sexual needs are not being met by the significant others in their lives. Or they will cause emotional pain in others when they fail to meet their psychological needs. Therapy is a process which helps clients to identify and express their psychological needs, and to change their relationships with others to insure their needs will be better met.

4. Following Maslow's (1954, 1968) classification of needs—physiological, security, love and esteem—we believe that except in cases in which child protective services are required because of parental abuse or neglect, most family therapists do not have to concern themselves with the physiological and security needs of the families they're treating. Instead, we usually treat family members whose love and esteem needs are not well met. For example, at the Family Teaching Center, we diagnose the target child in terms of how much familial love he is, or is not, receiving.

5. Healthy parental love for children consists of three abilities, any one of which may be lacking in one or both of the parents and so should be the target of your therapeutic intervention. A deficiency in one or more of these abilities represents a parental inability to meet the psychological needs of the children. These abilities are:

—the ability to express love for their children through nurturance, emotional support, praise and appreciation,

—the ability to support each other in disciplining their children firmly, fairly and flexibly using more rewards than punishments and

—the ability to let go of their children when they come of age to function more independently.

In short, effective parents are loving parents who give their children plenty of hugs, kisses, verbal expressions of love, praise and appreciation. They are also parents who back each other up in specifying clearly to their children what are acceptable and unacceptable behaviors and in following through consistently with rewards for acceptable behavior and penalties for unacceptable behavior. Yet these same parents are able to allow their children more independence as each demonstrates he or she can handle it. Since they are high in self-esteem, they do not have to live vicariously through their children or expect their children to meet their needs.

6. The keystone to family functioning is the marital relationship which, in turn, depends upon the psychological health of the spouses. If they are emotionally healthy, the family will be healthy. If they are troubled or the marriage unhappy, the chances are one or more of the children will display behavioral or emotional problems. In a healthy marriage, the parents have love for themselves and for each other, which generates a surfeit of love for the children.

In a divorced family, the psychological health of the family depends upon the psychological health of the custodial parent or parents. If the parents have successfully completed the divorce adjustment process, if they both remain involved with the children in a loving way and if they can cooperate with each other for the sake of the children, the family, despite the pain of divorce, can remain healthy or regain its health.

7. Independent of their degree of psychological health, people differ in the relative strength of their need for other people. Some prefer more distance while others seek more intimacy. They will behave in such a way, even symptomatically, to achieve a level of intimacy or distance with which they are comfortable. If two spouses have roughly the same distance or intimacy needs, their marriage will have a better chance to be successful than if their needs differ.

In the latter case, usually one spouse wants more intimacy while the other is uncomfortable with too much closeness. Unfortunately, the more the spouse who wants intimacy presses for it, the more the spouse who prefers distance will retreat. This only worries the first spouse who redoubles her pressure for intimacy which only causes the second spouse to retreat even further, thereby setting into motion a self-perpetuating cycle.

8. There is a universal struggle all of us face between intimacy and distance, a struggle which can be especially difficult for the

young, adolescent who has been hurt by other people or the divorced parent trying to decide whether to remarry or not. It is a classic double approach-avoidance conflict between the advantages and disadvantages of intimacy and the advantages and disadvantages of distance, with the advantages of one side being the disadvantages of the other, and vice versa. To be intimate with people is to be loved and to belong, but it is also to be responsible to another person and to be vulnerable to rejection and hurt. Conversely, to be uninvolved with another is to be free to do as one pleases, and to be protected from the possibility of rejection, but at the cost of being lonely.

Since conflicts like this one are stressful, it is your function as a therapist to aid people in resolving them one way or the other. You may help the divorced person to decide she would rather remain single than risk another marriage, or you may help her to decide to take a chance and remarry again.

9. Psychologically healthy people have resolved this conflict between intimacy and distance in favor of both. They have struck a comfortable balance between their need for others and their need for time alone. But neither need is extreme in them. Paradoxically, the more independent they can be, the more they can rely upon themselves, the more intimate they are able to be with other people.

This is simply another way of saying that high self-esteem people usually achieve better marriages and friendships than low self-esteem people. There is psychological truth and perhaps a bitter irony in the New Testament parable which concludes that to those who have will more be given and to those who have not will more be denied.

A person who is high in self-esteem will be better able to give and receive love because she has plenty of love to give and because she believes she deserves to receive love in return. She can be more open, trusting and intimate with another because she is not as afraid of rejection as a low self-esteem person would be. By contrast, a person low in self-esteem would make a poorer marital risk for a number of reasons. He would come into the marriage with more needs to be fulfilled but with fewer emotional resources to share. He would be less willing to be open or honest with his spouse for fear of rejection. Not loving himself, he would assume, "If she really knew what I was like, she would reject me." Or he might assume she would leave him if he didn't cow her into remaining with him by his temper, intimidation and domination.

10. People at the same level of mental health or psychopathology tend to marry each other. Troubled people are attracted to troubled people while a healthy person, if he is truly healthy, would not want to be burdened with the problems of a disturbed spouse. If this assumption is true, it follows that in a marriage in which a seemingly high functioning person is married to an apparently low functioning individual, the former needs to keep the latter in her "lower" position in order to maintain his "higher" position and to perceive himself as healthier. As a result, the so called healthier spouse would be threatened by any drive for health or assertiveness on the part of the less healthy spouse as the following clinical example—an obvious failure—suggests:

> Molly was treated in individual therapy for a year by the author for depression with initially successful results. However, her husband became enraged because she was out one night a week in a Bible study group, which was really a support group for women, when he felt she should be at home.
>
> Upon questioning, the husband admitted in an individual session that one of the reasons he married Molly was because she was not too attractive and so he did not have to worry she would be unfaithful to him. Her improvement was too threatening to him, so he became angry and threatened divorce in an attempt to restore what for years had been the status quo. Like a teeter totter, his up position was maintained by her down position, while her attempt to move up was met by tremendous, and in this case successful, pressure from him to resume her down position.
>
> At the end of a year of individual therapy, Molly was as depressed as when she was first seen. This was a client I saw when I was first beginning as a psychologist and had not adopted a family systems approach to psychopathology. My treatment of this problem would probably have been through marital therapy today rather than individual therapy.

If it is true that two low self-esteem individuals will be attracted to each other, then the prognosis for such a marriage is obviously poor. Both spouses would probably expect more of the marriage than any marriage could possibly deliver—i.e., that it would be the perfect match which would meet all their excessive needs and make up for all their past hurts and rejections.

But both spouses would be limited in the capacity to meet the needs of the other. Lacking in self love, both would be limited in the ability to love the other. Thus, their marriage would begin on the basis of unrealistic expectations and excessive needs with limited emotional resources to meet those needs.

As the above clinical example shows, the need to see both spouses in such a marriage is imperative. To see one without the other is to risk straining an already strained relationship and possibly driving it to divorce. Any improvement in one spouse as a result of individual therapy could be misperceived as a threat to the other spouse who might then retaliate with anger or an attempt to sabotage the improvement.

11. Since marriage and the family are institutions which have evolved to meet our most important psychological needs, the failure of those institutions can precipitate strong emotional reactions. Emotions in the family can be so powerful because the family involves such basic needs. In few other situations can rejection be so devastating, loss so painful or anger so murderous as in the family. The existence of anger tells us that family members are hurt or afraid because they feel their basic psychological needs for love and esteem are not being met. Although the angriest member of the family may appear to be the most powerful or dominant member, in actuality he may feel quite powerless. His anger is really anguish. Nothing has worked for him in obtaining compliance from the family so he resorts to rage in an attempt to force what he believes they will not give him voluntarily.

At the Family Teaching Center, we assume the best way for clients to handle anger is either to cool it or convert it to the hurt and fear which usually underlies it. We're convinced that rather than reduce anger through catharsis, as some therapists believe, the expression of anger only serves to increase it. Anger can become a habit, so the more it is let loose, the easier it becomes to express it again the next time one feels angry. Even talking about that which triggered anger can increase the feeling of anger. A client can literally talk himself into a rage or maintain his anger long after it could have been dissipated.

12. The symptomatic behavior of the symptom bearer in the family serves several purposes:

—It is a way for the symptom bearer to proclaim his or her love and esteem needs are not being met.

—It is a way for the symptom bearer to attempt to have his needs met.

—It represents an attempt by the symptom bearer to act as an amateur family therapist in keeping the family together.

—It is an attempt to draw the family's attention away from other, potentially more serious problems.

—It is a cry for help for the family, a way to tell the outside world, "This family is not functioning properly."

In effect, the symptomatic behavior of the symptom bearer does two things: it expresses the emotional pain felt by him and his family because of unmet psychological needs, and it attempts to have those needs met either directly by seeking attention for himself or indirectly by insuring the family will continue to function so it can eventually fulfill his needs.

An example of the attempt to employ symptoms to have needs met directly would be the following:

> Barbara felt very isolated and lonely in her marriage. One way she could force her husband to respond to her was to become embroiled in a bitter fight with her son. Only after the fighting became especially loud and near violent would Barbara's husband step in to settle the argument between his wife and his son, thereby giving her some attention.

An example of an attempt to employ symptoms to keep the family together would be the following:

> Bill's parents have had marital problems for years but one day his father finally left his mother and moved to another town. A week later Bill was arrested for shoplifting. As a result of his arrest, Bill's father had to come back to town to be available to his son.

It should be obvious to you by now that the family members usually view symptomatic behavior as disruptive or maladaptive, something which is either "bad" or "sick" and in need of correction or cure. From a family systems point of view, however, symptomatic behavior is perceived as something potentially positive or adaptive, an attempt to change a situation which desperately needs changing. This is not to say that the symptom bearer consciously decides to behave symptomatically to save the family or force certain responses from the family members. Rather, the symptom bearer acts out his emotional pain in symptomatic behavior, the unintended effect of which is to bring him partial relief. In psychoanalytic terms, he receives secondary

gains for his behavior, while in behavioral terms, he is unintentionally reinforced for it.

Thus, symptomatic behavior works for the symptom bearer and
his family. If it didn't work, he wouldn't continue it. If it didn't
receive some reinforcement, it would eventually extinguish. But
the tragedy of the symptomatic behavior is that while it is
effective, it is only partially so. It brings relief but it prevents the
family members from finding other ways to interact with each
other more effectively. They cling to it because it does work—and
the more stress they're under the more they embrace it—but by
their very clinging they fail to search for better ways to function as
a family unit.

What you must do as a family therapist is help the family find
other, more effective ways of relating. Before you can ask them to
give up that which they are already using with limited success,
however, you must provide them with other ways to relate which
will be more effective for them. You must exchange the partially
successful methods they are using to function as a family for more
effective methods to achieve need satisfaction for all family
members, without the necessity of any one of them developing
symptoms.

COMMUNICATION

1. Every living system—be it a cell, an organ, a person, a family
or a nation—must maintain a balance between stability and
change if it is to survive. Change insures the system can survive in
the face of changing conditions while stability insures it does not
change too quickly. Too much of either could prove disasterous
for the living system.

As applied to the family, if the family members are too slow to
change in response to changing external or internal conditions,
they might not survive as an intact group. If the parents cling too
tenaciously to an adolescent driving for more independence, for
example, he may bust loose in a harsh, angry way from his
parents' control and sever all ties with them.

On the other hand, too rapid a change can weaken the family
also. A Vietnamese family which is suddenly uprooted and moved
to the United States, with its different language and customs,
would find itself severely strained. To slow down the pace of
change, the family members would probably settle near other

Vietnamese families with whom they could share their common language. Similarly, a laid off father who had been raised in a traditional home in which his father was the only breadwinner might find it extremely difficult to adapt to the idea of his wife now supporting the family while he stayed home doing "women's work."

2. The exchange of information through communication is what maintains the family's balance between change and stability. Such information relays one of two messages: "Change or don't change." Information which says "Change" is called positive feedback, while information which says "Don't change" is called negative feedback. Thus, positive feedback promotes growth or change, while negative feedback promotes stability and resists change. Parents who would encourage their adolescent's drive to independence would use positive feedback to do so, while parents who would discourage their adolescent's drive for independence would use negative feedback to do so. They would criticize or condemn any signs of independence in him.

Information is usually exchanged between the entire family system and the external environment, or between the subsystems of the family system. What typically happens in troubled families is that a conflict arises between two contradictory messages, between positive feedback and negative feedback. Perhaps the external environment is calling for a change in the family while the family members are resisting it, as in the case of the father laid off from work described above. Or perhaps one member of the family system is pushing for change while other members are resisting it, as in the case of the adolescent wanting more independence also described above.

As a family therapist we are usually, but not always, on the side of change. As change agents, we assume that families come to us because they are stuck at some point at which change is required but not forthcoming. However, there may be times when we oppose change and favor stability for the sake of the family. If we believe an adolescent is pushing her parents for more independence than she can handle, we would probably side with the stability represented by the parents and attempt to slow down the process of change.

3. Just as people cannot not decide, so people cannot not communicate. Not to decide is to decide to do nothing. Not to communicate is to communicate plenty. Silence can send a

message as powerful as any verbal message. It can signal anger, disapproval, disappointment, fear, hopelessness or depression. It can also frustrate another if he insists on communication from the one who is silent.

4. Analog communication is as important as digital communication if not more so. Digital communication simply refers to the verbal content of the messages while analog communication refers to communication which is a function of two factors: the context of the communication and the non-verbal cues associated with the digital communication. The context of the communication refers to who is speaking to whom in which situation. A compliment from a person one considers to be a superior carries much more weight and a different meaning than a compliment from a so called inferior. Similarly, criticism shouted in anger in front of peers can be much more devastating than caring criticism shared in private.

Non-verbal cues refer to the bodily gestures and processes which are employed in delivering a message: tone of voice, body posture, eye contact, use of hands, voice inflection and loudness. If a person grits his teeth, pounds his fist and shouts "I'm not angry," obviously he is delivering two contradictory messages, one of which—the digital—says "I'm not angry" and the other of which—the analog—says "Yes, I am." In this case, most people would assume the analog message that the speaker is angry is the correct one.

A conflict between the analog and digital messages creates a double message which is important in understanding disturbed family behavior. It sends conflicting communications to the receiver. A mother says she loves her son yet stiffens up and looks uncomfortable when he gives her a hug. A father pleads with a child to change yet immediately lists a number of reasons why he can't.

Watzlawick, Beavin and Jackson (1967) hypothesize that double messages occur frequently in schizophrenogenic families in which the schizophrenic-to-be learns to withdraw and become uncommunicative in the face of such conflicting messages. He learns not to trust what he is hearing. He also learns it is better not to communicate than to try to make sense out of what is so contradictory.

INTERPERSONAL POWER

1. We all seek what we can rarely or never have in this world: absolute certainty and security. Most of what we do—whether working, going to school, writing a book, falling in love, bearing children or going to church—is designed to promote our fortunes and protect our resources. Life is precarious and unpredictable, so anxiety is a powerful motivating force in human behavior. It is what pushes us to work hard, to get ahead, not to rock the boat when our jobs are insecure and to save for retirement.

In short, although occasionally we act from true selflessness, we are motivated by self-interest. We strive to secure the maximum rewards at minimal cost. Self-interest is the driving force in history and in contemporary life.

2. The major way most of us seek absolute security and certainty is through power and control. The more money we can make, the more degrees we can earn, the more power we can gain, the more friends we can surround ourselves with, the more love we can win from others, the more secure we believe we will be. Ironically, the more frustrated we are in our efforts to meet these goals, the more anxious we become and the greater becomes our drive for power and control.

Certainly, this is what can happen in troubled families. When family members realize things are not going as they believe they should, their usual response is to attempt to control other people and events more. But this strategy often makes the problem worse. The more a teenager rebels, the more the parents panic and try to control him, the more he rebels. The more a distant husband withdraws, the more his intimacy seeking wife presses him for intimacy, the more he withdraws. The more a man is unable to function sexually, the more he worries about it or tries to control his erection voluntarily, which, of course, prevents him from achieving an erection naturally.

3. Although there is usually a difference in physical power between a husband and wife, the psychological power in a marriage is usually equal, even if one appears to be more powerful or dominant. This is one of the reasons why some couples become stuck for years in seemingly unhappy and ineffective patterns of

behavior. Each partner is hurt, frustrated or afraid because each believes the other is not meeting his or her needs. Each attempts to coerce the other to change through anger, threats, silence, nagging, withdrawal or the withholding of love. Everything may be tried to force behavior change in the other but nothing works, further adding to each partner's hurt, frustration and anxiety.

The reason why change is not forthcoming in such a marriage is that the power of the spouses is roughly equal, even if the power of one spouse is to do little or nothing. The attempt by one spouse to control or change the other is met with resistance or a counter demand that the other change. It is as if the spouses were standing apart, pointing angry, accusing fingers at each other and shouting, "It's all your fault. You have to change." And, of course, in such a situation of mutual blaming, the chances of change occurring are practically nil. Each spouse tries to make the relationship unilateral which is impossible because it is bilateral. But neither would want to admit this for fear of admitting to a lack of control in a frighteningly uncontrollable situation.

4. If psychological power is roughly equal in marital relationships, it follows that there is strength in what might appear to be weakness. Even though one partner may seem to be dominant and the other submissive, nevertheless the power between them is equal, so the seemingly submissive spouse may actually be in a position of strength. A student of mine illustrated this very nicely by describing what she called "the iron magnolias of the South." Even though these women appear to be weak, delicate and helpless, that posture exerts tremendous control over the men in their lives.

Madenes (1981) describes a case in which a social worker wife had been trying to help her depressed husband for years. Being a social worker, treating her husband for depression put her in a superior position to him. However, for the years she treated him, his depression never lifted, thus putting him in a superior position and her in an inferior position. What seemed like weakness—i.e., depression—was really strength because by it he had been able to frustrate his wife. And what appeared to be an unequal relationship actually involved roughly equal power between the spouses.

It should be obvious to you by now that the power which lies in weakness is very subtle. It is not the power to bluster, bellow or threaten but the power to sabotage or to do nothing. It is the power of the wife who says "Yes, dear" to her domineering husband but then turns around and does exactly what she wants to do. It is the power of the adolescent whose parents want him to be admitted to a good school but whose grades are so poor he'll be lucky to be accepted at any college. It is also the power which enables adolescents to completely ignore their parents' warnings or prohibitions as soon as they leave the house for school or a night out.

5. Given that power is roughly equal in marriage, it follows that in the late twentieth century America most marital hierarchies won't work. The "one down" spouse either fights openly against her position or covertly attempts to undermine her husband's position. The only case in which a hierarchy may work is when a husband maintains it by threatening to use, or actually using, his greater physical power. But such a relationship is really no marriage if marriage is defined as a voluntarily maintained relationship between two people who care for each other.

6. In some situations, the best way to gain the power to influence someone is to relinquish it. This is an assumption which underlies the paradoxical techniques to be discussed later in this book. As therapists, perhaps we can learn something about the art of influence from the iron magnolias of the South. To pressure people to change can backfire and stiffen their resistance to change. With chronic or resistant clients, the best we can do for them is encourage them not to change or declare our powerlessness to help them change. They may then either resist our directives or feel sorry for us and change.

There's an ancient wisdom that underlies this assumption which is summed up in the Taoist poem:

By letting go it all gets done,
The world is won by those who let it go.

Chapter 3

HOW FAMILIES FUNCTION

The primary purpose of this chapter is to discuss the functioning of troubled families. However, before we do that we must discuss two other topics: the functioning of the healthy family and the developmental stages through which every family passes.

The reasons we should talk about the healthy family before proceeding to a discussion of the dysfunctional family are twofold: to provide a standard of comparison by which you can assess the troubled family and to provide a goal you can strive for in your treatment efforts. In our discussion of the healthy family, however, please bear in mind that we will be describing an ideally healthy family which probably does not exist in the real world. If such a family did exist, we would be envious of its members. The fact of the matter is most of us have, or have had, problems in our families of origin and our families of procreation. Life is too complicated and stressful for any of us to sail through it unscathed or untroubled.

In considering the ideally healthy family, we will be describing an intact, two parent family. This is not to say, however, that a divorced or stepfamily cannot be healthy. They certainly can be but the reality is they have suffered a loss through death or divorce from which they must recover to be ideally healthy, and that process takes time. Later in this book, we will discuss in detail what it takes to successfully restructure a disrupted family. Suffice it to say now that like the intact, first marriage family, the health of the divorced or stepfamily depends upon the health of the parents and their relationship.

THE HEALTHY FAMILY

The family serves two basic functions, the first being primary to the second. It provides a structure to meet the social, emotional, financial and sexual needs of the spouses and it provides a structure to meet the physical and psychological needs of the children. Since we believe the marriage is the keystone to family functioning, we believe the parents' first loyalty should be to each other and secondarily to the children. However, we also assume that a good marriage is important for the mental health and well being of the children.

One characteristic of parents in an ideally healthy family is their high self-esteem. We have already noted in the last chapter how this contributes to a better marriage. Now we should note how it contributes to better parenting also.

Coopersmith (1981) found that high self-esteem in parents is positively correlated with high self-esteem in their children for several reasons. High self-esteem parents model this type of behavior, are better able to accept their children's differing ideas and emotions and do not have to live vicariously through their offspring. They also tend to be stricter, more effective disciplinarians who set firm but flexible limits with their children and who use more rewards than punishments in disciplining them. These firm limits give the children a sense of security since they know what is acceptable and unacceptable behavior. In addition, such limits let the children know their parents care for their welfare.

Parents in an ideally healthy family have positive, caring relationships with their own parents. They have been able to emancipate themselves from their parents yet still maintain a loving contact with them. The grandparents are involved with their grandchildren, perhaps providing them with more unconditional love than can the parents. However, the grandparents do not spoil their grandchildren too much by being in coalition with the children against the parents. They do not interfere with the legitimate executive authority of the parents.

Similarly, the grandparents are not in coalition with one spouse, usually their own offspring, against the other spouse.

They do not take sides in any marital disagreements. Each generation seeks its primary source of support and need satisfaction within its own generational level and does not cross generational boundaries to have their needs met.

As we have said before and will say again, the parents in an ideally healthy family have a good marriage. Since we define mature heterosexual love as mutual need fulfillment, two people love each other to the extent they give each other pleasure, reward each other or fulfill each other's needs. The pleasure they give to each other is the bond which keeps them together. Whatever pain or problems are in the marriage, they are far outweighed by the satisfaction it provides.

In addition, the sex life of the parents in an ideally healthy family is satisfactory. There are no major problems and the frequency of intercourse is acceptable to both partners.

Lest this description becomes too idealistic, there are problems in our ideally healthy family. The difference between a healthy family and a dysfunctional family is not in the presence or absence of problems but in their respective abilities to solve problems. Both families have problems; the healthy family is simply better equipped to handle them.

Two factors which make this possible in an ideally healthy marriage are the ability to communicate and the ability to problem solve effectively. Happily married couples can communicate effectively with each other and with their children. They are able to state their needs, emotions and ideas clearly and succinctly and are willing to listen to the expressed requests, feelings and opinions of their spouses. Even in the midst of an argument—and healthy spouses will have arguments—they can still empathize with each other. Even though she really doesn't want to, one spouse can say to the other, "O.K. I can understand what you're saying. I can see your point of view."

Communicating effectively with each other will not be enough to solve the problems of our ideal family, however. To do so, the family members must be willing to compromise and to be flexible. At the Family Teaching Center, compromise is something we often encourage family members to do. We explain to them that, in compromising, people do not necessarily receive what they want but what they can live with for the sake of family harmony.

The relationship between parents in an ideally healthy family is non-hierarchical. Both recognize the relationship is bilateral. Decision-making power is shared equally by them either because they can reach a joint decision on important issues, because one can give in gracefully at some times while the other can give in at other times or because they can comfortably divide decision-making responsibilities into different areas.

The relationship between the parents and the younger children is hierarchical in an ideally healthy family in that the parents are firmly in charge of discipline and comfortable with their executive authority. However, as the children become adolescents, the parents are willing to share more of their decision-making authority in negotiating and contracting for family rules and consequences.

Discipline in the ideally healthy family is firm, fair and flexible. Rules are clearly spelled out and automatically backed up with consistent consequences, both positive and negative. However, since they know the rules and consequences, the children realize it's their own fault whenever they are punished. They do not perceive their parents as arbitrary, capricious or unfair.

More rewards than punishments are employed in the ideally healthy family because the parents realize rewards are a more effective way to discipline children. In general, the atmosphere in the family is much more positive than negative. The children, being children, have to be corrected at times but there is more expression of love, praise, appreciation and support than criticism. There are problems and conflicts but there are far more good times. Affection and appreciation are expressed easily, freely and daily so all family members know they are well loved.

Another way to conceptualize the ideally healthy family, or any family, is to look at the boundaries which surround and differentiate it. In our hypothetical family, there are clear but flexible boundaries between the individual and his family, between the various subsystems in the family, between the nuclear and extended family and between the family and the larger society.

Firm, flexible boundaries are boundaries which hold up under most stressors. They give people a sense of separation and security but they are not completely rigid or impermeable. Family members can permeate them on occasion for a short time but then must slip back across to their rightful places in the family. It's acceptable for the children to jump in bed with the parents in the morning, for example, but it's not healthy for them to sleep with their parents all night long. It's appropriate for an older sister to babysit her younger siblings on occasion but she should not be expected to discipline or babysit them all the time. It's fine for a parent to have a friend and advisor in her mother but her first loyalty should be to her husband and not her parents.

The boundary between an individual and her family is such that she feels accepted, loved and supported in the family as an individual. Her unique personhood is respected. She has to conform to certain behavioral standards, but she does not necessarily have to conform cognitively and emotionally. Her feelings and ideas are accepted as legitimate for her, even though others may not agree with them. She does not have to live her life for her parents, be the kind of person they would want her to be, have the career they would choose for her or marry whom they would like her to marry. In short, she is loved in her family, can leave it when the appropriate time comes but still maintain ties of support to the members of her family.

In any family, there are three subsystems to consider: spousal, parental and sibling. Again, the boundaries between these three subsystems are firm but flexible. There are no parental children or consistent blurring of the boundary between the parental and sibling subsystems. Since the parental subsystem is functioning effectively, no child is expected to assume a parental role. There are also no role reversals between parents and children. The parents are expected to fulfill the needs of the children and not vice versa. The spousal subsystem is working well so neither parent has to turn towards a child to serve as a confidant or meet his or her needs. In addition, the spousal and parental subsystems do not interfere with each other. In the midst of a marital spat, the parents can still support each other in their disciplinary efforts and, conversely, not allow a disagreement about discipline to interfere with their married life. In a divorced family, the ideal is that the parental subsystem will continue to function smoothly even though the spousal subsystem has been dissolved.

In an ideally healthy family, there are firm but flexible boundaries between the nuclear and extended families. The relationships between the parents and the grandparents are neither too distant or too interfering. Contact is maintained with the grandparents but they do not interfere with either the disciplining of the children or the parents' marriage. The parents' first family loyalties are to each other, secondly to their children and thirdly to their own parents. In other words, there are no crossings of generational boundaries to form coalitions between the grandparents and the grandchildren against the parents or between the grandparents and their adult offspring against the other spouse.

Finally, the boundary between the family and the larger society is firm but flexible. The family is not so disorganized that it is splitting apart. It has a secure, separate identity and heritage which gives the family members a sense of rootedness. Yet the ideally healthy family is still open to information and influence from outside itself. It can change to meet changing external conditions. It can accept and incorporate new information from the outside. It is not isolated but connected to the larger society. The family members realize the family cannot possibly meet all of their needs so they are able to seek friendships and sources of need satisfaction in the wider world and not thereby be disloyal to the family.

DEVELOPMENTAL STAGES

Just as developmental stages have been identified in the life of the individual, so developmental stages have been identified in the life cycle of the family. And just as the failure to master the developmental tasks at one stage can lead to problems at another stage for the individual, so the same failure can spell trouble for the family. As a family therapist, you should be aware of these stages because family members will seek you out either when they are faced with an unexpected crisis or when they are stuck at one of these stages and can't progress satisfactorily beyond it.

What follows is a description of the developmental stages of the family as experienced by the parents. This is consistent with our view that the parents' psychological adjustment and marriage set the tone for the functioning of the entire family.

Leaving Home

The first stage in the development of the family comes before the formation of the family but it may still be the most important stage in its life cycle. A failure here can portend grave consequences for the functioning of the future family. To successfully establish a marriage, both spouses-to-be must emancipate themselves emotionally and financially from their parents. However, that emancipation, to be effective, must be based upon a secure, loving relationship with their parents. Such a relationship serves as a sound springboard for the children to be launched into healthy adulthood.

There are two major problems which can occur at this stage. The first is that the young person is unsuccessful in his attempt to emancipate himself from his family of origin. Either he doesn't leave home, or he keeps failing in life and so retreats to the security of home. Haley (1980) argues that this behavior may serve a homeostatic function in the family. The parents usually have marital problems which they avoid confronting by worrying about their troubled offspring. According to Haley (1980), therapy consists of helping the parents take a united stand against their child to gain control of his failure-laden behavior.

The second major problem which can occur at this stage is the opposite of the first. Instead of remaining at home, the young person angrily tears away too abruptly and severs all ties with her family of origin. Although she may feel she has gained her independence, psychologically she has not. By her action she has left herself with unresolved dependency problems which she may struggle with for the rest of her life. Without a secure, loving and supportive relationship with her parents, her chances for finding contentment in life and marital satisfaction will be diminished.

Courtship

During the courtship, the spouses-to-be may struggle with a number of tasks simultaneously. In addition to finding and starting their careers, they must choose a mate to marry. A major problem which can occur at this stage is the failure of the prospective spouses to honestly communicate to each other their expectations for the proposed marriage since they are both trying to win the love of the other. There may be an irresistible tendency for both to put their best selves forward, to hide their more undesirable traits and to avoid bringing up issues which might cause an argument and threaten the continuation of their budding relationship. It is as if each lover thinks, "Now is not the time to bring up potentially serious disagreements. Besides, as soon as we're married, I can get the other person to change." Needless to say, this kind of thinking can create false expectations and lay the groundwork for later serious problems. No one should enter a marriage thinking, "This person is not fully acceptable to me now. He or she will have to change."

Early Marriage

There is much to be done during the early marriage. After the delights of the honeymoon, the couple has to settle down to the very serious business of learning to live together. They must define the nature and parameters of their relationship, and this they may do through many fights and tears. Both partners must state and accommodate their positions. Both must make some major adjustments as they integrate two sets of values, past experiences and behavior patterns into a smoothly functioning unit which will be capable of meeting the needs of both. And they had better accomplish this before their first child commands so much of their time, energy and attention.

Birth of the First Child

Alas, the birth of the first child is not always the blessed event we imagine it to be. The new mother and father have major adjustments to make. They have to make room for another human being who is totally dependent upon them for her very survival. They have to create an effective parental subsystem which will drain time and energy from the newly formed spousal subsystem. They have to nurture an infant yet continue to insure their own needs are met.

If the foundation for a good marriage has not been set during the preceding early marriage stage, the stress at this time could be more than the marriage could bear. And if the couple conceived a child in the hopes he or she would save their troubled marriage, the chances are good their marriage will be further strained, and perhaps cut asunder, by the birth of their first born.

Middle Childhood

The middle childhood stage, which includes both the pre-school and school age years, begins the process which hopefully will result in the successful emancipation of the child during the leaving home stage. This is the time when the child begins to develop and test his separate sense of identity. Although this is a healthy, normal process, it can be very stressful for the parents as every parent of a two year old knows. At this stage, mother and father must respect the growing sense of selfhood of their child but still remain in control. They must establish firm discipline with their child yet provide a loving atmosphere in which he or she can grow. In effect, they must balance the seemingly conflicting requirements of providing love and discipline for their child.

It is at this stage that many families will be referred for problems with a child. Any unresolved marital problems which may exist at this time will only exacerbate whatever problems they are having with a child.

Adolescence

Although it doesn't have to be and sometimes is not, adolescence is often the period of storm and stress we read about. There are major changes taking place at this time to which everyone in the family must adjust. As the children mature, they will naturally seek more independence from their parents which may result in more conflicts between parents and offspring. As an example of how critical it is to master the tasks of one stage before proceeding successfully on to the next, if the parents have not established firm disciplinary practices with their children during the middle childhood stage, they'll have a much more difficult, if not impossible, time controlling their offspring during adolescence.

Rarely can the parents of an adolescent give him the commands they could when he was a child. The most they can do is to set certain limits and serve in an advisory capacity. They can warn him of the risks to health of smoking, for example, and forbid him to smoke in the house but they can't forbid him to smoke all the time and back up that prohibition since he can light up as soon as he is out of sight. Similarly, parents cannot absolutely forbid their adolescent to see certain friends. Again, they can express their concern about the potentially negative influence of those friends, and forbid them in their home, but they cannot prevent her from visiting with them in school.

As if it is not enough that the parents may be having more conflicts with their teenagers, they are probably also struggling with their own midlife adjustments at this time. While their children are young, healthy, possibly sexually active and full of excess energy, the parents may be feeling more tired and becoming more aware of their own physical decline. They may also be facing the end of the occupational dreams of their youths through the growing realization they've gone as far as they can in their careers. This may also be a time when they begin to face the loss of their own parents through death, leaving them as the older generation.

Leaving Home

Leaving home is the stage which began this series, but this time we shall consider it from the point of view of the parents and not their offspring. If it is the task of youth at this stage to emancipate themselves from their parents, it is the task of the parents to let them go but still provide them with a home base of love and support. To do this successfully, the parents must be able to accomplish two tasks: to adjust to the loss of their roles as fulltime parents and to re-establish their marriage in a home that is much quieter and perhaps less stressful. In other words, they must find something else to do with the time and energy which are no longer devoted to full time parental duties. And they must maintain their spousal relationship in the face of the diminution of their parental responsibilities. If they have stayed together "for the sake of the children," they may divorce at this time.

Retirement

There are two major adjustments to be made during the retirement years. The first is a reduction in prestige, a sense of usefulness and income associated with the loss of employment. Both spouses are home now and must become accustomed to spending more time together. Both must find alternative interests to occupy their time and attention. Successful retirees are those who are able to stay busy and become involved in hobbies or work other than their lifetime careers.

The second adjustment during the retirement years may be the most difficult to make. Parents must adjust to the death of friends, spouses and themselves.

TROUBLED FAMILY FUNCTIONING

We have already noted in the last chapter how the behavior of the symptom bearer is potentially adaptive. It represents an attempt by the symptom bearer to express the family's pain, to have his needs met and/or to insure the continued functioning of the family. We assume that everyone suffers from the behavior of the symptom bearer yet everyone benefits from it also. The symptomatic behavior is painful to all family members yet somehow they derive some advantages from it otherwise the behavior would not be maintained.

A few examples should suffice to illustrate this:

Mother is caught between her husband who complains to her about the children and the children who complain to her about their stepfather. While this middle position can be extremely uncomfortable for her, at the same time it provides her with tremendous leverage in the family. She is the central switchboard through which most of the communication in the family flows. As such, she is placed in a very important position in which she is needed by both sides.

The symptom bearer usually receives much blame and anger from the family because of his misbehavior. However, at times this places him at the center of attention which may be better than no attention at all. Moreover, if he is perceived as "sick" by the family members, rather than "bad," he may receive sympathy and care from one or more family members.

If the symptom bearer is a child, her siblings may be embarrassed by her problems and resent the extra parental attention she receives. However, they may be glad the spotlight of parental concern or anger is not on them. The target child also provides them with a standard by which they can favorably compare themselves.

The parents may be genuinely worried about the misbehavior of one of their offspring but relieved their worries prevent them from facing their own very serious marital problems.

A socially isolated, single-parent mother may have horrendous discipline problems with her children. As each reaches a certain age, each either runs away or has to be placed out of the home. Mother is genuinely stressed by the misbehavior of her children, but it rouses her from her periodic bouts of depression, provides her with a sense of purpose and gives her her major social contacts with other people at the helping agencies she has been going to for years.

If it is true that there are benefits to the family members provided by the behavior of the symptom bearer, then it follows that there may be some risks in family therapy. The cure may be worse than the disease. To make some improvements in the symptom bearer may expose other, more serious family problems or precipitate another family crisis. Mother could become depressed, for example, the marriage could be severely threatened or another family member could become the symptom bearer. As a family therapist, you must be prepared to deal with these other problems should they surface.

Hoffman (1981) addresses these possibilities and raises some questions which all family therapists must consider in dealing with each case:

> A new problem may be a less life-threatening or serious problem than the first, *or* (a very big *or*) it may not. Will the "good" sibling become a "bad" sibling if the "bad" sibling reforms? Or will the marriage which seemed to depend for its unity on the worry caused by the sick child, go on the rocks? Or will the mother become seriously depressed if the psychotic son regains his sanity and moves toward independence? The negative consequences of not having a symptom can be (although they don't have to be) at least as serious as the seriousness of the symptom, and any therapist who works with an entire family begins literally to ask: Is it better or worse for this family not to have this problem? If I tamper with it, will I be able to handle the consequences?

These are very serious and weighty questions indeed.

Here in all its stark power is the concept of homeostasis which many family therapists assume operates in the life of the family. The symptomatic behavior of the symptom bearer is maintained because it serves some useful function in the family. Thus, attempts to change the behavior may be resisted by the family. The family members may not want to change for fear of the consequences of changing. And as Hoffman's quote above suggests, *that fear may be realistic.*

As a family therapist, you must look at the concept of resistance from the family's point of view. You must see it not as stubbornness, stupidity or problems with authority but as a process which is motivated by fear of the unknown. The family members are not necessarily being obstinate, ignorant or resistive; they're being cautious and perhaps for good reasons. They have something which has worked for the family in the past, and they're not as convinced as you are that something else will work better in the future.

Change is threatening for everyone. None of us changes unless we have to. But it is probably safe to assume that the more dysfunctional the family, the more resistant the members will be to change.

Not all family therapists accept the concept of homeostatis, however. Jacobson (1981), for example, maintains that "resistance" is not a valid process, that the family must be motivated to change by the skill and enthusiasm of the therapist. And with mildly troubled families, he may be right. In other words, it may be that the more troubled the family, the more powerful is the operation of homeostasis and so the more you will have to work to overcome it. By contrast, the less disturbed the family, the less the fear of change and so the better the prognosis.

If it is true the family resists change and if the symptomatic behavior serves some type of homeostatic function, what finally forces the members to seek the professional help they would rather not have? The answer, perhaps harshly but simply put, is emotional pain. The family finds itself in a crisis in which what has worked in the past is no longer as effective. The crisis may take several forms: mother's depression becomes worse; mother and father have an argument and father leaves; the oldest son is arrested for shoplifting, expelled from school or charged with drunken driving; mother begins to beat her daughter and can't stop until the middle child intervenes.

In contrast to the family's view of it, crisis is a positive event, your therapeutic ally in the battle for change. It is rarely possible to bring about change in a family's functioning without it. Crisis and the pain which accompanies it are what motivate the family members to come to and remain in therapy. Just as physical pain worries people and tells them something must be done medically, so emotional pain signals to them something must be done psychotherapeutically. Emotional pain says to the family, "It's no longer working for us. We have to find other ways to function."

If a family is not in crisis, their motivation to change may be minimal. Although you can point out the consequences of not changing to a family headed for a crisis, there is probably little else you can do until that crisis arrives as the following clinical example suggests:

The Smith family was seen for problems with their teenage son, Bill. The therapist suspected some serious problems in the family and set up another appointment with them. However, the family did not show up the next week. When telephoned, mother gave a weak excuse why they missed their appointment and indicated she was no longer interested in therapy.

Six months later, a surprised and sleepy therapist was awakened by an early morning call from the mother who was frantic because her son was in jail for running away. Since the entire family was in crisis, the members were willing to work hard to make some needed changes in the family. What would have been impossible six months before—the successful completion of family therapy—came to fruition this time because of a crisis situation.

In effect, the family has been doing fine until the moment of crisis. Their family functioning may not have been optimal but it has been adequate for them. The family members have been able to limp along until some added stress is too much for their resources to bear. That stress can come in one of two ways: either an unanticipated event such as father being fired, mother coming down with a serious illness, a divorce or an unexpected death, or a developmental task the family is unable to master. It is the latter category of unresolved developmental tasks that explains why a knowledge of the developmental stages in the family life cycle is essential for you as a family therapist. The following examples should illustrate some of the crises which may occur at a particular developmental stage:

An able and intelligent twenty-one-year-old won't find himself a job or leave home so he lies around most of the day while his parents continue to support him.

The fighting of newlyweds becomes frequent and intense because their expectations for the marriage are not being fulfilled.

Father feels left out after the birth of his first child and so withdraws from his wife sexually and emotionally. Just recovering from a post-partum depression, she feels overwhelmed by her new responsibilities.

A school-age child develops a school phobia. His mother, a lonely and depressed woman, really doesn't mind his staying home to keep her company.

The arguing between the parents and their rebellious adolescent is becoming more bitter. The more they crack down on him, the more he rebels especially since he is not accustomed to consistent discipline from them.

An unhappy marriage of twenty-five years verges on the brink of divorce after the youngest child goes away to college.

A husband becomes depressed after he retires because he has so little to do. His wife becomes depressed after his death and dies soon afterwards.

What these examples illustrate is the failure to master the developmental tasks of one stage may be due to the failure to master the tasks in the preceding stage or stages. To be alive is to be stressed and subject to pressure to change. Life moves along its inexorable course. Those who cannot keep up with its demands fall behind. It is your function to attempt to prevent this from happening by getting the family unstuck and flowing with life again.

At these times of crisis—whether expected or developmental— change is required but resisted because it is unknown and therefore frightening. Paradoxically, at a time when it is resisted, change may be exactly what is needed to keep the family intact. The behavior of the symptom bearer may be calling for change when the family homeostatic mechanisms are pressuring for stability.

The degree of dysfunction in the family will be a function of two factors: the general level of health of the family and the intensity of the crisis to which members are subjected. Even the healthiest of families will develop some symptoms if they are subject to enough stress. However, they will be able to bounce back more quickly once the stress is removed than dysfunctional families will be.

In considering dysfunctional families, Skynner (1981) distinguishes between three types: those which produce severely dysfunctional children, those which produce midrange functioning children and those which produce healthy children. Severely dysfunctional children are those who are labeled as chronic schizophrenics or sociopaths. They come from chaotic families in which the dysfunctional child is usually aligned with the mother to the exclusion of the father. Communication in such families is vague, confused and contradictory. Burdened by a highly unsatisfactory marriage, there is a pervasive mood of hostility, depression and/or hopelessness in the family.

Midrange functioning children are those who are labeled as reactive psychotics, behavior disorders or neurotics. Control in the midrange family is usually rigid with the parents either competing for power or one of them dominant. The marriage is poor while family members feel isolated from one another.

Communication is better than in the families producing severely dysfunctional children but still troubled. A mood of unhappiness pervades the family atmosphere.

The point of this description of the two types of disturbed families is that the severely dysfunctional families usually display problems which require treatment most, if not all, of the time. They're usually known by several helping agencies and their files at each agency are at least an inch thick. These are the families with chronic problems who may have to be continually treated or monitored.

The midrange families, by contrast, can function adequately most of the time and do not seek or require treatment until a family crisis forces them to do so. The members can usually be successfully treated and then terminated as a case until another crisis arises.

What this analysis of family pathology and family stress suggests is that the diagnosis and treatment of any family problem should be threefold:

—You should do whatever you can to work directly on the specific presenting problem. It is the reason why the family came in to therapy in the first place. They'll expect the presenting problem to be the focus of your concern. If you do not pay sufficient attention to it because of your belief that other family problems are more important, the family members may soon find another therapist or drop out of therapy altogether.

—You should do whatever you can to reduce the stress the family is experiencing. To do this, you may have to refer them to another agency such as an employment agency if father needs a job, a relief agency if they need financial support or a drug and alcohol counselor if alcoholism is a problem in the family.

—You should do whatever you can to strengthen the coping and problem solving skills of the family. To do this, you may have to work on communication skills, negotiation skills, discipline or the expression of love in the family. Ideally, your goal should be to move the severely dysfunctional family to the midrange level of functioning so it won't have to be monitored most of the time, or to move the midrange family to health so it can handle most crises by itself.

By way of an analogy, the capacity of a dam to contain the water behind it depends upon two factors: the strength of the dam and the level of the water. Engineers can prevent the dam from breaking by insuring it remains strong and by preventing the water behind it from getting too high. Similarly, you can prevent the family from breaking down by strengthening it and by helping to reduce the stress on it.

Interestingly, in a dysfunctional family not all of the children are affected by the family pathology in the same manner or to the same degree. For whatever reasons, the other children do not become the target child or are not involved in the parents' conflicts. The target child may fall into his position because of factors over which he has no control: his sex, age, birth order or resemblance to someone else of significance to his parents. In addition, the other children learn what to do to avoid trouble by observing the frequent punishment of the target child. They may also have sources of support outside of the family or simply try to withdraw from the family.

PATTERNS

One of the most important concepts for you to understand about families is that the members become stuck in almost lawful patterns of behavior which they repeat over and over again. These patterns are usually beyond their awareness which is why it is so difficult for the family members to change them. Often, they have been passed down from previous generations so the patterns found in the family of origin may also be found in the family of procreation. The effects of early modeling on human functioning are powerful. When under stress, people cling to what they've witnessed or done in the past, no matter how ineffective their behavior patterns may be. Your function as a family therapist is to identify these patterns and attempt to modify them especially if they are preventing the family from finding better ways to relate to each other.

The patterns to be discussed below are cycles, rules, roles, triangles and relationships.

Cycles

Our Judeo-Christian heritage has accustomed us to think in terms of linear causation but to be an effective family therapist, you should think in terms of circular causation. In linear causation, time and causation flow in a straight line. The past is replaced by the present which will flow into the future. Moreover, human history moves in a linear fashion as humankind progresses in its journey through time.

By contrast, Eastern philosophies are more attuned to the idea of circularity in human history. Events re-occur in cyclical manner. Life involves endless rounds of birth and death until it finally ceases in Nirvana.

In linear causation, A causes B which causes C. The pool player pushes the cue stick which strikes the cue ball which hits the eight ball. In linear causation, A is at fault; A can be blamed. After all, he started it all. Johnny is at fault for hitting his little sister. Mrs. Smith is to blame for filing for a divorce from her husband.

In circular causation, by contrast, A causes B and B causes A. A and B reciprocally influence each other. Johnny hit his little sister but she poked him in response to his teasing. Mrs. Smith is the one who filed for a divorce but she and her husband have been hurting each other for years.

Circular causation plays a prominent role in family functioning. It accounts for the "stuckness" family therapists see in many families. It is what drives the repetitive patterns of behavior from which family members are unable to entangle themselves.

Circular causation also means that in families there are no heroes and villians, no good guys and bad guys. One cannot point a finger at A and say he started it because his behavior has been influenced by B. Conversely, one cannot point to B and say she started it because she has been influenced by A. The concept of blame, though foreign to most therapists, is an important consideration to family members coming to therapy. They would like to blame someone for the family's problems, usually the symptom bearer, or they are afraid they will be blamed by the therapist. However, because of his knowledge of circular causation, the therapist, as we have said before, believes either no one is to blame or if blame must be ascribed, everyone is to blame.

Although there are undoubtedly more, we have identified five patterns of circular causation—which we call cycles—in many troubled families who come to the Family Teaching Center.

Probably the most common cycle in pained human relationships is what we call the mutual hurt, anger and blaming cycle. This cycle is commonly seen in deteriorating marital relationships and in strained relationships between parents and their adolescent or adult offspring.

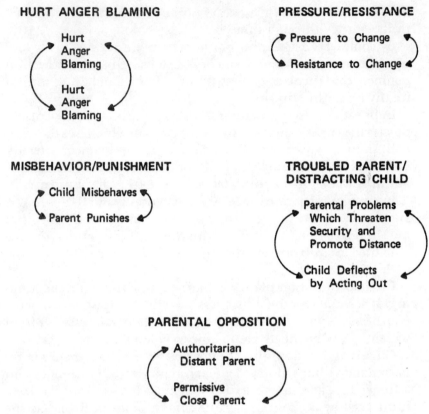

Figure 1. Five types of family cycles in which family members reciprocally influence each other's behavior.

It doesn't matter who started this cycle or how it started. The point is it has now become self-perpetuating. Each person in the cycle feels hurt but that hurt is expressed as anger and blaming. When emotional pain is strong, each victim believes the best defense is a good offense. To admit to hurt would take courage because it risks the possibility of further hurt, so each attacks instead. Such an attack only hurts the other person who attacks in return. Each becomes more defensive as the attacks escalate. With increasing defensiveness, the possibility of empathizing with the pain of the other, and of breaking out of the mutual hurt, anger and blaming cycle, becomes greatly diminished.

A second cycle we see at the Family Teaching Center we call the pressure/resistance cycle. Pressure for change is met with resistance to change which further increases the pressure to change and so on. The more the intimacy seeking spouse pressures her spouse for closeness, for example, the more uncomfortable he becomes and so the more he withdraws. The more he withdraws, the more anxious she becomes and so the more she pressures for intimacy. The more that worried parents pressure their rebellious adolescent to conform, as another example, the more she rebels which frightens them into pressuring her to conform even more. Or the more they criticize her boyfriend, the more attractive he becomes in her eyes.

It is this type of cycle which underlies the paradoxical techniques to be discussed later in this book. (See Chapter 13.) The best way to handle this cycle is either to back off on the pressure to change or go to the opposite extreme of encouraging the behavior you want changed.

A slight variant of this cycle is what we call the punishment/ misbehavior cycle. When a child misbehaves, most parents will punish him. If he misbehaves more, they'll punish him more. And if he continues to misbehave, they'll continue to punish him but with increasing frustration, anger and harsher punishments. Soon, the child may perceive himself as isolated, picked on and blamed in the family, which he acts out in more misbehavior, which brings more punishment and anger from the family.

What we frequently find in families with misbehaving youths is that they do receive more negative responses from their parents—anger, yelling, criticism, correction and punishment— than positive responses—hugs, kisses, I love you's, praise, appreciation and rewards—so their perceptions of themselves as isolated and picked on is accurate. What they fail to see is how their behavior contributes to reactions they receive. Frankly, some of these children can be brats. At times, their behavior hurts their parents as much as they feel their parents are hurting them.

Obviously treatment of the punishment/misbehavior cycle must be twofold: the disruptive behavior which brings so much punishment must be brought under control using behavioral technologies but the pained parent-child relationship must be changed as well. Although we don't abandon the use of punishment at the Family Teaching Center, we do try to reverse the preponderance of negative parent-child interactions over positive interactions. In effect, we have the parents say to the child, "We love you very much, and we want you to be a part of this family, but your misbehavior must stop."

Yet another variant of the pressure/resistance cycle is the troubled parent/distracting child cycle. In contrast to the punishment/misbehavior cycle in which the parents attempt to change the behavior of the child, in this cycle the child tries to change the behavior of the parent. Unfortunately, in both cycles, the attempted solution to the problem only tends to make things worse.

A common example of this cycle is when the parents are having marital problems, the child draws their attention away from those problems by misbehaving. Their fighting threatens his security, so whenever they have a bad argument he becomes anxious and acts out his anxiety in misbehavior. Although not consciously planned by the child, the effect of his misbehavior is to bring the parents together to respond to him. They can't simultaneously deal with their marital problems and his misbehavior. This tactic may work for awhile in keeping the parents together to help their child, but in the long run it puts more strain on an already strained relationship.

The same situation occurs with a depressed parent and an acting out child. The child's behavior may succeed in rousing his mother from her depression for awhile but it may also contribute to mother's sense of despair and powerlessness. With an ambivalent or rejecting parent—one who either has strongly mixed feelings about being a parent or wishes she never had a child—a young child will either cling to her or misbehave to get her attention. Either strategy will only serve to drive the parent further away, thereby increasing the insecurity of the child and escalating his attempts to get a response from her. Exactly at a time when a depressed or distressed parent needs a break is when a child is most likely to act out his anxiety over his parent's troubles.

The fifth type of cycle we frequently see at the Family Teaching Center is the parental opposition cycle. Troubled families often contain extremes but nowhere can this be more apparent than in the parents' attempts to discipline their children.

In the parental opposition cycle, the parents simply do not support each other in their disciplinary efforts. One parent is usually too authoritarian while the other is too permissive. One is strict and distant with the children while the other is protective and overinvolved. The behavior of each parent stimulates the opposite behavior of the other, however, so their different parenting styles become a self-reinforcing cycle. The authoritarian parent feels he has to be strict because the other is too lenient, while the permissive parent feels she has to protect the children from the harshness of the authoritarian parent.

Meanwhile, the children grow up without the consistent discipline of united parents.

Both parents care about their children but express that caring in opposite ways. He's convinced he's doing what's best for the children, while she's equally convinced she's doing the right thing.

Looking at such a family, it would be easy to blame the authoritarian parent for the children's problems because he is too strict and distant. It would also be easy to blame the permissive parent for being too lenient and overinvolved. But examining this family from a systems perspective, and being aware of the nature of circular causation, you would have to take the position that both parents contribute to their failure to achieve agreement about disciplinary matters. Obviously, one of the things we try to do with such families at the Family Teaching Center is to have the parents agree about rules and consequences. The more they can support each other in their disciplinary efforts, the better their chances of gaining the children's compliance to family rules.

Rules

Another type of pattern found in families are the family rules. These are not the explicit, agreed upon or written down type of rules which say the garbage goes out on Tuesdays or Dad plays golf every Saturday afternoon. Rather they are the unspoken, implicit, covert rules for family conduct. No one has ever spelled out these rules in detail but everyone knows about them. They are designed to deal with conflict or strong emotions in a homeostatic way. To violate a family rule is to be met with pressure from the family members to return to "normal" or expected behavior.

A good way for you to uncover some of the family rules is to ask yourself what is forbidden in this family. What does this family do when faced with too much conflict or emotions which are too strong to restore its previous level of functioning? What homeostatic pressures are used to change the deviant behavior? Some examples of family rules are:

1. Don't express strong emotions in this family.
2. Conflict is to be avoided at all costs. We're a happy family.
3. Don't argue with your father, especially when he's upset.
4. Don't take responsibility for your own behavior. When blamed, blame someone else.
5. When in doubt, blame Joey.
6. Don't make any decisions or take responsibility for your decisions.
7. Don't talk about certain issues.
8. Don't be different.
9. Don't leave the family.
10. You must live the life we have planned for you.

The problem with these rules is the same as the problem with all symptomatic behavior: they work to keep the family functioning by avoiding conflicts or strong emotions but they prevent the family members from developing more effective communication and problem solving skills. Like any other symptoms, they are effective but only partially so. Thus, the members cling to them but miss the opportunity to discover new ways to interact as a family.

As a family therapist, it's not easy to deal with family rules. Once you've recognized them, you should begin to violate them, otherwise you won't help the family change, but if you violate them too quickly or too frequently, the family may drop out of therapy claiming you're weird or don't understand them. Your job is to help the family become aware of and change its rules but to do so slowly and gradually.

Roles

Roles are behaviors covertly assigned to, or assumed by, individuals in the family which they are expected to display with regularity. Most family members have roles assigned to them which are relatively benign: the family jokester, the scholar, the athlete, the messy one, the neat one, the chatterbox or the quiet one. However, the more disturbed the family, the less benign these roles may become.

Satir (1972) has developed a model of troubled family functioning which involves four roles. The blamer is the angry one who defends himself by his blustering and blaming of others. The placater is the one who tries to please others and avoid conflict at all costs. The super-reasonable person in the family coolly brings dispassionate reason to situations which are anything but dispassionate or subject to reason. The irrelevant person tries to distract the family from its serious problems by her silly antics.

Wegscheider (1981) describes five roles in the alcoholic family. The enabler is usually the non-alcoholic spouse who enables the alcoholic to keep drinking by unintentionally protecting him from the negative consequences of his alcohol consumption. The hero is usually the oldest child whose high grades, outstanding achievements and exemplary behavior give the family members a source of pride to distract them from the pain of the alcoholic's drinking. Likewise, the negative behavior of the scapegoat draws the family members' attention away from the real source of their pain. The lost child is the quiet child who withdraws into solitary pursuits to escape the unhappiness in her alcoholic family, while the mascot is similar to Satir's (1972) irrelevant family member.

Two roles we see in troubled families which concern us are what we call the blamed scapegoat and the good child. The word scapegoat is an old Jewish term which refers to the ancient Hebrew practice of placing the sins of the community unto a goat and driving it into the desert. In the modern troubled family, however, the family members do not want the scapegoat to go away for she serves a useful function. Typically, most of the family problems are blamed on the scapegoat as a way to avoid responsibility for them. The blamed scapegoat usually, but not always, falls nicely into this role by becoming the symptom bearer for the family. Feeling isolated and scapegoated, she may act out in anger or withdraw in depression. In either event, she may be labeled as disturbed, the cause of all the family's problems and in need of individual treatment.

Lest it sound as if the role of blamed scapegoat is entirely burdensome, it must be remembered there are advantages to this role as there are to every symptomatic behavior. The scapegoat receives much attention, even if it is negative in nature, but negative attention is better than no attention at all. Moreover, the scapegoat has considerable control in the family. Her misbehavior can usually elicit immediate and powerful responses from the family members.

In dealing with the blamed scapegoat, we try to spread the family's problems around and not have them lodged in one person only. We can't do this too quickly or too radically, however, otherwise the family might decide we really don't understand their situation. Two things we do are to look for other problems in the family—and they're usually there—and to relabel the scapegoat's misbehavior as both positive and interactional rather than negative and individual. In other words, we attempt to point out that the symptomatic behavior has some positive benefits for the family and indicate by our insisting on seeing every one in the family that the problem is the family's problem, not just the scapegoat's problem.

Another family role we're concerned about at the Family Teaching Center is the good child or what Wegscheider (1981) calls the hero. She is usually a sibling who obeys her parents explicitly, does all her chores on time and earns straight A's. Although she may not appear to have any problems of her own, and indeed is often held up as a good example to the target child, we assume she's under pressure to behave. If she doesn't, she may fear losing her parents' approval as has the scapegoat. She may also feel that she has to be good to make up for all the pain the target child has caused their parents. She also unwittingly plays into the misbehavior of the scapegoat by her good example. He may also compare himself unfavorably to her and decide either he can't match her achievements, or to be just the opposite of her because he'll be damned if he'll ever be like her!

With the good child, we try to lighten her burden somewhat by letting her and her parents know she doesn't have to be perfect to be loved and that she can make mistakes and still be O.K.

Triangles

According to the theory of triangulation, whenever two people are in conflict, they will tend to involve a third person either as a scapegoat to avoid the conflict or as an ally to help them win it. The third person does not have to be present to be part of the triangle as the following clinical example shows:

> A single parent mother and her oldest teenage daughter were in the midst of a fight when the therapist arrived for a home visit. Sensing the tension between them, he asked the other, younger children to leave so he could deal directly with the conflict without interruptions. However, both mother and daughter began immediately to talk about one of the mother's other children as a way to avoid dealing directly with one another. The therapist stopped this

interaction and asked them to come back to a discussion of their
disagreement. This they did for awhile but then both switched to
complaining about the father who lived in another town and
hadn't contacted the children in months.

In the first instance, mother and daughter triangulated a family
member who was still in the family but not physically present,
while in the second instance, they triangulated someone who was
no longer a committed member of the family.

Assuming the conflict is between mother and father, as it
usually is in troubled families, there are three types of triangles
which can be stressful for a child caught in them.

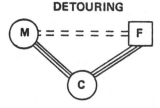

Figure 2. Three types of family triangles. Broken line represents broken
communication, triple lines represent overinvolvement, single line represents underinvolvement and double dashed lines represent pseudo-intimacy.

In the double bind triangle, both parents are overinvolved with
the child. Because of their frustration with each other, both
parents implicitly ask the child to be either a confidant to comfort
them in their marital troubles or an ally to side with them against
the other parent. Whatever their parents' request, the effect of the
double bind triangle on the child is devastatingly the same. She is
placed in an impossible, no win situation in which she is asked to

choose between two people both of whom she loves. If she's young, she cannot withdraw from the field of battle because she is dependent on both her parents. But if she chooses to side with one, she is, in effect, rejecting the other.

This is the type of triangle which can be especially deadly in divorces or bitter custody battles. Sometimes, the parents will use their children to retaliate against or spy on each other. When the children visit father, for example, he may want to tell them "what your mother is really like" or how she's to blame for the divorce. Of he'll grill them about what their mother is doing or who she's dating. Of course, mother may do the same thing as soon as the children arrive back after their visit with father. The children soon receive the message they're weapons in their parents' continuing battles. In effect, they're being used as objects of war rather than being cared for as persons with feelings and needs of their own.

In the odd person out triangle, one parent is overinvolved with the triangulated child, while the other is underinvolved. Because of her marital dissatisfaction, mother may be overinvolved with her son, while father, feeling left out of the family, may have buried himself in his work. Or he may be overinvolved with another child with whom the mother is underinvolved, causing a split in the family with one child siding with one parent and the other child siding with the other.

In the detouring triangle, both parents deny there are any problems in their marriage. Everything's just fine with them; it's Johnny who has the problem. He's either "sick" or "bad," so they both must be overinvolved with him. What you should suspect in this type of triangle are marital problems which are either being covered up or avoided by the child's problems. Mother and father can't possibly find the time to deal with their own problems when they're spending so much time on Johnny's problems. In point of fact, they may be frightened to face their marital difficulties for fear they might prove insurmountable. Better that Johnny should be troubled than that they might split up.

There are certain things you should do in working with family triangles. First and most important of all, don't become triangulated yourself. To do so would be to lose most, if not all, of your effectiveness as a therapist to the entire family. If you must take sides, be on the side of mental health.

Second, you should try to reduce or eliminate all triangles since they are ineffective ways to solve conflicts and stress on children who are caught in them. To do this, you want to weaken some dyadic relationships and strengthen others. First and foremost, the marital dyad should be strengthened if possible. Its dysfunction is often the root cause of the excessive need to triangulate the children in families. Then work to have the underinvolved parent become more involved with the child and to help the overinvolved parent or parents become less involved. Ideally, a good family structure would involve a strong bond of love and respect between the parents with each parent having a secure, caring relationship with each child.

In weakening some dyads and attempting to strengthen others, however, you must be careful. You cannot ask someone to become less involved in one relationship without gaining or strengthening another relationship. If you want mother to be less involved with a child, for example, you must help her have her needs met in another relationship, ideally with her husband if she is married.

Relationships

At the Family Teaching Center, we find certain relatively constant parent-child relationships in disturbed families which we label enmeshed, distant, ambivalent and rejecting.

An enmeshed parent-child relationship is one in which the implicit message to the child is usually, "Don't grow up and leave me for then I'll be all alone." Because of her own social isolation—due either to her single state or an unhappy marriage—the parent is overly dependent upon her child for the satisfaction of her social and emotional needs. This makes it difficult, if not impossible, for the child to grow up to be a healthy, independent adult as demonstrated by the following clinical example:

As a socially isolated, single parent, Jill's mother was extremely overprotective with her. For years, she missed many days of school, allegedly because she was ill but actually because mother kept her home whenever she complained of not feeling well even though two pediatricians diagnosed her as a medically healthy girl.

Finally, because family therapy failed to do so, the school authorities recommended residential treatment to disrupt the enmeshed parent-child relationship. In a humorous vein, the consulting psychiatrist stated that what was needed in this case was a "parentdectomy."

Although usually overinvolved and overprotective, the enmeshed parent-child relationship may involve extreme hostility, especially if the enmeshed parent depends upon his child for his sense of worth. The following clinical example illustrates this process:

> Father was extremely critical of his ten year old son which resulted in bitter conflict between them. In an individual session, he admitted he thought of himself as a failure in his job and marriage and was frightened if his boy turned out badly, he would really consider himself to be completely inadequate.

Your treatment of an enmeshed relationship should involve the attempt to create some distance between the parent and the child. To do this—and frankly, it is not easy—you have to help the parent find other sources of satisfaction and worth in life and to encourage the child to behave more independently.

A distant parent-child relationship is one in which the implicit message to the child is, "Don't be a bother." The parent cares about the child but does not express his caring fully either in words or attention. Often, when one parent is enmeshed with a child, the other is distant, creating the odd person triangle described above. In contrast to your attempt to weaken an enmeshed relationship, your treatment of a distant relationship should consist of an attempt to strengthen it, to bring the parent and child closer together.

An ambivalent parent-child relationship is probably the most distressing for the child. Since the parent is truly ambivalent in her feelings towards her child—part of her wanting to be a loving mother and part of her wanting to party instead—the child receives double messages from her, one which says, "I love you" and the other which says, "Go away." Insecure because he is not sure how she really does feel, the child may act out to gain attention from his parent, an action which only serves to drive her further away.

Outpatient treatment of an ambivalent parent-child relationship is usually twofold. First, you may be able to strengthen that part of the parent who wants to be a good parent by empathizing with her difficulties with him. Give her permission to say she doesn't want her child and she may come to realize she does love him. Go after the negative and you may draw out the positive in her.

In no case, should you insist that the ambivalent parent love her child and be a more responsible parent. Such an action would probably stiffen her resistance to your suggestions or make her feel even more guilty than she already does.

Second, whatever you can do to reduce the misbehavior of the child using behavioral technologies will strengthen the parent's sense of herself as a competent parent and reduce the tension between her and the child. Failing these strategies, the child in an ambivalent relationship may have to be treated intensively in an inpatient setting.

The rejecting parent-child relationship is one in which the implicit message to the child is, "Don't be." The parent wishes he never had the child and has no real interest in being an effective parent.

Like the child in the ambivalent relationship, the rejected child may require intensive inpatient treatment because of the magnitude of trauma to him. But unlike the partially loved child, at least he has something concrete to work on since he knows how he stands with his parents. Treatment should involve an attempt to help him realize he is not responsible for his parents' rejection of him. Because he is not loved by his parents does not mean he is unloveable, an attitude which may take years to develop.

Chapter 4

HOW FAMILY THERAPISTS FUNCTION

Y ears ago, a friend of mine courted a young woman hoping she would marry him. She would not. Later, she agreed to his proposal but he had changed his mind and didn't want to marry her. So she began to pressure him to marry, whereupon he decided he would wed her. However, she then changed her mind and didn't want to marry him!

Watzlawick, Weakland and Fisch (1974) call this an example of first order change. In first order change, although there may be a flurry of activity and the appearance of change, there really is no change. In effect, the more things change, the more they stay the same.

First, my friend pursued his girlfriend, then she pursued him, then he pursued her. Despite all the pursuing, their relationship remained the same. They always stayed the same distance from each other—intimate but not intimate enough to marry—no matter whether he was courting her or she was courting him.

Another example of first order change involves the nuclear arms race. Each side builds up its weaponry in response to a perceived increase in nuclear weapons by the other side. An increase by one side is matched by a buildup by the other side which spurs an increase by the first side. But the more things change—i.e., the more each adds to its arsenal—the more things remain the same—i.e., neither side gains an advantage. Although there are many more weapons in the world, the difference in the nuclear arsenals of the two superpowers remains slight or non-existent.

A third example of first order change is described by Watzlawick, Weakland and Fisch (1974) and involves a nightmare in which the dreamer is chased by a bear. No matter how hard he runs to get away from the bear, he can't as long as he keeps dreaming of being chased. But let him wake up and, poof, the bear and the danger will be gone. Which brings us to what these authors call second order change.

In second order change, there is a change which is introduced from outside the system. The introduction of change may seem paradoxical or contradictory to those inside but that is because it is introduced externally. The same rules no longer apply because new rules have been introduced, allowing for genuine change.

In the case of my friend, he found another girlfriend and so broke off completely with his first girlfriend. In the case of the nuclear arms race, if alien beings from outer space were to threaten an invasion of the earth, the Soviet and American governments would become instant allies, united against a common foe as we were in the period, 1941 to 1945. In the case of the dreamer who can't escape from the charging bear, he can do so by waking up.

The point of this discussion is that the interactions we have been describing above cannot change without some external intervention. Second order change, which is a genuine change, is not possible without it.

So it is with families who come to family therapy. If they were able to change by themselves, they wouldn't need a family therapist. But they can't change for a number of reasons. In family crises, emotions are usually running too high for people to be objective or fully rational. When they're upset, it is more difficult for family members to really listen to each other and to problem-solve effectively. In addition, as we noted in Chapter 3, they are afraid of change and for good reason. Change could be worse than what they have now. Their interaction may not be that good but it is partially working for them. They are understandably reluctant to give up the familiar and partially effective for the unknown and untested.

Since the family in crisis cannot change by itself, it is your function as a family therapist to create the conditions to bring about change. Entering the family system initially as a stranger from outside of it, you are a second order change agent. Families come to you with a need to change which is not forthcoming because the members don't know how to change or are afraid to change. You may run into strong resistance if you demand change or attempt to force it, but you certainly can encourage change, teach the family members how to change or point out the negative consequences of not changing. If all else fails, you can use paradoxical techniques and encourage the family not to change in the hope the members will resist your suggestion and change.

Before giving you guidelines to do family therapy, we need to talk about the differences in functioning between individual and family therapists.

INDIVIDUAL AND FAMILY THERAPY

Although there are many similarities between individual and family work, there are also major differences. While there can be some transfer of training from individual to family therapy, there also can be some interference. If you are an individual therapist making the transaction to family therapy, you must guard against the very strong temptation to do individual therapy in a family setting. Your goal should be to change the interactions among family members, in the belief that these changes will eventually benefit the individual family members. Your goals should not be to change the individual in the hope of adapting him to the family or to bring about family change through individual change.

To be effective, both the individual and family therapists must have the relationship skills necessary to form therapeutic alliances with their clients, and both must believe in themselves and their therapeutic strategies. Obviously, where they part company is when it comes to technical knowledge and skills. For the most part, the individual therapist assumes that the client's problems lie within himself, in his beliefs, memories, perceptions, emotions and behaviors. Her focus is on studying, understanding and changing an individual's internal states.

By contrast, the family therapist perceives psychological problems as lying within the interactions of the client with both her family of origin and her family of procreation. His focus is on studying, understanding and changing family patterns of interactions which, he assumes, will affect the client in a positive manner.

Because of the differences in the focus of their work, individual and family therapists also differ in whom each sees in therapy.

Although she may occasionally have collateral visits with other family members, most of the sessions provided by the individual therapist are with the individual client. The family therapist, by contrast, usually sees more than one family member in various combinations. Some family therapists insist on seeing all family members for all sessions. Others—probably the majority—will see the entire family at times, certain subsystems of the family at times and individual family members at times.

This is not to say, however, that individual therapy cannot be provided using a family systems perspective. Family therapy is as much a way to conceptualize problems as it is a treatment strategy. Although family therapists usually involve all relevant or accessible family members in treatment, sometimes this is not always possible as with, for example, a college student whose parents live five hundred miles away or an adolescent in a residential treatment program whose family has abandoned him.

In doing individual therapy with these clients, however, you can still assume a family systems perspective. You can have the client draw his family of origin, sculpt them using chairs or speak to each family member in empty chairs. In a group setting, you can ask other members of the group to play the part of different members of the client's family as he sculpts or talks to them. In these settings, you cannot change family interactions as you would attempt to do so if you were meeting with the entire family, but you can help to bring about insight and attitudinal and emotional changes as would any individual therapist.

Another difference between the family therapist and the individual therapist is that the former is usually much more active than the latter. Family therapy as practiced by most family therapists is an active, directive, take charge type of therapy. It is not a passive, accepting, client-centered, let-the-individual-enfold-at-his-own-pace type of therapy which is more often practiced in individual therapy. In contrast to the individual therapist who may be gentler and more accepting with clients, the family therapist can be perceived as downright rude and obnoxious. He is on the move, getting close to some family members at one time and to others at another time. He tells people when to talk and what to say. He interrupts some family members and ignores others. He moves people around, asking them to switch seats or sculpt how they see the family.

The family therapist can also be more forceful, deceptive and manipulative than the individual therapist. Family therapy involves not only a caring, trusting relationship between the therapist and the family members; it can also be a power struggle which the therapist must win if therapy is to be effective. It is he who may attempt to induce people into behaving in certain ways or to trap them in situations in which they may be forced to change.

Make no mistake about it. Our task as family therapists is to get people to change, to do things differently, because what they are doing now as a family is not working well for them. Being nice, using our therapeutic skills to establish therapeutic alliances, are usually not enough to get the job done. We want to come to care about people, for our caring is therapeutic, but we also want to influence, persuade and manipulate them.

Another difference between the individual therapist and the family therapist involves therapeutic caring. As the individual therapist comes to know her client deeply and intimately, she learns to like and respect him more. This enables the client to better like and respect himself. Despite the fact that he has revealed the worst in him to her, the therapist still retains a positive, accepting attitude towards him. She has not judged him in any way, except, perhaps, for his behavior. Having done so, the client can then begin to develop a positive, accepting attitude towards himself.

Although not absent in family therapy, this element of caring cannot be as strong as it is in individual therapy simply because there are more people to receive it from the therapist. Instead of trying to provide that therapeutic caring himself to all family members—an impossible task anyhow—the family therapist attempts to change the family relationships in such a way that the family members learn to care and interact with each other more effectively. In effect, the therapist wants the members of the family to meet the love and esteem needs of each other rather than his doing it for them.

It is also reasonable to assume that transference reactions are not quite the same in family therapy as they are in individual therapy. For one thing, they may not be as intense simply because there are more people interacting with the therapist. No family member has the opportunity to develop as strong a transference response to the therapist as each would in individual therapy simply because each has to share him with others. Also, the therapist's behavior discourages transference reactions simply because he attempts to have family members interact primarily with each other and secondarily with him.

For another thing, transference reactions in family therapy may differ qualitatively from transference reactions in individual therapy. Rather than develop strong emotional reactions to him, or project repressed elements upon him, what families typically do is attempt to entice the therapist to behave in ways which are consonant with their usual patterns of behavior. They will want him to confirm these patterns rather than challenge them. Or one or more of the family members will want him to take their side against other members of the family.

As a family therapist, you must resist both of these family transference reactions. Your function is to identify and disrupt those patterns of behavior which you believe are preventing the family members from finding more effective ways to interact with each other, not to confirm them. And if you consistently take sides with one or more family members, you could lose your therapeutic effectiveness with the entire family.

A problem common to both the individual and family therapists is that of countertransference responses. But perhaps the family therapist may experience them more strongly since he may deal with an entire family that reminds him of his family of origin rather than with one client who reminds him of a parent or sibling. It is in treating such families that you may not be able to be as objective as you might be with other families. Two ways for you to guard against such a possibility are to have had therapy yourself for your family of origin problems and to be in consultation with colleagues who can provide you with greater objectivity and help you to separate the past from the present.

If you experience any strong emotional reaction in your sessions with a family—be they countertransference in origin or not—we would advise you not to comment on it directly to the family member who stimulates it. Rather use your reaction to sense how other family members may feel towards one another. Two clinical examples should illustrate this process:

> The family therapist found himself intensely angry at a father who claimed he had only come in for one family session to see what

family therapy was all about and then would decide whether or not he would continue to attend further sessions. This put some performance pressure on the therapist but also gave him some empathy for the mother who had been attempting to get father into therapy for years. Not believing this to be a countertransference reaction to his own father, the therapist assumed, and later confirmed, that the anxiety and frustration he felt in dealing with the father was similar to the emotional reactions the mother had experienced in trying for years to get him to come to therapy.

It was with some anxiety that the family therapist realized he was treating a family which was uncomfortably similar to his family of origin in having a controlling mother and a passive, quiet father, but it helped to discuss it with his colleagues. Later in an individual session with the male target child, the therapist recalled what it was like for him to grow up in such a family. By doing so, he was able to elicit an agreement from the target child that their reactions to their families were similar.

GUIDELINES FOR THE FAMILY THERAPIST

Whether you are a clinician with years of experience in individual therapy or a graduate student new to the field, how can you get started in family therapy? How can you avoid making mistakes as you begin to see families?

There are four things you can do to learn the art of family therapy: receive training through workshops and courses, read as much on family therapy as you can, find an experienced family therapist who will consult with you and then start seeing families. We believe that constant consultation with colleagues is essential for the practice of family therapy. There is usually so much going on in family sessions, so many dyadic, triadic and family interactions, that consultation is necessary to help you wind your way through the mass of information, dynamics and interactions you confront in your office each day.

What follows is a list of general guidelines which we have found useful in our work with families and in our training.

1. **Join the family but do not become enmeshed or triangulated.**
In some ways, you must walk a tightrope between a therapeutic alliance with the family and triangulation. The family members should come to feel comfortable with you but they must not be able to manipulate you in the ways they manipulate each other.

Two ways the family members may attempt to manipulate you are by pressuring you to confirm rather than challenge their usual patterns of behavior or by pressuring you to take sides. We have already discussed these maneuvers above.

Joining the family, inducing the family to like and trust you, may take considerable skill and effort. It is especially important that this be done during the intake sessions so the family will be willing to come back for treatment. There are several things you can do to promote this joining process:

—Make contact with each family member at the beginning of the first session by introducing yourself and asking something about each member—e.g., name, age and what each does. At the beginning of each following session, greet each family member, ask how things are going or in some way acknowledge each member's presence.

—Whenever the chance arises, but especially initially, comment on whatever you may have in common with the family. Perhaps you're a skier also, or from the same state they're from or have children the age of their children.

—Speak at the family's intellectual, educational and social levels, using their idioms and peculiarities of speech. Be scholarly with a scholarly family and be willing to talk sports with an athletic family. Don't use terms such as reinforcement or contingencies with an intellectually limited family who might not understand what you're talking about.

—Whenever possible and appropriate, use humor with the family. It can be very therapeutic. You don't have to go telling the family members jokes but you can share a laugh with them whenever possible.

—Be pleasant, friendly and positive but don't overdo it. The family may not want to meet with you again if you are unfriendly, cold, distant, withdrawn or depressed.

However, there will be times when you will be tired, discouraged or stressed, especially if you've had an especially trying last session. Telling the family members how you feel may take the pressure off you to cover your reactions and give you a chance to ventilate. In addition, this may prevent the family members from thinking they've done something to upset you. They may realize you have the problem, and may come to appreciate you even more as a human being with feelings like their own.

Of course, you should not carry this sharing too far. Saying something to the family such as the following will probably suffice:

> If I seem a little down right now, it's because I've had a long day (or a particularly stressful session the last hour). I tell you folks this so you'll know that if I seem distant to you, it's not because of anything you've done. It's me. I'll be alright in a few minutes.

My experience has been that most clients are very accepting of this kind of confession. Many claim they appreciate my sharing my humanness with them.

In sum, as a family therapist, you must be part of two worlds: the family's world and the world of greater health. One part of you must be with the family, empathizing with their struggles and feeling their emotional pain. But another side of you must be on the side of change and greater family effectiveness. And you must not allow the family to suck you too far into their world of pathology. Instead, it will be your function to bring them over to the world of greater health.

2. Proceed slowly with haste.

This guideline is purposefully written in a contradictory manner because it indicates another difficult position you can encounter in family therapy. Just as you must walk a tightrope between joining the family and not becoming enmeshed in it, so you must walk a tightrope between setting an acceptable pace in therapy and not moving too fast. On the one hand, you must deal directly and effectively with the family's presenting problems if the members are to experience some success or relief and keep coming in for further sessions. They must see some progress, however slight, if they are to maintain hope. On the other hand, if you proceed too quickly in touching upon some very sensitive or difficult problems, you may scare the family members off as the following clinical examples demonstrate:

> Mother brought in her 11 year old son because he was having nightmares. The therapist soon discovered that mother had recently left father but then had returned to him even though she claimed she did not want to. Father knew nothing about the mother's appointment for the boy. When the therapist insisted he be invited to the next session, mother dropped out of therapy. Apparently, it was too threatening for her to deal directly with her marital problems.

The Browns were seen for problems with their adolescent daughter. The initial interview revealed long standing marital conflicts about which the parents appeared to be embarrassed. The day after the initial interview, mother called to ask if the therapist would see the target child only, as the rest of the family did not want to be involved in any further sessions. She also revealed that she and her husband were staying married only for the sake of the children and would probably divorce once they were grown.

When the therapist refused to see the girl for individual sessions, the mother refused to have the entire family come in to finish the diagnostic sessions. At that point, the family therapist referred the daughter to an individual therapist.

After you have obtained the basic information, your best strategy in working with any family is to explore the presenting problem in depth, then explore other areas of family functioning. If you meet serious resistance, make a mental note of the area you're exploring, back off and plan to come back to it at a later date if necessary.

For example, if you're seeing a family about problems with the children and you stumble upon serious marital problems which the parents don't want to discuss in front of the children, go on to something else. But ask again about the marriage when alone with the parents. If they still resist your inquiries, you may have to drop the subject for now. Instead, work on the presenting problem. If the children's behavior improves as a result of your work, you will have strengthened the marriage without having done marital counseling per se by having gotten the parents to agree about discipline and by having provided them with a jointly successful experience. But if your efforts to ameliorate the presenting problem do not bear fruit because of the interfering effects of the marital problems, you may then have to confront them about this interference.

If you suspect the presenting problem is a function of other problems, as it often is, it is not a good idea to present this diagnostic formulation to the family or the parents at first unless you think they're ready for it. If, for example, you suspect the target child's problems are a reflection of the chronic tension between the parents, but the parents perceive the child as "bad" and treat him like a blamed scapegoat, don't share that opinion with them yet. They would find it too threatening and would probably drop out of therapy with you. But if you sense the parents are already aware of the connection between their marital problems and their child's problems, and are willing to do something about the former, then give that interpretation with an offer of marital counseling.

3. Don't consistently take sides.

This is another way of saying don't become triangulated by the family members or enmeshed in the family pathology. As a family therapist, you must realize all members of the family are in emotional pain, even the angry, abusive father who is so difficult to like either because he won't come in to see you or when he does, he snarls at you that family therapy is "a bunch of crap." If you are going to work effectively with this family, you have to see beneath the nasty exterior of father and be in touch with his pain and frustration, as difficult as this may be to do.

The advice not to take sides doesn't mean that you shouldn't take sides at times; rather it implies that you shouldn't consistently take sides with one person or subsystem against another. If you do, you run the risk of alienating one or more persons in the family. Perhaps a few times you can agree with one spouse against another, or with the adolescents against the parents, but make sure you offset these maneuvers at other times by agreeing with the other spouse against the first, or with the parents against the adolescents.

At no time is this rule more important than in marital and custody counseling. Couples in painful conflict can be especially prone to seek allies and exquisitely sensitive to side taking. To a couple in marital conflict, you are on the side of them both working out their problems; to a couple in a bitter custody battle, you are on the side of their children. What is best for the children is that mother and father work out their custody dispute themselves to the satisfaction of them both.

Like any rule, there are exceptions to this one. There are times when you may have to take sides, to support one person or subsystem against another, even at the risk of alienating other members of the family. Some of these times may be:

—When the family interaction is stuck and going nowhere. For example, as we saw in Chapter 3, psychological power in a marital dyad is roughly equal even though one spouse may appear to be dominant and the other to be submissive. To the frustration of both spouses, the relationship between them may not have changed for years because of the equality of their power.

To change this system, you may have to lend the weight of your authority to one side against the other to unbalance the distribution of power which is making change impossible. There is a risk in such a maneuver—the risk of alienating one of the spouses— but if the marital problems have been going on for years, and if you have tried everything else, you may have to take that risk.

—When one member of the family is too disruptive or intrusive in the family sessions. Again, taking sides entails the risk of alienating that person but if you can't proceed in your sessions because of her behavior, what else can you do? With a mother who keeps answering for her son, for example, or who keeps interrupting as you try to strengthen the father-son relationship, you may have to ask her to be quiet, sit between her and her son or schedule an appointment with the father and son alone. Similarly, with an adolescent who is too angry in a session, you may have to ask him to leave the room and cool down.

—When one family member's behavior is harmful or life-threatening to himself or to others. If there is irrefutable evidence that an adolescent is chemically dependent, although she angrily denies it, you may have to side with the parents to have her committed to a chemical dependency unit for an evaluation. By doing so, you may ruin your chances of ever working with that adolescent again, but there's little sense in working with anyone on an outpatient basis who is abusing drugs. Again, if mother is depressed and seriously suicidal, you will have to arrange for her to be hospitalized despite her loud and angry denunciations of you.

—When the children's behavior is out of control. In some of the families with young children we see, the children are in charge because the parents have relinquished their rightful parental authority. They are not disciplining their offspring consistently or effectively. To reverse this situation, to put the parents back in charge, we usually see the children once for diagnosic purposes, and then work with the parents to teach them discipline skills. Similarly, we support parents who set reasonable age-appropriate rules for their adolescents, yet the latter are still out of control.

Clearly, in these cases, we side with the parents against the children because we believe in firm, consistent discipline for youth. We are convinced that such discipline builds the self-discipline and self-control which is necessary for successful adult functioning.

4. Study the family's usual patterns of behavior but don't let them continue long in your office.

As they come to feel more comfortable with you, the family members should begin to revert to their usual patterns of behavior in your office. Mother and son may begin to argue while father withdraws. Or mother and father may disagree vehemently, then switch to a discussion of the target child. Or the target child may act up as mother and father start to fight. Or father may harshly criticize his daughter while mother rushes to her defense.

Diagnostically, it is helpful for you to observe these patterns. If the family members do not display them spontaneously, you should attempt to induce them by encouraging an argument or giving the family a difficult problem to solve. But once you've studied these patterns, you should interrupt them or change them in a therapeutic way. The family is in your office because their usual behaviors are not working for them or working only partially. Although the family members would insist they're in therapy only to change the behavior of the symptom bearer, they are also in therapy to modify these patterns. If you let them continue long in your office, you will be inadvertently reinforcing what needs to be changed.

In the examples above, when mother and son begin to argue while father withdraws, encourage father to support mother in disciplining their son. When mother and father avoid an argument by talking about the target child, interrupt them and have them come back to the subject of their argument in an attempt to resolve it. If the target child tries to stop his parents fighting by misbehaving, intervene to stop his disruptive behavior. Ask him to be quiet, have him sit next to you rather than in between his parents or send him from the room. If father continually criticizes his daughter while mother defends her, ask them to switch roles. Have mother be critical of her daughter while father defends her. If father can't or won't give up his critical stance, you may be able to get him to defend his daughter by criticizing her yourself:

> Boy! Her behavior sounds awful! I've never heard of such obnoxious behavior in all my years as a family therapist. I'm beginning to doubt if we'll be able to help.

Such an attack by you may compel father to abandon his criticism and begin to defend her.

5. **Be active and directive.**

As noted above, family therapy is usually much more active, directive and manipulative than individual therapy. The goal in family therapy is to change the way the family functions and not just emotional release or cognitive restructuring. And to bring about change, you will have to be an investigator, director, instructor, consultant and monitor.

As an investigator, your function is to probe, ask personal questions, observe certain patterns and ask the family to do certain tasks. As a director, you are in charge of the flow of the family therapy. You are responsible for the progress of the sessions. You are the expert to whom the family has come for help. They are to behave according to the rules established by you. Like a director, your function is to get people to behave as you want them to behave. You ask the family members to switch seats, to be quiet, to say things you tell them to say, to speak directly to one another, to stand up and sculpt the family, to draw pictures, to solve certain problems and to do homework assignments.

All the time you're doing this, you may be moving around. You rise as you ask people to stand up; you position yourself between people to create an artificial barrier; you wheel around in your chair to be closer first to one person and then to another; then you wheel back as the family members begin to work on their problems themselves.

As an instructor, you teach the family members new skills, run them through certain drills, give them homework assignments, ask them to practice certain behaviors in your office, model the skills you want them to learn and reinforce them for whatever progress they make.

You become a consultant to the family in the later stages of therapy as the members begin to make some changes, to use the skills you've taught them and to work directly and effectively on their problems. In your role as a consultant, you don't have to be as involved with the family as you were earlier in their treatment. Instead, you can sit back and be available for advice and occasional reinforcement.

As a monitor, your function is to check up on the family to insure they're doing their homework assignments and to follow them up after termination. At the Family Teaching Center, we monitor the families we see in two ways. During the treatment proper, we call them in between sessions to see how things are going, to find out if they're doing their homework assignments, to be available to answer their questions and to make any necessary adjustments. After treatment, with certain difficult cases, but especially those involving child abuse or bitter custody disputes, we continue to see families once a month for up to six months to insure the continued implementation of the changes they have made.

6. **Reduce the fear, guilt and blaming.**

Family members who come to see you are usually afraid and defensive. They are entering into an unknown process which they would rather not go through. The parents may be especially worried you may hold them responsible for the family's problems. They may be feeling guilty, inadequate and blamed.

As a family therapist, you must take the position that everyone has tried their best and that either no one is to blame or everyone is to blame. If despite your best efforts to reassure them, however, you still find the family members feeling blamed and defensive, there are several things you can do to reduce their sense of guilt:

—Slow down. Maybe you're going too fast and exploring some sensitive issues before the family members are ready to face them.

—Let the family know your views about family functioning. Tell them that you believe it follows certain patterns into which family members easily fall. Explain to them that you assume everyone has tried their best and state that the concept of blame is foreign to you.

—Discuss the fact that behavior is multi-determined. Explain to the parents how the children turn out is a function of many factors over which they have no control.

—Find the strengths in the family and emphasize them. Let them know you see love in the family even though it may not be fully expressed. Tell them that you admire them for being able to bear up so well despite the incredible stress they're under.

This emphasis on strength is an extremely important stance for you to take. You could become lost in the family pathology if you chose to explore it in depth. But attention to symptoms may be what helps to keep them going. By emphasizing the strengths in the family, you may help the family overcome the many problems all families face.

At a workshop in Great Falls, Montana, in September, 1982, Virginia Satir told a wonderful story about a family she saw in which the father was having sexual relations with the family cow. During the first session, Satir commented that she was aware of what the father was doing, then stated that perhaps through family therapy, he could find better ways to have his needs met. She briefly acknowledged the pathology in the family but then used it as a springboard to greater health. She did not go into it in depth because of her belief that such a strategy would have been counter-productive. She said, in effect, to the family, "So Dad is screwing the family cow. Let's get moving and find better ways for him to relate."

Of course, the blaming can go the other way in which most, if not all, of the responsibility for the family's problems are dumped on the target child who is a blamed scapegoat. Again, you may want to reduce this blaming and can do so in several ways:

—Insisting that the entire family be present at the intake interviews gives the family the message that the symptom bearer's problems are everyone's problems. It implicitly conveys to the family members your belief that everyone contributes to the problems.

—If there are other problems in the family—and there usually are—explore these if the family allows you to do so and suggest the family consider working on them. A clinical example should illustrate this process:

When the family was seen for the first interview, only about fifteen minutes time was spent discussing the target child's problems. It soon became apparent that mother suffered periodic bouts of depression, for which she had never been treated, and that father was very unhappy in his work. In addition, the oldest son, who was not the target child and had strongly resisted coming to the first session, wound up in tears complaining he could do nothing to please his parents. At the end of the first session, all the family members agreed they had other problems to work on in addition to the presenting problem of the target child.

—Relabel the symptom bearer's problems as positive rather than as negative. In other words, suggest to the family members that the presenting problem is a family problem which, crazy as this may sound to them, may have done them some good. The following clinical example can demonstrate how you might relabel the symptom as positive rather than negative:

The family came in because their daughter, Sally, had been arrested for being drunk and disorderly over the weekend. Later in the first session, the family members agreed they needed to work on communication in the family and accepted the therapist's interpretation that Sally had done them a favor by getting drunk and bringing them the counseling they needed.

7. Concentrate on the family process rather than the content.

Content is what the family members tell you about themselves. Father reports that his son has stolen three bicycles in the past three weeks, although mother claims it was only two bicycles. Stepfather complains to the mother about the mess in his stepdaughter's room, while she complains to mother about him being on her case all the time. Mother complains that father had six drinks at a party last weekend and watched four football games this past weekend.

Process is the how of family interactions. It is what underlies the content. It is the way the content is expressed. Specifically, content includes the patterns of behavior we discussed in Chapter 3—the cycles, rules, roles, triangles and relationships—which you attempt to modify.

In the first example above, the process is that father criticizes the son while mother defends him, creating a parental opposition cycle. The more he criticizes, the more she defends, so the more he criticizes. What father specifically complains about his son constitutes the content.

In the second example, mother is the switchboard through which communication flows. She is caught in the middle between two people, both of whom she loves. The specifics of the complaints she receives from both sides constitute the content while her being caught in the middle switchboard position is the process.

In the third example, whenever mother attacks father, he withdraws in stony silence, which only motivates her even more to increase the pressure for him to change. Again, the specifics of mother's complaints about her husband constitute the content, while the pressure/resistance cycle which has developed between them is the process.

For the family therapist, the content can be overwhelming since it can be so endless, complex and varied. You can become lost in it as you can become lost in the family pathology. This is why you must concentrate on the process rather than the content. Process enables you to make sense out of the complexity and variety of the family interactions and their statements about content. It limits your scope so you can see more clearly. It is the map which enables you to find your way through the maze of content.

Your function as a family therapist is not only to work directly on the content-laden presenting problem but also to change the family process. You want to ameliorate the family's problems as well as change the patterns which maintain them. You also want to teach them new skills so they'll be able to solve other problems as they arise. If you didn't do this, if you only solved the presenting problem without changing other aspects of family functioning, the family would have to come running back to you each time the members were confronted with another problem.

My wife has a poster hanging on her office wall which perfectly expresses the point being made above. It states: "Give me a fish and I eat for a day. Teach me to fish and I eat for a lifetime."

Our job is to teach families to fish.

8. Avoid all secrets.

This may be a controversial guideline. Not all family therapists would agree with it. Karpel and Strauss (1983), for example, are willing to accept secrets from family members even though they're aware of the risks that entails.

At the Family Teaching Center, we believe it's safer not to accept secrets. To do so is to put ourselves in an alliance with one family member which could reduce our maneuverability and effectiveness in treating the family. This is not to say, however, that we will automatically reveal all secrets which are revealed to us. On the contrary, we may decide not to reveal a secret but we reserve the right to discuss it with other family members in some future sessions if we think it is important to do so.

If we decide to see family members individually, we guard against being triangulated by secrets by saying something to the members of the family such as the following:

> I would like to see some of you (or all of you) individually to give
> you each a chance to talk about some things you may not be

comfortable discussing in front of the whole family at first. However, I don't want to hear any secrets you wouldn't want me to discuss with the rest of the family.

Since we apply this rule to everyone, most family members see it as fair and reasonable and are willing to abide by it.

Sometimes, however, we don't have the chance to lay down the rule described above to the family, and find ourselves in an individual session with a family member who wants to tell us something important but doesn't want the family to know about it. At this point, it is extremely tempting to agree to the conditions to hear the secret. After all, it really may be important diagnostic information! However, we would still tell the person the following:

> What you have to say to me may be extremely important but I can't agree to your conditions. If I think it's important to bring up to other family members what you'll have to say, then I would reserve the right to do so with your help. This is not to say I will share what you have to say. I may decide not to. But I don't want to accept any secrets I've promised not to reveal.

Usually family members are dying to tell the secret, so they'll reveal it despite these conditions.

Obviously, there is some information the other family members don't need to know or have a right to know. The parents' sex life does not have to be discussed in the family, for example. Or mother doesn't have to know about the affair father had years ago. Or father doesn't have to know about mother's sex life before he met her. Or the parents don't have to know their teenage son has experimented with marijuana or their daughter had intercourse with her boyfriend.

However, if you suspect the adolescent son is abusing drugs, and not just experimenting, you have a responsibility to tell the parents. Similarly, if the daughter becomes pregnant, it will be your responsibility to help her tell her parents.

9. Determine what is the client's position and use it in your therapeutic efforts.

Fisch, Weakland and Segal (1982) define the client's position as the assumptions the client has about the causes and treatment of her problems. To persuade a client to do what we want her to do, you should determine what her position is and use it to secure her consent to treatment.

To make their point, these authors present the example of a car salesman selling a car. With the customer who is interested in economy and dependability, the salesman emphasizes the high mileage and low repair rate of the automobile he is trying to sell. With the customer who is interested in status, he emphasizes the comfort and distinctive features of the car.

You should learn something from these salespersons. Like them, you too are in the business of persuasion. It's your function to sell the family on family therapy. Since parents generally take one of two views about the target child—either he is "sick" or he is "bad"—you should determine what is their view of the child and use it to get them to commit to family therapy. The following two clinical examples should illustrate these differing approaches:

> Although he was doing well at school and had plenty of friends, the parents are still concerned about what they considered to be the self-esteem problem of their son. The therapist did find some evidence of a slightly lower than average level of self-esteem on a self concept scale, but he didn't think it was significant. To induce the parents to agree to the child program for their son's somewhat disruptive home behavior, however, the therapist labeled the boy as having a borderline self-esteem problem. He then explained to the parents that the best way they could help him with his self concept problem would be to provide him with security afforded by consistent discipline.

> Mother and father were very critical of their son, explaining that they spanked him often but to no avail. The boy never minded, rarely did his chores and was mean to his siblings, according to the parents. No intervention by the therapist was successful in breaking the parents out of their perception of their child as totally "bad." Consequently, the therapist began to agree with them that their child's behavior was quite a handful. He empathized with their frustration and stated they had to become stricter with him by learning some new disciplinary techniques.

10. **Help the family members obtain what they want from each other in positive, healthy, more effective ways.**

This is what family therapy is all about. This is our major goal for the family. Although the family comes to therapy because of specific problems in one or more of the family members, we assume they're also in therapy because their love and esteem needs are not being met.

We would work to secure the greater independence an adolescent seeks from his parents, for example, but we believe the best way he can accomplish this is not by rebelling but by conforming. The more he follows the rules he and his parents have set up in their sessions with us, the more trust his parents will have in him and the more freedom they'll allow him.

With a wife who wants more intimacy from her husband who is comfortable with distance, we would attempt to have them compromise in such a way that both have their needs met although not to the degree each would like. If the husband agrees to go out every other Friday night with his wife, and if he further agrees to spend Saturday afternoons with the children, then the wife agrees to his going fishing by himself on Sundays. Or they can agree to go fishing as a family, thereby satisfying his love of fishing, her wish to be with him and the children's desire to spend time with their father. We would also encourage the wife to seek sources of support outside the family in friendships and constructive activities.

However, if the need satisfaction of one family member could prove harmful to one or more other family members, then we would play no part in it. If an insecure mother wants to remain very involved with her adolescent son, for example, our function would be to encourage her to find other ways to meet her needs than through her relationship with her son. We might try to improve her relationship with her husband or encourage her to date if she's a single parent. We might also refer her to a support group or suggest she take a course at the local college.

Chapter 5

THE INTAKE INTERVIEWS

THE TELEPHONE CONTACT

It begins with the first telephone contact when someone in the family calls for an appointment. It's critical you begin to establish your ground rules at this time.

At the Family Teaching Center, most of the calls we receive are for problems with the children so we have some idea why a family member is calling. All of our initial calls are answered by our secretary who has been trained to handle them appropriately. Her function is twofold: to gather some information and to set up an appointment with all family members. She asks the usual questions about names, ages, address, telephone numbers and presenting problems. She also asks briefly about referral source, previous counseling, medical problems, school problems and involvement with juvenile probation. She ends this information gathering process by asking what brings the family to the Family Teaching Center at this time.

Then our secretary asks that all members of the family who are living at home come in for the first session. She explains the family counselor will need to find out as much about the target child as possible and this can be best done by meeting with everyone in the family. This explanation usually suffices to satisfy the caller.

We insist on family diagnostic interviews as forcefully as we can for a number of reasons. Such interviews do, in fact, give us more information about the target child. Not only can we hear everyone's view of the presenting problem, we also have an opportunity to observe family interactions with each other and with the target child.

Family diagnostic interviews also take some of the pressure off the target child. They convey to the family members our belief that all of them are involved in the target child's symptomatology. They also better insure the cooperation of all family members in treatment and enable us to become aware of any other problems in the family should they arise during the intake interviews.

Typically at the Family Teaching Center, with families with young children we usually meet with the parents first, then with the children. With families with adolescents, we usually meet with the family together, then with the adolescents alone and finally with the parents alone. We feel these separate sessions with the parents and the children may provide us with information we may not obtain by meeting with everyone in the family for every session. We believe we can discover more about the children's behavior and the parents' marriage this way.

If you're in private practice or work for a comprehensive agency which doesn't specialize in children's problems, whenever anyone calls for an appointment, you won't have any idea what is the presenting problem as we do at the Family Teaching Center. If you are to take a family systems approach to psychological problems, you'll first need to find out exactly what is the presenting problem. This can be accomplished either by you or by your secretary. If you do it, have your secretary obtain the name and telephone number of the person calling and call him or her back when you have time to do so.

When you call back, first ask about the presenting problem. If the caller hesitates to discuss it in detail on the telephone, ask if it is a personal problem, a marital problem or a problem with the children. You'll need this information to decide how to proceed to set up the first appointment. Then ask if the caller is married, divorced or single.

If the presenting problem is a personal one and the caller is single and living alone, then you can simply set up an appointment to see her only. If there are significant others in the picture— parents, siblings, friends or a lover—you can make arrangements to see them later for diagnostic or treatment purposes if you think it is necessary. If the single person is struggling with some family of origin problems, for example, and her parents or siblings live nearby, you can suggest having some joint appointments with them at a future date. One or more sessions with parents and an adult child in which they talk with each other may be worth many individual sessions in which a client only talks about her parents rather than with them. By actually facing her parents in sessions with you, your client could clear up some misconceptions she may have about them, finish any unfinished business, gain some valuable insights about herself and learn to give and receive the love which is usually there in most families even though it is not fully expressed. The following clinical example should illustrate part of this process:

> Even though she was twenty-eight years old, Barbara was still not sure of her father's love since he was a quiet and undemonstrative man. However, one session with Barbara and her father was sufficient to prove to her and her therapist that father did, in fact, care for her very deeply. By contrast, no number of individual sessions with Barbara without the involvement of her father would have been able to demonstrate his caring.

If the presenting complaint is a personal problem in someone who is married, you might ask to see both spouses together at first, but you needn't insist on it. However, you would want to meet with the client's spouse later on to gather diagnostic information from him.

If the caller indicates the problem is marital, you or your secretary should insist that both spouses come in together at first. You could simply explain that if the problem is marital, the best way to solve it is by both spouses working on it.

Sometimes, however, the caller in a marital crisis may insist on being seen alone first to tell you her side of the story. This is usually an opening move to triangulate you on the caller's side. You can agree to this only if you've made it clear you'll want to see the other spouse also in an individual session:

> O.K. I'll see you first for one session, but then I'll want to see your spouse alone for one session. If I'm to be of service to the two of you, I have to talk with both of you and I like to make sure you each have equal time to talk to me.

If the caller claims the problem is with the children, you should insist on seeing everyone living at home for your diagnostic interviews. If there are significant others living near by—grandparents, adult siblings or a divorced parent—you can ask to see them in later sessions with or without the other family members being present. For example, if the parents are divorced and living in the same town, we may try to see them together if they have been cooperating fairly well for the sake of the children. If the parents don't get along, we may see them separately at first and later try to get them together to talk about the children if we think it is necessary. If the parents are in need of custody counseling, we'll insist on seeing them jointly at some time to work out their custody disputes. We may allow them a few individual sessions to work into joint sessions but eventually we have to get them together.

Our policy about whom we expect to see at the Family Teaching Center is somewhat flexible but within limits. We want to interview as many people in the family as we can but we don't always insist on it. We'll see the family if not all the siblings attend the intake interviews or one of the parents refuses to come. However, we'll warn the family members that without the participation and cooperation of everyone, the prognosis for improvement cannot be as good. We may be willing to see one spouse who complains of marital problems individually but only after we've made every effort to see the other spouse and have warned both spouses of the risks of individual counseling for marital problems—i.e., it can put a strain on an already strained marriage and possibly end in divorce. Probably the only absolute we have is we won't see the target child alone for individual counseling if the family refuses to become involved. We feel that whatever good we can do for the child in individual sessions would be undone by the family pathology.

How flexible you might be in deciding who in the family to see would depend upon a number of factors:

—Your agency's policy. Perhaps it specifies whom to see under what conditions as we do at the Family Teaching Center.

—How busy you are. If you're busy, you'd probably be more willing to insist on your rules for family involvement. If you're not that busy, you may be willing to be more flexible.

—Whether you're in private practice or not. If you're in private practice, you can function as you choose without having to follow any agency policy about family involvement. Also, you may be more willing to see the family under their conditions since they're paying your fees. You may be willing to see the target child alone, although we hope you'd still want to see the parents periodically, if only to give them reports about the progress of therapy. Perhaps that way you can surreptitiously entice them into therapy.

—Your own theoretical orientation. Perhaps you don't take as hard a family systems line as we do. Perhaps you're willing to see the target child alone in the belief you can be of some benefit to him. Maybe you can, although we would take the position that seeing the child alone only tends to reinforce the family's scapegoating and does little good without a change in the family interactions.

THE FIRST SESSION

The ideal seating arrangement for family therapy is one containing a number of comfortable, single chairs placed in a circle. As they enter your office, allow the family members to sit where they choose. Where they sit should give you diagnostic information you'd never obtain if you didn't see all of them or if you saw them separately. If the target child sits between mother and father, for example, he may serve as a buffer or mediator in his parents' arguments. If mother and father sit as far away from each other as they possibly can, suspect marital problems. If the target child sits on one side of the circle while the rest of the family sits on the other side, she may feel isolated and unsupported by the family.

If everyone whom you asked to come in does not show up for the first interview, there are several things you can do. If you want to take a hard line family system approach and insist that everyone participate, as does Napier and Whitaker (1980), you could refuse to see the family members and reschedule them for another time when they can all come in. You'd risk losing them by doing so, but you would have given them a strong message you expect everyone to be involved in the family sessions. Your chances of treating the family effectively might then be improved.

Or you could agree to see the family members who did show up but insist that the missing members come to the next scheduled session. This is probably what we would do at the Family Teaching Center if most of the family members show up. Whoever is missing, we designate an empty chair as representing that missing member. This indicates to the family we consider him to be a part of the family and expect him to be present at our next meeting. We'd probably say something such as the following:

I'm sorry Dad couldn't make this appointment today. Tell you what: let's use this empty chair to represent him. Let's pretend he's sitting there. Next time we meet, I assume he will be here.

In using an empty chair to represent a missing member, however, we would not allow the other family members to talk about him unless we were preparing them for an intervention for chemical dependency. We convey to them that anything they want to say about him should be said in his presence.

When there are one or more missing members for the diagnostic sessions, there are several things we do at the Family Teaching Center to attempt to get them in. First, we instruct the other family members to ask the errant member to come in. We request the one spouse to ask the other spouse to attend the next session or we instruct the parents to have the siblings come in. Failing our request, we call the person ourselves and make an appeal to him such as the following:

I try to talk with everyone in the family to get everyone's opinion. I'd sure like to meet with you to hear what you think about this family. You could be a source of valuable information to me.

One reason we like to call the missing family member is to insure that, in fact, the other family members have asked him to come to therapy. The importance of this maneuver can be seen from the following clinical example:

Jane was seen in individual therapy for marital problems. On two different occasions, both of which, fortunately, were documented, the therapist instructed Jane to ask her husband to call for an appointment. Each time, she claimed he refused to do so.

A few months later, Jane sued her husband for a divorce. He went to court to block the divorce and attempt a reconciliation. On the witness stand, Jane's husband testified she had never asked him to attend marital counseling sessions.

If a phone call still doesn't bring the errant member in, we may then follow it up with a letter explaining the disadvantages to him of his not attending the family sessions. We may point out to him the other family members may decide to make some changes without input from him. As a result, he may have a difficult time adjusting to those changes and may feel even more isolated in the family than we imagine he feels now.

After the usual greetings, introductions and small talk, we like to begin the first session by constructing a genogram of the nuclear and extended families. A genogram is simply a schematic diagram which gives basic information about the family members such as names, ages, occupations of the adults, grade levels of the children, where living, marriages, divorces and remarriages.

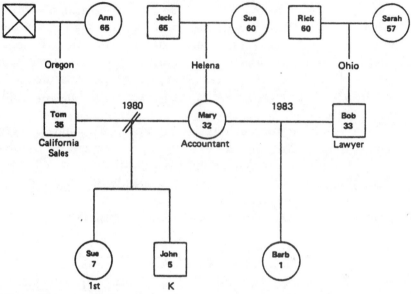

Figure 3. A sample genogram which gives the name, age, occupation or year in school and residence of each family member.

In our genograms, females are designated by circles and males by squares. The names and ages of each family member are written in each's circle or square while their grade level, occupation and city or state of residence are written below. Divorces are indicated by double slanted lines while separations are shown by a single slanted line. The dates of marriages, divorces and remarriages are written over the horizontal line connecting the couple. Deaths are indicated by X's in the circles or squares.

In the family in Figure 3, although it is not shown in the genogram, the target child is John who is 5 and in kindergarten. His older sister is Sue who is 7 and in the first grade. His father is Tom, age 35, a salesperson living in California. His mother is

Mary, age 32, an accountant. Tom and Mary were divorced in 1980. Mary remarried Bob, age 33, a lawyer, in 1983. They have one child, Barb, age 1. This is Bob's first marriage. Tom did not remarry.

The grandparents are Mary's parents, Jack and Sue, living in Helena and Tom's mother, Ann, living in Oregon. Tom's father is deceased. Bob's parents, Rick and Sarah, live in Ohio.

Constructing a genogram gives you the opportunity to make contact with each person in your office as you ask their names, ages, occupations or grade levels. Then by extending the genogram to the entire family, you will convey to the family members present in your office your belief that there are persons outside the immediate family who have an influence on them and on the target child.

After you have completed the genogram, you should spend the next twenty to thirty minutes exploring the presenting problem in detail. It is that which brought the family to you in the first place and it is what they are anxious to talk about. Then spend the rest of the time exploring other areas of family functioning, a process which may take one or two more sessions to complete.

FAMILY DIAGNOSTIC QUESTIONS

At the Family Teaching Center, we have designated nine areas of family functioning which we explore after we have investigated the presenting problem. What follows is a list of those areas with questions designed to elicit information about each area. Which of these questions you may use would depend upon how much time you want to take for your intake interviews and how open the family is with you. You don't have to ask all of them.

Presenting Problem(s)

In exploring the presenting problem, ask about its definition, frequency, antecedents, consequences and immediate and past precipitating causes. Also, ask about the changes the family members would like to make and assess their degree of motivation to change. The following questions should give you this information:

How do you see the problem?
What exactly happens?

How often?
What happens before? After?
When did it start? What was happening in the family then?
What brings you in now?
Who referred you?
What would you like to change about the problem or the family?
How do you feel about coming to my office? Whose idea was it?
Who didn't want to come?

Other Family Problems

After you have explored the presenting problem in depth, note and possibly explore other family problems. If your intake form indicates there are other problems with the symptom bearer—e.g., medical problems, recent arrests or chemical abuse—ask about these in detail. Then inquire if there are any other problems of concern to the family members.

In exploring other family problems, proceed as gingerly and sensitively as you can. Most likely, there are other problems in the family but the family members may not want to talk about them. If you meet some resistance, anxiety or embarrassment in asking about other problems, your best strategy is to note the area, back off and go on to ask about something else.

If the family doesn't describe any other problems in the family, you may want to ask specifically about them:

Does anyone in the family have a medical condition we should know about?
Has anyone had any emotional or behavioral problems before?
Have any of you been to a therapist like me? Who? When? For what?
Has anyone been in trouble with the law?
Is there a history of mental illness or alcoholism in the family?

If you stumble upon a present drug or alcohol problem, you may want to discreetly ask about it in detail. For example, if you suspect father has a drinking problem, ask him about it alone or in the presence of his wife only. Similarly, any questions about drug use are best addressed to an adolescent alone. The following questions should give you the information you need:

How often do you drink (or take drugs)?
How much each time?
How long have you been drinking?
Have you had any blackouts or bad reactions?

Has your drinking caused you any problems at work, with friends, with your family or with the law?

Have you ever tried to stop?

Do you drink to forget your worries or to help yourself relax?

Do you sometimes drink more than you intended to?

Do you ever drink alone or in the morning?

Do you gulp your drinks?

To help shift some of the focus from the target child and to gather more family diagnostic information, ask about the other children:

How are the other children doing?

Any problems with them?

Do they have any problems with grades, peer relations or discipline?

Try to make a quick assessment of the individual functioning of the parents. To do this, consider their intellectual level, level of self-esteem, occupational functioning and existence of psychiatric symptoms. You can ask them about their jobs, if they're employed, and psychiatric symptoms, but you can only infer intellectual level and level of self-esteem by observation.

Also, attempt to assess the marital functioning. This you may have to do very carefully so as not to discourage the parents from returning for further diagnostic sessions or therapy. If the parents are coming to you specifically for marital problems and not for problems in one family member, then you can ask them the following questions without the children being present:

How would you characterize your marriage?

Any serious problems? Known affairs? Problems with in-laws? Money problems?

To what extent do you agree about raising kids? To what extent do you differ?

How do you get along sexually? How often do you have intercourse? Are there any specific sexual problems: vaginal pain, lack of orgasm or lubrication, premature ejaculation (come too soon), retarded ejaculation (can't come), or difficulty getting or sustaining an erection (can't get it up or keep it up)?

How do you show love to each other?

How satisfied are you with your married life? What, if anything, in your marriage would you like to see changed?

With a single parent family, ask the parent without the children present about his or her adjustment:

What's it like to be a single parent?

How do you manage it all? How do you find time for yourself? How do you insure that your social, emotional and sexual needs are met?

Family's Relationship with Target Child

Here again observation will give you as much information as direct questions. Where does the child sit in relation to each member? How does each parent interact with him or her? Does one seem close and the other distant? Does one attack the child while the other defends? Who supports the target child?

To explore the family members' relationships with the target child, ask the parents:

How's your relationship with (child's name)? How are you at giving her praise, hugs and kisses? When's the last time you told her you loved her?

How do you correct her?

Ask the target child:

Who in this family could you talk to if you had a problem? Who's interested in what you're interested in? Who cares about what you do?

How's Mom (Dad) for giving praise, hugs and kisses? When's the last time she (he) said she (he) loved you?

How does she (he) correct you?

Obviously, these questions could, and perhaps should, be asked of each child in the family and not just the target child.

Emotional Communication

There are three areas to explore under this category:

—The emotional climate in the family. Is it positive? Anxious? Depressed? Resentful? Lonely? Observation should give you this information.

—The expression of emotions. Is it open, inhibited or repressed?

—The expression of emotional support. Do members feel loved, valued and supported? Or do they feel smothered? Are there more positive interactions than negative, or vice versa?

Again, both questions and observations should elicit the information you need. Ask all family members:

How does this family show love? How does it handle negative feelings like anger, anxiety and sadness?

What feelings are easiest for you to handle? What are the hardest?

Who's the most expressive member of the family? Who has the most trouble expressing feelings?

How much time does this family spend together? Doing what? Is it enough time? Not enough? Too much?

What does this family do for fun? With whom? How often?

Who fights with whom? Who avoids fights?

If we could secretly observe this family at home and could count the number of positive interactions (hugs, kisses, praise and appreciation) and the number of negative interactions (anger, criticism and correction), which would be higher? How much higher?

This question could also be asked about the relationship between the parents and the target child. Along with other questions about love, hugs, kisses, praise and appreciation, it suggests to the family what they may need to change without directly saying so.

Conflict Resolution

There are three areas to explore under this category:

—Instrumental communication. Can the family members express their ideas, needs and proposed solutions, and listen accurately to what the others have to say?

—Conflict resolution. How effectively can this family handle conflict and solve problems? Can the members work out compromises, or do some have to give in? Do they try to ignore problems? How many unresolved conflicts are there in this family?

—Decision-making power. If problems aren't solved through compromise, how are decisions made? Who holds the most power? Is power equally shared by the parents, or is this a father-dominated or mother-dominated family?

Ask all family members:

How do you communicate your needs and ideas? How well does this family listen to each other? How well do you compromise?

What happens if you can't reach a solution? Does someone usually give in? Who?

Who decides if a solution can't be found? Do some people usually get their own way? Who?

Is decision-making authority shared or is there a boss? Who is it?

Discipline Enforcement

Three areas to explore in this category are:

—Family rules. Are there too many rules or too few? How clearly are they stated or known? Are they rigid or flexible?

—Rule enforcement. How consistently do parents follow through in enforcing rules? How effectively do they support each other in formulating rules and applying rewards and penalties? How comfortable are they with executive authority? Are there any parental children?

—Enforcement strategies. What strategies do the parents use to enforce discipline? What rewards, if any, do they use? What punishments? Do they use more rewards or more punishments?

Address to all family members:

What are the rules in this family? What's unacceptable? Who does what chores?

How are the rules made? Who determines them? Do Mom and Dad agree on the rules?

How are the rules communicated? Do you understand what they are?

How are the rules enforced? By whom? What happens if you keep a rule or do your chores? What happens if you break a rule or don't do your chores?

Relationships with the Extended Family

Under this category, explore the impact of the extended family members on the nuclear family. Specifically, examine the influence of grandparents, a biological parent living outside the home, other relatives and significant but non-related others.

Ask the parents about their parents:

Are your folks still living? Where?
How often do you see them? How do you get along with them?
How do they get along with the children?

If there has been a divorce in the family, ask the parent:

What was the divorce like?
How did the children react to it? Did they blame themselves?
How did the divorce affect you? How did it affect your relationship with your children?

How's your relationship with your ex-spouse? Are there any problems in your relationship? Any custody disputes or legal battles?

How often does Dad (Mom) see the children? How does he (she) get along with them?

How do the children get along with Dad (Mom)? Do they say they miss him (her)? Do they show any distress about the divorce?

Ask the children about the divorce, either alone or in front of the parent:

What was the divorce like for you? How do Mom and Dad get along now? Do you feel to blame for their divorce in any way? Do you think it's your job to get your parents back together again (or to stop fighting)?

If any of the children answer "Yes" to either or both of these last two questions, assure them they're not responsible for their parents' divorce or possible reconciliation.

Ask the family members if there are any other relatives or friends who have a significant impact on the family.

Family Stresses

Under this category you need to specify exactly what are the stresses this family is under—and there will be many—and what can be done to reduce them. By the time you've come this far in the intake process, you'll have a good idea of the extent of family stress but you might ask if there are any other problems or stresses you've not discussed. Also note the developmental stage the family is in and how well they're handling it.

What's it like having a new baby after four years together without children?

What's it like to see your son no longer a little boy but becoming a man?

How did you react when your daughter went off to college? How did it affect your marriage?

Family Strengths

Under this section specify the family strengths, reinforce them whenever possible and determine what else can be done to strengthen this family. Consider these categories of strengths:

—All of the categories above.
—Financial resources.
—Non-family support systems and interests.
—Spiritual support.

Since we use a sliding fee schedule at the Family Teaching Center, we learn something about each family's financial status at intake.

To assess social and spiritual support, ask:

How often do you entertain or have friends over?

What does each of you like to do independently of the family? What hobbies, sports or interests do you each enjoy?

Do you belong to a church? How often do you attend? Separately? As a family? How does God fit into your life?

Family Changes

There are two types of changes under this category:

—Those the family has agreed to work on.

—Those you feel need to be made.

Obviously, you want most of the changes to be those the family members want to make so their chances of success will be greater. Accordingly, in your diagnostic interviews you should emphasize that the family is in your office to make some changes since things haven't been working too well for them.

Ask all family members:

What changes would you like to make in this family?

What are your goals for this family? How would you like to see it a year from now? Two years from now? Five years? Ten years?

Is this something you'd all like to work to change (as you cover each diagnostic category)?

You might also ask the family members what each perceives as the goals of family counseling and how each sees it working. You don't want them to agree to family counseling under some false assumptions—e.g., that you will hear about their problems and tell them what to do. Instead, you want the family members to realize that you can only act as a teacher and facilitator, and that they will have to do the work to make the needed changes in their family functioning.

THE INTERPRETATIVE INTERVIEW

Our intake process at the Family Teaching Center takes two to three sessions and possibly more. We believe the more thorough we are in our diagnostic work, the more effective our treatment will be in fewer sessions. At the end of our intake sessions, we meet with the parents of young children, and with everyone in the family with adolescents, in an interpretative interview. In our child program, to be described in the next chapter, we work only with the parents to teach them discipline skills so we need to obtain only their agreement for treatment. In our work with families with adolescents, we usually treat everyone so we feel we should include everyone in our interpretative interview.

In our interpretative interview, we present our findings and recommendations for treatment to the family members. We may then warn them of the risks in therapy, if there are any, but our major goal is to get them to agree to treatment.

Motivating family members to accept and remain in treatment is not always an easy thing to do as our 40% discontinuation rate shows. However, there are several things you can do to involve a family in treatment and keep them involved:

—Use all the relationship skills you can to establish a thera- peutic alliance with the family members. If they like and trust you, they'll be more willing to keep coming back to see you.

—If there are several presenting problems, start with the easiest problem first to obtain some success. Make sure you reinforce the family members verbally for any improvements they do make. This should encourage them to continue working on their other problems.

Success can be a two-edged sword, however, and work against you as well as for you. Once the family members begin to experience some success, once their problems begin to clear up, they may lose interest in continuing therapy. Although you may want to do more to help them make changes in the way they function, with many families perhaps the only thing you can hope for is the reduction or elimination of the presenting problem.

—Do what you can do to increase the external pressure on the family to continue in therapy. In a case of suspected or confirmed child abuse, for example, perhaps you can ask the child protective services to keep after the parents to remain in therapy. Or you can talk with your local judges about the possibility of court ordering families to you.

—As we saw in Chapter 3, crises and the pain which accompany them are your allies in your therapeutic work. As harsh as this may sound to say, whatever you can do to increase the pain of family members who are not in a crisis but headed for one may be for their benefit. One way you can do this is to point out to the family members the consequences of their not accepting or completing therapy. At the Family Teaching Center, we feel it is our professional responsibility to do this. With families who are about to drop out of therapy, we may do this in person, while with families who have already dropped out, we may contact them by telephone or letter. A clinical example should illustrate this process:

> To induce a single parent mother with a disruptive six year old
> to remain in therapy, the therapist pointed out two consequences

of her inability to gain control of her son's behavior. First, he would become harder to handle as he grew older and would probably be unmanageable by the time he became an adolescent. Second, the example of disruptive, undisciplined behavior he would set for his younger siblings would also make it more difficult for mother to discipline them as they grew older.

Since mother agreed with both of these dire predictions, she decided to remain in therapy until she had gained better control of her son's behavior.

—At the Family Teaching Center, we do not provide once-a-week, face-to-face, outpatient therapy only. We are also in frequent telephone contact with many of the families we see. We believe calling families in between weekly sessions serves in several ways to keep them committed to therapy. It tells the family members we will stay with them until they have worked through their problems. It makes us more available to monitor and reinforce their completion of homework assignments. It is a way for us to remind the family members of their next appointment, and it enables us to intervene and resolve any crises which may arise during the week. An unresolved crisis may discourage a family from continuing with us since they may decide therapy is not working.

—Finally and paradoxically, with quite resistive families or families who have been to many therapists, the best way to keep them in therapy may be to be willing to terminate with them. If you put pressure on a reluctant family to accept therapy, they will probably resist your pressure and drop out. However, you may be able to induce them to agree to treatment by suggesting that perhaps they're not ready for therapy or that you can't help them in a type of reject-them-before-they-reject-you maneuver. The following clinical example demonstrates how this can work:

Mother came in complaining about the behavior of her six year old son. She had been to the Family Teaching Center when he was four years old, but had dropped out after one session. She explained she had not wanted to do the homework assignment but now heard our program had changed.

Sensing her continued ambivalence about therapy, the therapist explained the program had not changed, so perhaps he should refer her to the local mental health center. The mother balked at this and said she was willing to try our program again.

Mother then began to complain bitterly about her son's disruptive behavior. The therapist responded to her criticism by stating her boy sounded like a very difficult case and by wondering if our program would work for him. This made mother even more anxious to start therapy. Although the child program was streamlined somewhat to accommodate her, mother remained in therapy until her boy's behavior was brought under better control.

Of course, as will be explained in Chapter 13 on paradoxical techniques, you should use this approach only as a last resort when everything else has failed or you are dealing with a family which has a history of jumping from therapist to therapist.

In presenting any recommendations for treatment, you should warn clients of the risks, if any, involved in therapy. Clients have the right to know the benefit/risk ratio. They assume there will be benefits in treatment, but they should also be aware there may be some risks.

Certainly, the major risk every client faces is that treatment will not work at all or will be only partially effective. You cannot guarantee success. In presenting our treatment recommendations for our child program, we may warn parents their children's behavior may become worse as discipline becomes tighter. Children may test this new system of discipline, but we predict their behavior will improve if the parents remain united and consistent in their disciplinary efforts. In our work with families with adolescents, there is also a risk the program will not work. If our program fails, and if the youngster continues to misbehave, we may have to recommend an out-of-home placement.

In marital counseling, the risk of therapy is that it could end in divorce. The spouses may decide they don't want to stay together so marital counseling can become divorce counseling. In custody counseling, the risk is that the parents will have to go to court to settle their differences if they can't do so in their counseling sessions.

Chapter 6

THE FAMILY WITH YOUNG CHILDREN[1]

Some children may consider us "mean" at the Family
Teaching Center. We believe in firm, strict discipline for
young children and we give parents the tools to enforce that
discipline. We're convinced that such discipline, when combined
with plenty of love, is not only beneficial for the parents but also
beneficial for the children. It gives them a sense of security since
they know what are their behavioral limits. It contributes to better
parent-child relationships since there is less conflict in the home.
It helps the children develop high self-esteem since they receive
more rewards and praise from their parents than correction and
criticism. And it enables them to gain more freedom from
parental control since effective discipline when they're younger
contributes to greater responsibility and self-control as they
become older.

WHY YOUNG CHILDREN MISBEHAVE

Even though they have greater physical and psychological
power, there may be several reasons why parents are unable to
effectively discipline their young children:

[1]Our child program described in this chapter was first developed by Gerald Patterson,
Ph.D., taught to staff of the Family Teaching Center by Matthew Fleischman, Ph.D. and
Robert Conger, M.A. and further developed by our second Director, Steven Szukula, Ph.D.
The Weekly Observing Sheet (Figure 4), Point Incentive Chart (Figure 5), Point Incentive
Chart with Time-Out (Figure 6), Back-Up Rewards and Time-Out Review are used with
the permission of Dr. Fleischman.

—Since we all tend to raise our children the way we were reared, some parents may not have the skills to effectively discipline their children because of their own deficient upbringing. Without a conscious effort to change, parents can only give their children what they received from their parents. Parents who were spanked often as children usually see nothing wrong with the frequent use of this type of punishment. After all, they've turned out all right, haven't they? Similarly, parents who were abused as children tend to be abusive parents themselves.

In these cases, our function as therapists is to rectify these skill deficits by teaching the parents effective parenting skills. But we must also change their attitudes and induce them to try something different with their children. With parents who have been referred to us for suspected or confirmed physical abuse, we tell them not to spank their children while they're counseling with us. We ask them to suspend their judgment and see how our program works for the next several weeks. If it does work, as it usually does, we will have demonstrated to them that they can discipline their children more effectively with techniques other than physical punishment.

—The parents may have the skills to be effective disciplinarians but be unable to successfully apply those skills because of their own serious personal problems. A parent who suffers from untreated psychosis, alcoholism or moderate to severe depression will probably not be able to carry through with our program. In such cases, you should refer the parent for treatment of her personal problem, or provide that treatment yourself, before proceeding with our child program.

—The parents may have severe marital problems which make effective discipline difficult, if not impossible, to implement. This is one of the more common reasons why parents referred to the Family Teaching Center are having behavior problems with one or more of their children. Severe marital problems contribute to discipline problems in two ways: they prevent the parents from supporting each other in their disciplinary efforts and they create anxiety in children which may be acted out in misbehavior. Ironically, behavior problems in the children can contribute to marital stress, so that each type of problem can exacerbate the other in a vicious, self-perpetuating cycle.

At the Family Teaching Center, we note the existence of such marital problems but usually proceed with our child program in the hope the parents will be able to overcome them enough to present a united disciplinary front. Their marital problems do not have to spill over into disciplinary problems unless they allow them to do so. If the parents can agree on discipline in spite of their marital difficulties, then we will have strengthened their marriage without actually doing marital counseling. If they cannot, then our function is to point out to the parents how their marital problems are interfering with good discipline and to encourage them to do something about those problems, not only for their own sake but also for the sake of their children.

—The grandparents may interfere with the legitimate executive authority of the parents. Although it is the function of grandparents to "spoil" their grandchildren in the sense of giving them the unconditional love parents can't always provide, this can go too far. In a continuing conflict with their own adult children, grandparents can undermine the discipline of the parents. This is why we ask about the influence of grandparents on the family at the Family Teaching Center and do what we can to negate that influence if we think it is harmful to the children as the following clinical example shows:

> Despite her most determined efforts, a single parent mother was unable to bring the behavior of her ten year old son, Bob, under control. Her situation was becoming desperate as Bob's misbehavior at home was beginning to spill over to school. Bob freely admitted that his grandparents "spoil me rotten," so he received one message from mother to behave, but a stronger message from his grandparents, who were in conflict with the mother, not to behave. Moreover, Bob hoped if he behaved badly enough, his mother would send him to live with his grandparents.

—The parents may have the skills, the emotional strength and the interpersonal resources to discipline their children but are still reluctant to do so for a number of reasons. A parent may not make her children mind, for example, because she is still rebelling against what she considers to be her own harsh upbringing. She may assume that to be strict with her children is to be "mean." Or she may want to be friends with them and not risk their displeasure or anger. Or she may feel guilty about having divorced the children's father and not want to further burden them with firm discipline.

In these, and all cases involved in our child program, our function as therapists is not only to teach the parents specific discipline skills but also to strengthen their rightful, parental, executive authority. To the parent who thinks being a strict parent is being a "bad" parent, we counter that good parenting involves effective discipline. To the parent who wants to be friends with her children, we say that parents and children have more fun together when the children's behavior is under control. To the parent who feels guilty about the sadness expressed by her children after she divorced their father, we point out that children feel more loved and secure when they are well disciplined.

What this means is that at the Family Teaching Center we are not behaviorists only. A behavioral approach is our first approach in treating children's discipline problems, but if it does not work, we assume there are underlying causes for the failure of our program which we attempt to uncover and treat. If the reason our child program doesn't work lies in the marriage, we offer marital counseling; if it lies in relations with the extended family, we try to change these relations; if it lies within the individual parent, our treatment becomes psychodynamic and insight-oriented as the following clinical example shows:

> The child program was not working with a single parent mother of two children, of whom the oldest son, Robert, was the target child. The therapist's hypothesis was that mother had had problems with all the significant men in her life—her father, stepfather and two ex-husbands—so she simply expected and created problems with another important male in her life, her son.
>
> The therapist shared this interpretation with mother who rejected it in favor of two other reasons why the program was not successful. One, she did not want to rear her son as strictly as she felt she had been reared. And two, she felt considerable guilt about having divorced Robert's father since the boy claimed he missed his Dad. As a result, mother found it very difficult to send him to time-out for misbehavior. With the therapist's support, mother became a more effective disciplinarian as soon as she became aware of these dynamics operating within her.

—Finally, the parents may have the necessary skills, knowledge, resources and attitudes to effectively discipline their children but have borne a child who is temperamentally difficult to discipline. In their longitudinal studies of several populations of children, Thomas and Chess (1977) found that children differ in nine categories of temperament—activity level, regularity, avoidance or withdrawal, adaptability, responsiveness, intensity of reaction, quality of mood, distractibility and persistance—which are independent of parental styles of relating and disciplining. Based on these temperamental differences, these researchers then identified three types of children.

The Difficult Child is irregular in his biological functions, slow to adapt to new situations, intense in his emotional reactions and generally negative in his moods. The Easy Child, by contrast, is regular in her biological functions, highly adaptable, mild to moderate in her emotional reactions and generally positive in her moods. The Slow To Warm Up Child displays mildly negative reactions to new stimuli but eventually adapts to new situations with time and repeated exposure to them.

Thomas and Chess (1977) found that about 10% of the children they studied were Difficult, 40% were Easy and 15% were Slow To Warm Up. What is important in considering these children is not only their unique temperaments but how the temperament of each interacts with the values, hopes, fears and attitudes of their parents.

The behavior of the Difficult Child, for example, would be stressful to any parent, but more stressful to the parent with little tolerance for disruptive behavior or unrealistic hopes of raising "the perfect child." The Slow To Warm Up Child may present no problems to her parents as an infant but she may worry them as she grows older and does not adapt to new situations as quickly and as confidently as they would like. Any undue pressure they may place on her to adapt quickly may exacerbate her temperamental tendency to initially hang back. And although the Easy Child may be a delight for most parents, he may be a source of concern to the competitive, ambitious parent who would like to see more spunk and assertiveness in his child.

If you encounter a Difficult Child in your practice, your task is twofold: to educate the parents about the temperamental basis of their child's behavior and to help them to realistically adjust their emotional and behavioral responses to him. Although the Difficult Child may require firmer, more consistent discipline, his parents may also have to lower their expectations for him and themselves. They must not burden themselves with the unrealistic belief that they are fully responsible for their child's behavior. No matter what they do, the Difficult Child will never be a perfect, well behaved child.

There are three skills we want the parents of children, ages three to ten, to learn at the Family Teaching Center: the use of clear, specific commands; the use of rewards to strengthen acceptable behavior and the use of time-out to weaken unacceptable behavior. We take six sessions to teach parents these skills. The first three sessions are devoted to presenting them, while the last three are devoted to the review and consolidation of any gains the parents have made. What follows is a description of each of our six sessions.

THE FIRST SESSION

The purpose of the first session is to help the parents to become aware of the antecedents of their children's behavior, to teach them to give clear commands and to have them chart the target child's behavior for one week. If you have not already done so, you might at this time explain to the parents that they will be meeting with you for six sessions to learn new skills. Tell them also that you will be giving them weekly homework assignments and keeping in telephone contact with them.

Next, give the parents a mini-lecture about social learning principles. We do this at the Family Teaching Center by talking about the A B C's of behavior change using the following diagram:

A	B	C
Antecedents	Behavior	Consequences
1. Set up for success		1. Reward—behavior is strengthened
2. Decide on acceptable behavior		2. Punish—behavior is weakened
3. Give clear commands		3. Ignore—behavior is weakened

Explain to the parents that antecedents are what comes before the behavior while consequences are what comes after the behavior. We can change behavior by changing the antecedents and the consequences.

Under antecedents tell the parents that during this session you will be helping them to set up for success, to decide on acceptable and unacceptable behaviors for their children and to give clear commands. Then explain to them that after the behavior occurs, three things can happen: the behavior can be rewarded and thereby strengthened, or the behavior can be punished or ignored and thereby weakened. Tell them you will be teaching them to strengthen their children's acceptable behavior using rewards in the second session and to weaken their children's unacceptable behavior in the third session using a procedure called time-out.

Set Up for Success

To teach the parents how to set up for success, give them the following examples, ask them to identify the problem in each example and discuss what the parents can do to change the children's behavior.

> Mother has problems with her five year old when she takes him on a long shopping trip.

In this example, the parents should recognize that a five year old can behave for a short time only and that a long shopping trip will make him irritable and fussy. The way the parents can change their child's behavior is to shorten the shopping trip.

> Following a three hour nap in the afternoon, the parents are having difficulty putting their child to bed at night and getting her to fall asleep.

In this example, the parents should recognize the child doesn't go to sleep at night because of the long nap she has in the afternoon. The way to get her to go to sleep at night is to shorten or eliminate her afternoon nap.

> The parents promised a reward to their children but then withdrew it as a punishment. One hour later, the children had a bad fight.

In this example, the parents should recognize that the children were probably frustrated and angry because they were denied the reward they were promised. This may have led them to fight. Explain how this example shows that a reward which has been earned should not be later taken away as a punishment.

Now ask the parents if they can think of ways they can set up for success with their children. In effect, have them look at the antecedents of their children's misbehavior and discuss ways they can change those antecedents. Of course, they should talk about some of their own behavior in this exercise.

Decide on Acceptable Behavior

To teach the parents how to decide on acceptable behavior, explain that they will both have to determine the rules for their children's behavior. The important dividing line is between what is acceptable and what is unacceptable behavior. Once a child crosses the line, he or she should be punished using a technique called time-out which you will teach them in the third session.

For example, what is the dividing line between the children's legitimate expression of complaints and back talk. Can they complain to their parents and, if so, how in an acceptable manner? Similarly, what is the dividing line between the children's teasing or horseplaying with each other and unacceptable fighting? Is it when one child is hurt or starts to cry? Is it when the horseplay becomes physical?

Each parent may have different ideas about acceptable and unacceptable behavior. Your job will be to have them agree on the rules for their children's behavior, by compromise if necessary, and to state those rules clearly to their children.

Give Clear Commands

To teach the parents how to give clear commands, first explain their children won't be able to mind if they don't know exactly what is expected of them. Once the parents have decided on acceptable behavior, they must communicate the household rules to the children as clearly as possible. Give them the following examples of poor commands, ask what is wrong with each and discuss how each can be improved:

> Sue is listening to her stereo in her bedroom. The parent calls out from the kitchen, "I want you to do your homework now."

In this example, the parents should recognize that Sue may not have heard what she was told to do. In giving good commands, the parents should insure they have their child's attention.

> "Your bedroom is a mess. You're such a slob. Now get it cleaned up."

The parents should describe this as a very rude command which will probably elicit more resistance than compliance from the child. Explain that they should be polite but firm in giving their commands.

"I'm tired of how you've been acting all day. I want a better attitude out of you right away."

Parents should define the behavior they want from their children in such a way that it can be seen, heard or counted. They should specify exactly what the behavior is they want from their children. Commands to be good, play nicely, behave yourself or change your attitude are not specific enough.

"Bob, please pick up your room." Five minutes later mother returns and says in a louder voice, "Bob, pick up your room!"

Parents should not only specify exactly what they want done but when. In this example, Bob was not given a deadline.

"Will you get off the telephone and do your homework now?"

Parents should not ask their children to do something when they're really giving a command. If the child has no choice, he should not be given one.

After you have run through these examples with the parents, tell them it is a good idea with new commands and for young children to have the child repeat the command back to insure he understands it. Then ask the parents if there are ways they can improve their own commands to their children.

Chart the Target Child's Behavior

Your next task is to teach the parents to observe and chart the target child's behavior for one week. If they want to chart the behavior of their other children, allow them to do so as long as it will not make too much work for them. Whatever they learn from you about discipline by working with the target child will generalize to the other children, so it is not necessary that the parents do the child program with all their children at first.

Although it involves extra work for the parents, there are three advantages to charting. First, it gives you and the parents a baseline by which you can measure the progress of the child program. Second, it usually increases the child's positive behaviors and decreases his negative behaviors since he knows he is being watched and his behaviors counted. Third, it can give you some data which you can use to reassure the parents their child is not all that bad. In their understandable frustration and anger, many parents paint a completely negative picture of their child's behavior. If a week of charting reveals that he minded 40% of the time, you can point out to the parents, perhaps with an expression of delighted surprise, that he minded almost 50% of the time. Then remind the parents that their goal is to have their child mind *most* of the time—say seven out of ten times—rather than to have him mind *all* the time. The parents must set realistic goals for themselves and their children.

Before teaching the parents how to chart, explain the difference between minding and not minding. Tell them that minding involes the following elements:

—The child does what she is told to do when she is told to do it as well as she can.

—The child does not return to the prohibited behavior for a certain length of time. If she is told to keep her feet off the coffee table, she does so for the next hour or two. Whenever she and her brother are told not to fight, they play cooperatively for the next three to four hours.

—The child does what she is told to do without continually whining or complaining. She is allowed one reasonable question or complaint—e.g., "Ah, Mom, do I have to?"—but no more. Even if she complies while complaining or whining, she is still not minding according to our criteria.

Then instruct the parents to observe the target child for an hour each day for a week and to write down the number of times he minds and the number of times he doesn't mind during each hour. In a two-parent family, mother and father should observe at separate times. Also ask the parents to pick a positive daily behavior such as brushing his teeth, making his bed, dressing or undressing himself, and to count the number of times it occurs each day. Similarly, ask them to choose a daily problem behavior such as hitting his sister, not hanging up his coat or not going to bed on time, and chart the number of times it occurs each day. Along with minding, these are usually behaviors you will have the parents reward with points or stars after you have taught them the use of rewards to strengthen acceptable behavior during the second session.

To help the parents chart the target child's behavior, we give them a Weekly Observing Sheet. (See Figure 4.) On that sheet there are spaces for them to write out one command they have given each day which we then check at the beginning of the next session to insure they are giving good commands.

	S	M	T	W	TH	F	S
COMMAND - MINDING							
COMMAND - NOT MINDING							
POSITIVE BEHAVIOR							
PROBLEM BEHAVIOR							

Write out ONE command that you gave each day.

MON. _____

TUE. _____

WED. _____

THUR. _____

FRI. _____

SAT. _____

SUN. _____

Figure 4. Weekly Observing Sheet.

Next instruct the parents to explain to the target child what is involved in minding and to tell him they will be observing him for a week to see how he behaves. Then tell them to show the Weekly Observing Sheet to the child and post it in a prominent place where all in the family can see it. Finally, arrange for a convenient time to call the parents to see how their charting is going. In your telephone calls, answer any questions the parents may have, check to insure they're doing their homework assignments and reinforce them for any progress they claim they've made.

THE SECOND SESSION

The purpose of the second session is to introduce the concept of reward to the parents and to have them set up a reward system to strengthen acceptable behavior in their children. Before talking about rewards, however, first review the past week's activities with the parents. You want to insure they have learned to give clear, specific commands and to discuss with them the baseline data they have gathered on the target child.

Introduce the Concept of Reinforcement

Explain to the parents that rewards are the most effective way to change behavior permanently since it teaches children what behaviors their parents want them to display. Stress that another advantage of rewards is that it builds self-esteem in children especially if it is given in the form of praise.

At the Family Teaching Center, we encourage the parents to use three types of rewards: social, token and back-up. Social rewards are rewards such as praise, hugs, kisses, thanks, pats and participation in activities and attention. Although we stress to the parents that these are the rewards we want them to use primarily with their children over the years, we caution them not to make their love for their children contingent on certain good behavior. We want parents to love their children no matter how they behave or fail to behave.

Token rewards are the points and stars the parents give their children for acceptable behavior while back-up rewards are those the children can obtain by earning a specified number of points or stars. It is the use of these two types of rewards that you will teach the parents in the second session, although you will have them fade out the use of tokens after several weeks.

Before actually setting up a token reward system for the target child's behavior, however, stress to the parents the importance of rewarding their child as soon after the positive behavior occurs as possible. The sooner she is reinforced after an acceptable behavior, the more effective is the reward. If the parents don't reinforce their child immediately after the positive behavior occurs because of forgetfulness or unavoidable circumstances, tell them to reward their child as soon as they can by saying something to the effect, "I was really pleased with what you did last night" or "You really did a good job this morning. Thanks."

Also tell the parents it is important to keep rewarding a behavior on a periodic basis once it becomes established. You don't want them to take acceptable behavior for granted and begin to ignore, and thereby, weaken it.

Set Up a Token Reward System

To set up a token reward system, give the parents a Back-Up Rewards sheet which lists a number of possible back-up rewards and which is reproduced below:

BACK-UP REWARDS

Bedtime story
Later bedtime
Choice of TV program
Game or favorite activity
Undivided attention for 15 minutes
Special snack
Wrestling with Dad for 10 minutes
Choice of what is for dinner the next day
Helping to cook dinner
Going to friend's house after school
Ten cents

Explain to the parents that while social rewards are important, children do not always respond to them, so such rewards have to be supported by back-up rewards. Then ask them to list some possible back-up rewards the target child might enjoy.

Next give the parents the Point Incentive Chart (see Figure 5) and explain to them that the way the child can earn a back-up reward is through the use of points or stars. Stars are usually given to younger children and can, in some cases, be reinforcing in themselves without being paired with a back-up reward.

Then write down one or more daily chores or behaviors the parents want strengthened in their child and ask the parents to determine the number of points to be awarded each time the chore is done or the behavior is displayed. We usually list the positive behavior and the problem behavior the parents charted during the first week plus minding. By concentrating on strengthening minding behaviors in the target child, we believe we can clear up many, if not most, of the complaints the parents have about her.

CHORES/BEHAVIOR	DESCRIPTION	Value	Mon.	Tue.	Wed.	Thu.	Fri.	Sat.	Sun.
		TOTALS →							
		GOAL							

Rewards *(select one)*:

1 _____ 4 _____

2 _____ 5 _____

3 _____ 6 _____

Figure 5. Point Incentive Chart.

Next have the parents list three to four back-up rewards their child would like in the spaces provided below the Point Incentive Chart and instruct them to ask her to list two or three other back-up rewards she would choose for herself. Make sure these rewards are simple things the parents can do for their child, such as wrestling with Dad for fifteen minutes or having a bedtime story, rather than longer, more complicated activities such as going to the movies or going swimming at the YMCA.

Then have the parents determine the total number of points the target child must earn each day to earn a back-up reward. We instruct the parents to give the target child her points as soon as she does her chores or displays an acceptable behavior and to combine liberal praise with the granting of the points. If the child doesn't do all of a chore, the parents should praise what she did do, award any points she might have earned for a partially completed task and then point out what she can do next time to earn all of the points which can be awarded for that chore.

The target child can earn the back-up reward after an evening review—usually after supper—in which she and her parents go over the chart. Encourage the parents to praise whatever the child has done and have her choose one back-up reward if she has earned enough points for a reward. If she has not, the parents can point out what else she can do tomorrow to earn a back-up reward. If she goes for several days without earning a back-up reward, instruct them to reduce the number of daily points needed for such a reward. The program will not work if the child does not succeed at it.

Close out the second session of the child program by instructing the parents to explain the reward system to the target child and by setting up a time to call them again.

THE THIRD SESSION

The purpose of the third session is to teach the parents the use of time-out and to have them continue using a reward system now combined with time-out. Before you do this, however, review the past week's activities with them by reviewing the Point Incentive Chart which the parents should have brought with them.

Teach the Use of Time-Out

Explain to the parents that time-out is a consequence for not minding or misbehavior in which the child goes to a boring place away from people for five minutes (three minutes for children under age five). Time-out is used to decrease the occurrence of a problem behavior which occurs on a daily basis such as teasing, hitting or not minding. Stress to the parents that they should use time-out immediately after the problem behavior occurs so the child will make the connection between time-out and her behavior. It is also important that the parents use time-out every time the problem behavior occurs so the child fully establishes that connection as the following clinical example demonstrates:

> The first day she began to use time-out mother had to administer it twenty times to her very rebellious five year old son, Kevin. The therapist kept in frequent telephone contact with her to support her in her determination to gain control of Kevin's behavior. The second day she had to give Kevin ten time-outs while the third day he received only three. By this time, Kevin had received the message

that every instance of not minding by him would result in his mother putting him in time-out.

Having explained time-out to the parents, have them choose a boring place in their home which they can use for time-out. A bathroom, laundry room, hallway, or corner away from the rest of the family are acceptable. A closet or dark basement are not acceptable because they could frighten the child. His bedroom is not a good place since there are too many fun things for him to do in there.

Instruct the parents to use a timer when employing time-out. They can either purchase one or use the timer which is on most kitchen stoves.

Next stress to the parents that the target child may test time-out by misbehaving immediately after it is used, but assure them that it will work if they stick with it. Also discuss any problem which may occur while the child is in time-out. If he damages things or makes a mess, he should clean it up and/or pay for the damages with extra chores or an allowance. The parents should also consider selecting an alternative place for time-out. If the child screams while in time-out, the parents can add an extra minute for each minute of excessive noise.

To teach the parents how to use time-out, review the following Time-Out Procedure sheet with them:

—Label the misbehavior, not the child, and calmly tell him or her to go to time-out immediately—i.e., "(Child's name), that's not minding. Go to time-out."

—Send the child to a boring place for three to five minutes. Set a timer and allow the child to come out after it rings.

—If the child delays going to time-out by arguing or refuses to go, calmly say, "I'm adding on time." Add on one minute for each minute of delay. If after five minutes the child still refuses to go to time-out say, "If you do not go to time-out immediately, you will not be able to (loss of privilege) for the next day." Remove the privilege for the next twenty-four hours only and drop the attempt to get the child in time-out.

—Avoid any talking with the child while he or she is in time-out. You want it to be a boring experience for him or her.

—When the child comes out of time-out, thank him or her for going into time-out so cooperatively and regive the command, which was disobeyed. Avoid any "Now you had better behave" type of statements.

In giving time-out, it is important that the parents avoid labeling the child rather than his behavior. You don't want them to call the child bad, naughty or selfish, for example. If the child refuses to go to time-out after five minutes—a rare event in our experience—simply have the parents remove a privilege for twenty-four hours as a punishment for the child's refusal. If the parents object that they are then giving into their child, label their action as a strategic withdrawal rather than a defeat. They may have lost this particular battle but they will win the war. As soon as the child realizes the parents will take away a privilege each time he doesn't go into time-out, he should become more cooperative in accepting time-out as a punishment. If the child behaves beautifully for the next few hours after the parents have removed a privilege, still tell the parents to remove it. Just as an earned reward should not be taken away as a punishment, so an earned punishment should not be removed as a reward for good behavior.

Now tell the parents that since their child is allowed one reasonable question or complaint, they are allowed one reminder or warning before sending their child to time-out for not minding—i.e., "(Child's name), if you don't start to pick up your toys now as I've told you to do, I will send you to time-out." What you want to avoid is situations in which the parents warn the target child, usually with mounting anger, but do not follow up their warnings with specific consequences. The effective thing about time-out is that although it is aversive to young children, it is a relatively mild punishment so parents should be willing to use it frequently after one warning.

Continue the Use of a Reward System
Combined with Time-Out

Give the parents that Point Incentive Chart (see Figure 6) which now has spaces for the parents to chart the number of time-outs the target child receives each day. Have them list the same behaviors and chores to be rewarded they worked on last week. Now write in a behavior to be timed out which is the opposite of a behavior which is being rewarded. If playing cooperatively with sister is one of the behaviors to be rewarded, then fighting with her is the behavior to be timed out. We usually choose not minding as the behavior to be timed out as we believe a child who minds is a child who will not give her parents many disciplinary problems.

CHORES/BEHAVIOR	DESCRIPTION	Value	Mon.	Tue.	Wed.	Thu.	Fri.	Sat.	Sun.
		TOTALS →							
		GOAL							

Rewards *(select one)*:

1 _____ 4 _____

2 _____ 5 _____

3 _____ 6 _____

TIME-OUT BEHAVIOR	DESCRIPTION	Mon.	Tue.	Wed.	Thu.	Fri.	Sat.	Sun.

Figure 6. Point Incentive Chart with Time-Out.

Next explain to the parents that the best way to change behavior permanently is to combine rewards with time-out. We emphasize that effective discipline involves not only punishment for unacceptable behavior but also clear commands and rewards for acceptable behavior. Thus, ours is a two-pronged approach to misbehavior: we punish it while rewarding the acceptable behavior which is incompatible with it.

End the third session by instructing the parents to explain time-out to the target child and to show him the new Point Incentive Chart with Time-Out. Then arrange for another time to call them during the week.

THE FOURTH SESSION

If the parents are to encounter any problems in our child program, it is in applying time-out to the target child's misbehavior. Charting his behavior or awarding him points and a back-up reward for positive behavior do not involve any aversive control and so are usually not resisted by the child. Hence, at the Family Teaching Center, we devote two sessions—the third and fourth—in instructing the parents in the use of time-out. The purpose of the fourth session is to review the use of time-out, teach the parents to use it outside the home and have them continue using the Point Incentive Chart with Time-Out. Again, however, we review the past week's activities by reviewing the Point Incentive Chart with Time-Out the parents should have brought with them.

Review of Time-Out

To review time-out, simply give the parents the Time-Out Review sheet, which is reproduced below, and go over it with them.

TIME-OUT REVIEW

When giving time-outs:

Speak firmly.	VERSUS	Yelling.
Get near or call the child closer.	VERSUS	Giving time-out from a distance or standing eyeball-to-eyeball.
Briefly label the misbehavior.	VERSUS	Lecturing why the child shouldn't do what he or she did.
Correct the child as soon as he or she starts misbehaving.	VERSUS	Waiting until the child is really out of control.
Point out to a child	VERSUS	Threatening time-out

once that his or   or giving repeated
her behavior is not   warnings.
acceptable.

When the child is in time-out:

Leave the child alone.   VERSUS   Checking to see if he
                                                or she is all right.

Stop the clock if the   VERSUS   Calling to the child
child makes a big   or reminding him or
fuss while in time-   her to be quiet.
out.

If the child refuses to go to time-out:

Add minutes for   VERSUS   Trying to physically
delays.   make the child go to
                                                time-out.

Add minutes while you   VERSUS   Stopping everything
go about your   while you confront
business.   the child and add time.

Take away a privilege   VERSUS   Letting the conflict
after 5 minutes of   go on too long.
refusal.

If you have taken away   VERSUS   Giving in or backing
a privilege, stick to   down.
your word even if
the child is an angel
later.

After time-out:

Thank the child for   VERSUS   Carrying a grudge.
going to time-out.
Be pleasant or at
least matter of fact.

If time-out was about   VERSUS   Letting the child
a task, ask the child   trade time-out for
to do it again.   some chore or task.

After the child finally   VERSUS   Lecturing, explaining,
complies, drop the   justifying, etc.
issue.

Teach the Use of Time-Out Outside the Home

To teach the use of time-out outside the home, tell the parents they can put their children in time-out in the car, in the lobby of a theatre or restaurant, by a tree when outdoors or in the bathroom of someone else's home. In most of these situations, however, the parents should stay with the child to keep an eye on her. Parents should not leave their child alone in the car as a means of punishment, for example. Either they should sit in the front seat with the child in the back seat or stand outside the car while the child is in the car in time-out.

Continue the Use of a Reward System Combined with Time-Out

To close out the fourth session, tell the parents to explain the use of time-out outside the home to the target child and give them another Point Incentive Chart with Time-Out to use to reward and time-out the same behaviors they worked on last week. Then set up times for your weekly telephone calls.

THE FIFTH SESSION

By the end of the fourth session, you will have taught the parents all you can teach them about disciplining young children using the Family Teaching Center model. The remaining two sessions will be used only for review and follow up. The purpose of the fifth session will be to have the parents fade out the use of points or stars, if they choose to, but to insure they continue to reward acceptable behaviors with back-up rewards and to time-out unacceptable behaviors.

Fade Out the Use of Points

To teach the parents to fade out the use of points, instruct them to judge the acceptability of their child's behavior not just by the points earned, but also by her behavior in general. To make this global assessment, the parents should consider how well the child behaved or minded in general and how well she accepted correction. The parents can then rate their child's behavior for several days using this global assessment and match it with the number of points the child earned each day. If an acceptable global assessment matched, or closely matched, the number of points needed daily for a back-up reward for several days, then the parents are ready to drop the use of points and give back-up rewards simply on the basis of whether their child's behavior was generally acceptable or not each day.

Continue to Use Back-Up Rewards and Time-Out

The parents are to explain the fading of points to the target child but reassure her that she can still earn back-up rewards for acceptable behavior. The parents should also tell their child they will continue to use time-out for unacceptable behavior. At this time, they can discuss other behaviors which may be of concern to them with you. No further telephone calls need be made after the fifth session, although the parents should be told they can call you should any problems arise.

THE SIXTH SESSION

The sixth session can be held two weeks after the fifth. Its only purpose is to insure the gains the parents have made with their child are maintained. If there are no other problems the parents want to discuss, we usually terminate after the sixth session. However, if the parents have been referred to us by a child protective services for suspected or confirmed child abuse, we will most likely see them once a month for three to six months to further monitor their behavior.

COMMUNICATION SKILLS

Good communication skills are essential for effective family functioning. They enable family members to be emotionally intimate with each other, to express their love for one another and to solve the many problems which all families face. No group of people can solve their mutual problems if they can't effectively communicate about them.

In addition, communication skills are the major tools you have to treat your clients. It is through listening that you come to understand family problems and it is primarily through the spoken word that you treat those problems. What follows is a discussion of emotional communication, rules for communication and communication techniques you can use in your treatment of various families.

EMOTIONAL COMMUNICATION

Although it is an artificial distinction which is difficult to make in the real world, at the Family Teaching Center we distinguish between emotional communication and instrumental communication. Both involve two separate abilities: the ability to express oneself clearly and the ability to understand what the other person is saying. Emotional communication involves the ability to acknowledge, label and express emotions and the ability to listen to, accept and understand the emotional expression of the other. Instrumental communication, which we will discuss in the next chapter, involves the ability to formulate and clearly state one's needs, ideas and proposed solutions to a problem and the ability to hear what the other person has to say about a particular problem.

Emotional communication is important in effective interpersonal functioning for three reasons:

—It is what emotional intimacy is all about. It is what enables us to share our deepest, most intimate emotions with someone who cares. It is through emotional communication that we come to know and love another human being fully and intimately. The most comfortable relationship between two people—something which takes time to develop—is when both can express their innermost selves to each other and still feel accepted.

—Emotional communication of negative emotions is a way to recognize and express our deepest, most important needs. Fear, anger, guilt, hurt and depression are all signs that something is wrong in our emotional lives, that we feel unloved, that we are unhappy because our needs are not being met. By expressing these emotions appropriately and constructively, we can better recognize what our unmet needs are and let significant others know what they can do to help us meet those needs.

—It is through emotional communication that the love and support which is so important in healthy family functioning can be expressed. In addition to working behaviorally on the presenting problem, attempting to reduce the stress the family is under and strengthening their coping skills, we work hard at the Family Teaching Center to have family members express more love and support for each other, especially if love has not been well expressed.

A word of caution is in order here. When we talk about encouraging family members to express more love toward each other, we are talking primarily about family relationships in which there is little expression of love, as in the distant relationships discussed in Chapter 3. In enmeshed relationships— relationships in which family members are too close or too overinvolved with each other—rather than increase communication between family members, we may try to decrease it, to create more space between them. If mother is overinvolved with her child, for example, we may do what we can to create more distance between mother and child.

Probably the most visible emotion we work with at the Family Teaching Center is anger. We take the position that anger is a secondary emotion, an insight we frequently share with the family members. Beneath it, we usually see hurt, fear, frustration and/or helplessness. Anger is anguish, a loud bellow of pain and frustration. Although he may seem powerful and intimidating, we view the person who is angry as someone who is feeling weak, powerless, helpless and ineffectual. He is hurt because he believes he is being ignored. He may be afraid no one really cares about him.

Two clinical examples should illustrate this process:

> It would appear that the only emotion father shows his adolescent daughter is anger as he is always after her to behave. Actually, he is hurt she won't follow the family rules, afraid she is headed for more serious trouble and feeling absolutely helpless to control her behavior, all of which is expressed as anger.
>
> Meanwhile, the daughter is receiving the message her father doesn't really care about her since he is so "mean" to her. Not surprisingly, her reaction to his anger is to be angry in return, further straining the relationship between them.
>
> Mary angrily criticizes her husband because she feels he doesn't pay sufficient attention to her. Actually, she's deeply hurt by his limited attention and afraid he no longer loves her. Unfortunately, her criticism of him only serves to drive him away which confirms her worst case fears.

It should be obvious in the two examples above that beneath the hurt, fear and frustration which underlies anger, there is love and concern. Although it may not appear this way to its recipient, anger is a sign of love, a rough, crude and usually ineffective way to say, "I care about you." In families, people don't become angry about the behavior of others they don't care about. A lack of anger can be an indication of indifference. Behavior which is hurtful to self or others usually elicits anger in someone who cares but no response in someone who is indifferent.

The reason why hurt, fear and frustration may be expressed as anger is because it may be safer to do this. Sometimes people assume the best defense is a good offense. If they're feeling threatened or defensive, they attack. To express the hurt and fear which underlies anger would take an act of extraordinary courage. In a person who is already feeling vulnerable, it risks further hurt.

If the hurt person says, "I'm hurt," the recipient of this message, perhaps hurt and angry herself, may reply, "Tough."

At the Family Teaching Center, we don't believe anger should be acted out or directly expressed. We don't subscribe to the catharsis hypothesis which claims that expressing anger reduces it. Rather we hold the view, put forth by Tarvis (1982), that anger is a habit which is strengthened with use. We believe the expression of anger increases it. Even talking about anger can prolong it by keeping its stimulus in awareness.

Accordingly, in our treatment efforts, we do what we can to teach people to control their anger using some of the following techniques:

—When angry and nearly out of control, we advise people to separate, go for a walk, count to ten or do whatever else they can to cool down. Anger usually does subside after a time so the old fashioned advice about controlling it by distraction is still sound advice. If there's an important issue to be discussed by two angry people, as there usually is, we advise them to come back together later to discuss it.

—We ask angry clients to express the fear, hurt and frustration which underlie their anger. In other words, while discouraging as best we can the direct expression of anger, we encourage family members to express the emotional pain which causes their anger.

—Anger can be controlled by being charted. If a family member has a problem with temper control and expresses a willingness to do something about it, we may instruct the other family members to keep track of the number of times she loses her temper and bring that information to us the next session.

—Anger can also be controlled by rewards and punishments. If a family member keeps his temper for a day, he can be provided with a daily reward. Conversely, each incidence of temper loss can be penalized using some agreed upon penalty.

—A cognitive approach can be employed in anger control by teaching a family member to become aware of, challenge and modify the self statements she makes which contribute to her anger. If the critical wife in the example above is telling herself that it is horrible, catastrophic and unbearable that her husband is treating her as he is, that he shouldn't behave that way and that he's a S.O.B. for doing so, these thoughts would obviously fuel her anger. If you can teach her to replace these beliefs with others which say it's too bad her husband behaves the way he does, but she can learn to live with it, she may be able to thereby reduce her anger.

—Finally, the best way to reduce anger is to reduce the conditions which cause it: the inability to influence the behavior of other people which result in fear, hurt and unmet needs. In effect, at the Family Teaching Center, we try to insure that people's emotional needs are met so they don't have to resort to anger to express their anguish.

One way we try to do this is to have family members express more love, praise and support for each other, especially if the relationships between them are isolated or strained. In the example given above of the worried father whose concern about his daughter's behavior is expressed as anger, we would try to break through his anger to the love which underlies it. We would ask him to tell her of his worry and concern. We would instruct him to combine his attempts to control her behavior with a direct expression of his caring. We would have him say to her something such as the following:

> I love you very much but your behavior is not acceptable. I'm really worried about it. And it's because I love you that I must discipline you.

In addition, we would want the daughter to recognize that her father has been angry at her because he does care about her. She may not be able to see the connection between anger and love at this time in her young life, and she would probably not admit it even if she did, but we still want her to receive the message. Maybe it will bear fruit when she's older. To do this, we may say something to her such as the following:

> I know this may sound crazy, and I doubt you'll be able to see it, but it may be that your father's anger is a sign he really cares about you. Anyway, it is a pretty lousy way for him to express his love.

When we present our message with the caveat that we doubt the daughter will be able to see the connection between anger and love, we're challenging her to prove us wrong. And when we end our statement by saying that father's anger is a "pretty lousy way for him to express his love," our hope is that she will be more willing to accept it since our criticism of him fits with her anger towards him.

By encouraging the parents to express more caring for the target child, we hope to reduce the frequency of his unacceptable behavior. But quite frankly, this strategy doesn't always work, not because the parents won't express love, but because the target child won't signify acceptance of it by behaving himself. Despite the parents' sincere expressions of love and the establishment of reasonable rules and consequences, the youth still refuses to follow those rules, making it understandably more difficult for his parents to fully love him. By his misbehavior, he may create a barrier between himself and his family.

In such cases, we assume there are two possible explanations for the youth's continued misbehavior: either he is so unaccustomed to consistent discipline that he refuses to accept any reasonable limitations on his behavior despite the hurt he causes his parents, or he has been so hurt himself he doesn't fully believe his parents' expressions of caring. He is afraid to believe they love him or he believes himself to be unworthy of love. To conform his behavior to the family rules is to risk being accepted in the family, a risk he is not yet ready to take.

What you must do in this latter case is to encourage the parents to continue doing what they are already doing: providing their child with both love and discipline. If they are not yet ready to give up on him, he may eventually be willing to accept the reasonable controls on his behavior which is part of the price all of us must pay for being loved in a family.

COMMUNICATION RULES

As a family therapist, part of your job is to teach family members new ways to meet their needs and solve their problems. Specifically, you must teach them communication and problem solving skills. The way to teach any new skill is to instruct people in its application, model it yourself, have them practice it and reinforce them for any improvements they make.

One way to teach communication skills to family members is to have them communicate in your office under your direction. But to do this, you may need a set of rules with which to guide the family members in their efforts to talk with and understand one another. What follows is a list and description of communication rules you should enforce in your sessions with families. These are not rules which you need to make explicit to the family members although you may choose to discuss some of them with your clients.

1. Each family member is invited to speak although each can remain silent.

In your sessions with families, you should ask each family member's opinion on any particular topic but respect the right of some not to speak. Don't ignore or overlook any family members but don't force them to talk about something they may not want to discuss. In fact, the best way to deal with a silent family member— a sullen adolescent, for example—may be to advise her to keep quiet. Certainly, if you pressure a teenager to open up, you will only increase her determination not to cooperate with you. By telling her to remain silent, she may defy you and talk incessantly.

2. No one family member is to speak for another.

This kind of interaction can take place frequently in enmeshed family relationships. Since you'll want to create some distance in such relationships, one way to do this is to insure that each family member speaks for himself or herself. If you ask a child a question, for example, don't let his enmeshed mother answer it for him. You may have to interrupt her to do this but it is important to hear his view of the family as well as her's.

Another situation in which you may have to employ this rule is when meeting with two spouses in marital counseling. As you ask each what he or she feels or needs, each may begin to talk about the other. Since they are so accustomed to blaming or complaining about each other, discussing their own thoughts and emotions directly is not an easy thing for them to do. You may have to make a rule that when you ask each a question, each is to talk only about himself or herself, and not the other:

This may sound a little silly, but when I ask each of you a question about your relationship, I want you to answer it by talking only about yourself. Tell me what you want or how you're feeling.

3. No mind reading.

Mind reading is an insidious process in which one family member assumes what another family member is thinking or feeling and then acts on the basis of her unchecked perception. This practice can cause misunderstandings and can lead to serious problems as the following example shows:

John had had a bad day at the office so he was unusually quiet that night. His wife, Nancy, assumed he was still angry at her because of the fight they had had the night before. This was not the case, but since Nancy did not check it out, she became angry at him for his still being angry at her!

If at any time in your sessions someone begins to talk about what another family member is thinking or feeling, stop her immediately and ask her to check out her assumptions. If, for example, one spouse claims the other spouse hates to go to parties, have her ask her husband if this is the way he feels or ask him yourself. Either way, don't allow her to proceed on the basis of an unverified assumption about her spouse's thoughts or emotions.

This is one of the rules you may want to discuss openly with the family members. Define mind reading for them, give an example and explain how it can interfere with effective communication.

4. **No interruptions.**

Although you reserve the right to interrupt people when they're interrupting others or rattling on about an irrelevant topic, don't let family members interrupt each other. Explain to them that they can't be listening to what another person is saying if they're waiting to jump into the conversation with their own comments.

5. **No double messages.**

A double message sends two contradictory messages to the receiver at the same time. It is a confusing message because the receiver does not know to which message to respond. Some examples of double messages would be:

Be spontaneous.

Disobey me.

Don't read this.

What is so contradictory about these messages is that they put the receiver in an impossible double bind. If she complies with the message, she is not complying. If she becomes spontaneous under a command, she is not being spontaneous. If she disobeys the sender of the message, she is obeying him. If she reads the message, she cannot not read it.

In most double messages you'll see in your office, there will be a conflict between the digital (verbal) and analog (contextual and non-verbal) aspects of the message. The sender's words say one thing but his tone of voice and body posture send a conflicting message. Two examples of this type of double message would be as follows:

A husband grits his teeth and clenches his fists but claims he's not angry.

A wife has been unusually quiet and withdrawn all day. When her husband asks what's wrong, she replies with a sigh, "Nothing."

A common double message you may encounter in your practice is when one family member asks another to change but then begins to list all the reasons why he won't or can't. With this and any other double message, you should interrupt and point it out:

You're giving your husband two contradictory messages. You're asking him to change but then saying he can't. Which message do you want him to receive?

6. No switchboards.

To be more effective, all communication must be direct and not go through a third party or switchboard. If father has something to say to the children, he should talk to them directly and not through mother. If mother has a complaint about father, she should tell him directly and not complain to you about him.

When they first meet with you, family members will tend to talk directly to you and not to each other. This is what they believe is expected of them. They'll each tell you their view of the problem in the hope you will solve it!

Obviously, your view of how therapy works is quite different. You expect them to solve their own problems with your instruction, direction and encouragement. To help them do this, you'll eventually want them to talk directly to one another and not to or through you to each other. But at first, you probably should talk to each of them and gradually shift the flow of communication from you to the other family members. It might be too uncomfortable for them to begin confronting each other directly at first.

The best way to do this is simply and directly. If mother is complaining to you about father, tell her to tell him. Ask her to put it positively, however, by telling her husband what she wants from him rather than what she doesn't want him to do.

7. No zaps, putdowns, name calling or labels.

As they begin to talk directly to one another, make sure family members do not do this in angry, accusatory ways. In other words, do not allow them to say hurtful things to each other. Do not allow them to severely criticize, demean or negatively label each other.

At the Family Teaching Center, following the work of Gordon (1972), we teach family members the difference between "I" statements and "You" statements in order to avoid zaps, name calling or labels. We usually tell them something such as the following:

A "You" statement is an indirect expression of my feelings but a direct attack on the other person. By contrast, an "I" statement is a direct expression of my feelings which doesn't necessarily attack the other person. To show you the difference between these two statements, let me give you an example. Suppose I ask my wife to do something for me but she forgets. I'm really hurt and disappointed but my feelings may come out as anger in a series of "You" statements:

"You idiot. You're always forgetting to do what I ask you to do. You never do what I want. You're a selfish person who only cares about yourself."

In using "I" statements, I let my wife know exactly how her behavior has affected me without criticizing, labeling or attacking her directly:

"Mary Anne, I was really disappointed you forgot to do what I asked you to do. I was really counting on you. It was very important to me."

Later in this chapter under communication techniques, we'll discuss how we teach family members to use "I" statements.

8. **No past issues.**

Although we take a history of the presenting problem, we are initially present and future oriented in our therapy at the Family Teaching Center. We want people to decide what they can do about problems now and in the future rather than discuss what went wrong or who did what to whom in the past. Accordingly, after taking a history of the presenting problem, we encourage people to stick to the present issue only and not drift back into the past. Sometimes when people are stuck in the past, we may have to insist on enforcing this rule quite strictly:

I think we have a pretty good idea what went wrong so from now on I want you two to talk about what you can do to solve this problem or make it better. Let's concentrate on future solutions rather than past mistakes.

Just as we believe that talking about anger-producing situations can strengthen anger as a habit, so we're convinced that going over past conflicts or problems is usually not productive. Only if our initial approach hasn't worked might we decide to take a more thorough history of the parents' upbringing, courtship and marriage to gain some understanding of the present family dynamics. In other words, we don't usually take an extensive history until we feel we have to take one.

9. **One issue at a time.**

We not only want family members to discuss present issues, we also want them to stick to one issue at a time. Failure to do so can result in a failure to solve their problems. Usually people bring up other issues—past or present—when they feel they're losing in the present struggle. But such a strategy only serves to confuse the situation rather than clarify it. If you find the family members drifting to other topics, bring them back to the one issue until they settle it as much as they can.

10. **Express requests positively.**

Make sure that family members make requests for change from each other in a positive way. In other words, to get them away from criticizing or complaining about each other, have them tell each other directly and positively what each wants from the others. If mother says she wants father not to ignore her so much, have her say instead that she wants him to pay more attention to her.

COMMUNICATION TECHNIQUES

You now have a list of rules to enforce while working with a family on communication skills. What follows next are descriptions of some techniques you can use in helping the family members to communicate more effectively with each other and to strengthen their relationships.

Seating Arrangements

One way you can improve the family members' communication patterns is to rearrange the way they sit vis-à-vis each other. If you want father and daughter to talk more effectively and they're sitting on opposite sides of the room, have father switch seats with the younger brother who is sitting next to the daughter. If the target child is sitting between mother and father and a disagreement breaks out between them, ask the child to sit next to you so he no longer acts as a buffer between his parents. Then have mother and father move closer to each other.

Appointments

Appointments can also be used to work on communication patterns. If you think it's important to strengthen an isolated mother-son relationship, schedule an appointment to meet with the two of them without the other family members being present. Or if the marital relationship needs work, see mother and father together without the children.

Homework Assignments

Homework assignments can be used to work on family communication patterns and relationships. In the above examples, instruct mother and son to do one thing together this weekend for one hour. Or have the mother and father agree to spend twenty minutes every other evening discussing how the day went for each.

Seating arrangements, appointments and homework assignments are usually employed to strengthen certain distant relationships which need strengthening. However, they can also be used to weaken certain enmeshed relationships. For example, you can weaken a mother-son relationship by having mother sit out of the way while father and son sit closer, or by excluding mother from a father-son appointment or homework assignment. However, if you do this too prematurely or too frequently, without providing mother with something else to make up for the weakening of her relationship with her son, you may lose her and the family as clients. With enmeshed parents, you must proceed carefully and with empathy for the threatening nature of your distancing maneuvers.

Doubling

Doubling is probably the most effective communication technique you can use to uncover and express previously denied and unexpressed emotions. Rather than wait for the family members to gain the awareness and courage to express their deepest emotions, you can do it for them using this technique.

To use doubling, tell a family member you want to talk for her to another family member. Tell her also that she can let you know how accurate you were in expressing her feelings. Then either sit in your own seat, switch seats with her or stand behind her and express what you think are her feelings towards a particular family member.

If you are doubling for an adolescent who expresses much anger towards her father because of his constant criticism, for example, you might speak to father for her by saying the following:

Dad, it really hurts that you're always on my case. I feel like I can't do anything to please you.

Ask her how you did in expressing her emotions and invite her to speak for herself to father. Then ask father to respond to what you have said to him.

A variant of doubling is to put into words what you would like some family member to say to another. In the example above, you may want father to reply to his daughter in a certain way. Ask him if it would be accurate for him to say to her something such as the following:

If I've been on your case too much, it's because I'm really worried about your behavior. I'm frightened you're headed for serious trouble. Because I love you, I have to do what I can to prevent that from happening.

If father indicates this would be an accurant statement for him to make to his daughter, have him repeat it to her.

"I" Statements

We have already discussed above how we explain the difference between "I" statements and "You" statements to family members. What follows is a description of an exercise sheet we use with family members to teach them how to send effective "I" messages:

An effective "I" statement contains three parts:

1. A specific, non-judgmental description of the unacceptable or annoying behavior,
2. Its effect on you and
3. A specific, positive request for change.

For example, if Johnny uses the family car without putting gas in it, an effective "I" statement would be:

1. "Johnny, when you don't gas up the car after you use it,
2. I'm really hurt since I have to do it.
3. From now on, I want you to put gas in the car after you've used it."

Think of a behavior of a family member which annoys, bothers or worries you. Start with one you think would be easy to change. Then write an effective "I" statement below.

One way to teach family members "I" statements is to combine this exercise with doubling. In other words, use the doubling technique discussed above to demonstrate "I" statements to the family members. If you're working with a couple on their marital problems, for example, you can demonstrate the use of "I" statements by speaking for each of them to the other. If you start by talking to the husband for the wife, say something such as the following:

> When you read every night and rarely talk to me, I feel hurt and left out of your life. I want us to spend some time together talking with each other.

Check with the wife to insure that this is an accurate statement of her feelings. Then speak to the wife for the husband using another good "I" statement:

> When I'm reading at night and you want me to talk, I'm hurt because I feel you don't respect my desire to be alone. I want to have some time to myself each night.

If this is an accurate statement of the husband's feelings, you can then try to work out an acceptable compromise for this couple: if he agrees to spend ten to fifteen minutes each night talking with his wife, she'll agree to his spending the rest of the evening reading.

Rogerian Feedback

Named for the founder of client-centered therapy, Carl Rogers, Rogerian feedback is a technique in which family members learn to listen empathetically to each other and to paraphrase what they hear. Again, if you're working with a couple on marital problems, ask the wife to state her position on a particular issue. Then have the husband repeat back to his wife what he heard her say. Have him keep paraphrasing what she said until she is satisfied he accurately received her message.

Now have them switch roles so that the husband states his position on the same issue and she repeats back his message until he is satisfied she received the correct message.

Role Reversal

The role reversal technique is similar to Rogerian feedback in that you employ it to teach family members to empathize with one another. To use this technique, have two family members who are in conflict switch seats with each other. Then instruct both to imagine themselves as the other. Give them time to get into this role reversal. Ask them to consider what it would be like to be the other person.

Next ask one of them—the wife for example—to talk about a particular issue from her husband's perspective. Then ask him how well she did in expressing his views and emotions. Invite him to add or change anything she said about his position. Then have the husband speak from the point of view of his wife and invite her to modify what he said.

To introduce this technique to the family members, you can say something such as the following:

> Would you two mind switching seats?
> Thanks.
> Now I want each of you to imagine you're the other person. Carol, you're Jim, and Jim, you're Carol. Take some time to put yourself in the other person's place.
> Now Carol, I want you to tell me what it's like for you to be Jim in this family.

After she does this, ask Jim how she did describing the way it feels for him to be in the family. Give him the opportunity to modify what she said and then instruct him to talk about what it's like to be Carol in the family. As you did with Jim, give Carol the opportunity to say how he did and to modify what he said.

The role reversal technique can be used for both diagnostic and therapeutic purposes as you may encounter some family members who won't be able to do it. They'll sit in their seats and claim they can't speak for the other or they'll talk only about themselves, giving you an indication of what you'll need to work on to improve communication in the family.

The Hot Seat

If you use it, the hot seat is a technique which everyone in the family should be invited to do. In this exercise, one person is to speak and the remaining family members are to assume he is always right since his feelings are real and his viewpoint legitimate to him. He can talk about what it is like for him to be in this family or what changes he would like to see the family members make. The other family members are to listen to the person on the hot seat and to paraphrase what he is saying to his satisfaction.

A variant of this exercise is to have each family member in turn be on the hot seat while the other family members tell her what each likes or admires about her, to which she can only reply with a "Thank you." This technique can be used to create more positive feelings between family members as well as bolster each member's self-esteem.

Sculpting

Sculpting is another technique which everyone in the family should be invited to do. It is a non-verbal way for each family member to show how they each perceive the family.

Introduce this exercise by saying something to the family members such as the following:

> I want you all to pretend I can't hear but you're each to show me how you see the family. To do this, each of you will make a statue of your family using all the family members. Pretend each is clay so you can sculpt each in any way you choose.
> Who would like to go first?

At this point, if no one volunteers, you'll have to ask someone to go first. If someone does volunteer, you'll probably have to help her with this exercise by standing in the middle of your office with her. Instruct her to begin by sculpting how she sees one family member in the family. Next she can add a second member to the statue by sculpting him or her, then a third member and so on.

If the family members have trouble understanding this exercise, tell them to sculpt each other in terms of power or distance. Have them show you through sculpting the perceived distribution of power in the family or the perceived relationships in the family in terms of who is close to whom and who is distant. Then ask the family members how each feels in the position in which he or she has been placed.

Sculpting can be used for both diagnostic and therapeutic purposes. You can ask family members to sculpt how each perceives the family now, how it was to each five or ten years ago and how each would like it to be. You can also sculpt how you perceive the family and how you would like it to be.

Sculpting can also be used in individual therapy as you can ask a client whom you are seeing alone to sculpt his family of origin using chairs. You can also use it in group settings by asking a group member to choose other members of the group to be used to sculpt his family of origin. The problem with the use of sculpting in individual and group therapy, however, is you only obtain one member's view of the family without the possibility of challenging that view through sculpting by other family members. Although a young man may feel isolated in his family, for example, the other family members may not perceive him this way.

Family Drawings

A technique we use often at the Family Teaching Center—a family drawing is another non-verbal way for the family members to show how each perceives the family. Provide the family members with a pencil and paper and ask each to draw the family. If they press you with questions, say only you want each of them to make a map or picture of the family. While they're doing this, you can draw your impression of the family also and later share it with them.

Next collect the family drawings from the family members and discuss each with them. Sometimes family members will not give you much information in these drawings. They'll draw the family members lined up in a row with little indication of emotion or movement. There may be other times, however, when some of the family members will give you significant information, as when the target child draws herself separated from the rest of the family with a frown on her face and tears falling from her eyes. Using doubling and this drawing, you can speak for the target child and say to the family members:

> I feel very isolated and lonely in this family, and that makes me very sad. I want to be a part of this family.

History of Parents' Upbringing

At the Family Teaching Center, if we find our therapy is not working, we may take a history of the parents' upbringing for two reasons: to see if there are any unresolved family of origin problems which may be interfering with the parents' present relationships with their offspring and to provide the older adolescent with some insight into her parents' behavior. We usually find that parents who are unable to fully express their love for their children did not receive much expression of love from their own parents. We want children to understand that if their parents haven't expressed much love, it is because of the way mother and father were raised and not because of anything they've done or failed to do. In effect, we don't want the children to blame themselves for their parents' inhibitions in expressing affection.

The questions we usually ask to take a history of each parent are listed in Chapter 10.

Chapter 8

NEGOTIATING AND CONTRACTING

N egotiating and contracting lie at the heart of much of our
therapy at the Family Teaching Center. Our goal with
all the families we treat is to specify and implement those changes
which would improve family functioning. We often prefer to put
these proposed changes in writing to avoid later misunderstandings.

There are three problem areas in which we use negotiating and
contracting: in counseling families with behavior disordered
adolescents, in marital counseling and in custody counseling.
Since we have devoted separate chapters to marital counseling
and custody counseling, this chapter will concentrate primarily
on the use of negotiating and contracting in the treatment of
adolescent discipline problems. My hope is that once you have
acquired these skills in your work with families with adolescents,
you will be able to expand them to marital and custody
counseling cases.

Negotiating and contracting are the processes whereby all the
family members affected by a problem work together towards a
solution, write down their decisions as to who will do what and
sign their agreement. To be successful, everyone in the process
must have an equal say and equal power. No one family member,
or combination of family members, can be dominant. If the
members cannot arrive at a solution, no one shall have the
authority to impose a solution unless the other family members

agree to such a procedure. If they don't agree, the family members must keep working on the problem until they arrive at an acceptable solution.

In teaching families negotiating and contracting skills, we stress the importance of compromise, of giving in order to receive. We encourage family members to yield their positions a bit to arrive at a consensus. We point out they may not obtain what they want this way, but they arrive at a solution everyone can accept for the sake of family harmony. We jokingly say that if no one really likes the proposed solution but can live with it, it is probably a good compromise.

Before any family can negotiate and contract, however, the family members must have the skills to communicate with each other using instrumental communication. They must be able to express their opinions and proposed solutions clearly and to have these understood by the other family members. To teach these skills, we give the family members a list of negotiating rules, carefully explain each one and have them agree to the rules.

Whether or not we would have the family members work on emotional communication before proceeding with negotiating and contracting depends upon a number of factors. In custody counseling, for example, we avoid emotional communication because our goal is not to strengthen the relationship between two hurt, divorcing parents but to have them decide as calmly and rationally as they can what will be best for their children. By contrast, in a family in which there is obvious emotional pain or in which relationships are distant, strained or deteriorating, we would begin immediately to work on emotional communication and then proceed to negotiating and contracting as the following clinical example shows:

> Janet and her family were referred because she was disobedient and had recently been arrested for shoplifting. Her history revealed a caring but distant relationship with her depressed mother, a strained relationship with her stepfather and no relationship with her father who lived in another part of the state.
>
> The therapist diagnosed Janet as mildly depressed and decided to work on family support before proceeding with negotiating and contracting for her disobedience. He called the father to encourage him to re-establish contact with his daughter, held several sessions with mother and daughter to strengthen their relationship and

paradoxically instructed Janet not to become too emotionally close to her stepfather lest she be hurt again. In giving this last suggestion, the therapist hoped that Janet would resist it and allow her stepfather to care for her.

If the family members do not express much painful affect during the intake sessions and appear willing to work instrumentally on certain problems, we would proceed with negotiating and contracting. If we found this did not work, however, we would assume there are underlying, unresolved, emotional issues which prevent the members from working effectively together. It would then be our function to uncover these emotional issues and hopefully resolve them before proceeding to the negotiation of a behavioral contract. The following clinical example shows this process:

> Since James was not following the contract he had earlier agreed to, the therapist decided to explore in more depth the family pain. She explained to the family members her view that family counseling was not working because there was emotional pain in all members of the family which they were not talking about. She then indicated to James and his parents what she thought was their pain—i.e., the parents had struggled with marital problems for years, father felt like a blamed scapegoat and mother felt caught in the middle between her husband and son both of whom felt hurt because they were once close but now were estranged.
>
> The therapist then explained that several sessions would be required to share their mutual pain before a behavioral contract would work. They agreed to her proposal, worked on emotional communication and later successfully negotiated another behavioral contract.

TYPES OF CONTRACTS

There are two types of contracts we employ at the Family Teaching Center: contingent and non-contingent. Contingent contracts are those which depend upon the behavior of the signatories for their implementation. The contract breaks down if the parties to it fail to do what they have agreed to do. The parents will provide certain rewards and punishments, for example, for acceptable and unacceptable behaviors displayed by the adolescent. If they do not, the adolescent will have no incentive to behave. Husband and wife agree to do some nice things for each other if each reciprocates. If one fails to do this, the contract is no longer valid.

Non-contingent contracts are those which do not depend upon the behavior of all the signatories for their implementation. Husband and wife agree to do something nice for each other, for example, no matter what the other does. If one spouse doesn't follow through on the agreement, the other can still do what he or she has agreed to do.

At the Family Teaching Center, our contracts between parents and adolescents are contingent contracts. If an adolescent behaves appropriately, the parents will give certain rewards; if she breaks a rule, the parents will administer an agreed upon penalty. Our custody contracts are usually non-contingent. Each parent agrees to certain living, visitation, holiday and vacation schedules which apply to each only. If one parent misses an agreed upon time for visitation, this does not affect the other parent's time with the children unless both agree to rearrange visitation periods.

Though usually not written down, our marital agreements are often non-contingent. Contingent contracts in marital cases can be risky since they can break down so easily. Using non-contingent contracts, we can discover which spouse is not being cooperative and perhaps bring some pressure to bear on him or her to change.

Another reason we don't use contingent contracts in marital counseling is because unhappily married couples already interact contingently with each other before they arrive at a therapist's office. Jacobson (1981) reports that in contrast to satisfied couples, dissatisfied couples have more negative interactions with each other than positive interactions and, in their mutual hurt, anger and frustration, attempt to control each other contingently through punishments and the withholding of rewards. But such attempts at control only lead to mutual hurt, retaliation and even more negative interactions, creating what we call the hurt, anger and blaming cycle described in Chapter 3.

If the marriage is to survive and provide mutual satisfaction, this cycle must be broken. The partners must learn to give each other more pleasure and less pain, and to do so non-contingently. As therapists, we must not reinforce what they are already doing unsuccessfully. Instead, we should reverse their pattern of contingent interactions by having them behave non-contingently with each other. What we want to avoid at all costs are contingent emotional exchanges between spouses—i.e., she will show him love only if he will show her love, and vice versa.

Needless to say, we want the love of parents for children to be unconditional and non-contingent. Whatever they do or fail to do, we hope parents will always love their children even though they reserve the right to judge and discipline their behavior. Without the awareness that their parents care about their welfare, few, if any, resentful youths will be willing to follow the family rules no matter what rewards are provided. This is why at the Family Teaching Center we have parents express their love for their children before attempting a behavioral approach to their discipline problems.

NEGOTIATING WITH ADOLESCENTS

At the Family Teaching Center, we expect the parents of young children to be firm, effective disciplinarians. We encourage them to be in charge. We want them to establish clear limits for their children, and to back up their rules with automatic rewards and punishments. As the children grow older, however, our hope is that parents will begin to share some of their rule-making authority so that by the time adolescents leave home, much of their behavior will be under self-control. Although they may begin to use the negotiating process with their children when they're around eight or nine, we don't expect parents to use negotiating and contracting in earnest until the children are around eleven or twelve years old. Probably the ideal is that starting with limited use with children, parents use negotiating and contracting with increasing frequency with their adolescents.

Our use of negotiating and contracting to deal with adolescent discipline problems is based on Gordon's (1970) no-lose method of conflict resolution. We feel there are three advantages to this method. First, since adolescents are involved in the process of resolving family conflicts, they are more willing to comply with the solutions to those conflicts. There's a better chance that family rules will become internalized by teenagers as their own since they had a say in formulating them. And the more internalized rules are, the more likely they'll be obeyed without external pressure.

Second, negotiating gets to the heart of a problem since each member of the family feels free to share his or her honest reaction to the conflict. All have the right to speak out without fear of ridicule or reprisal. As a result, the best solution to the problem, acceptable to all, will be found.

Third, the effects of this method are to treat adolescents with dignity, to show respect for their needs and opinions and to express faith in their integrity and good judgment—sure ways to help them become self-respecting, considerate and responsible adults. This treatment of teenagers should also result in less hostility and better parent-child relationships.

In teaching these skills to families with adolescents, you want to guard against the parents' agreeing to negotiating and later changing their minds when a solution is not forthcoming, or when they don't like the solution which appears to be emerging from the negotiating process. In effect, you don't want the parents to assume control of rule-making authority once they agreed to share it with their adolescents. Such a maneuver would only make the teenagers angry and mistrustful of their parents' word, and rightfully so.

To avoid this possibility, insure the problem areas to be discussed are ones about which the parents are willing to negotiate. Explain to the family members the difference between negotiable and non-negotiable items. Define negotiable items as those items—e.g., chores, hours, grades, use of the family car or use of the telephone—about which the parents are willing to share rule-making authority and to compromise with their offspring. Non-negotiable items are those such as attending drinking parties or driving without liability insurance about which there is no room for compromise. These are areas in which the parents retain their rightful, executive authority.

However, you may point out to the parents that non-negotiability can be a two-edge sword. Their adolescents may have some non-negotiable items also, such as choice of friends. Realistically, parents cannot forbid their offspring to associate with certain friends. They can express their concerns once about those friends and forbid them to visit their home, but this is all they can do. As soon as the adolescents leave the house, the parents have no control over their offsprings' associations, and nagging will only make undesirable friends more attractive in the eyes of rebellious adolescents.

In actually doing negotiating and contracting, include in your sessions only those family members—usually adolescents and parents—who will abide by the finished contract. You do not have to include younger brothers and sisters in the sessions, for example, if the rules decided upon will not directly affect them.

Start by stressing the idea of compromising, of giving in order to receive. If parents who were raised in an authoritarian manner object to this concept, agree with them that parents should be in charge with young children, but that research shows adolescents will better follow rules they've had a part in formulating. If the parents still object, ask them to try this method for several weeks since what they've been doing up to now has not been working for them. Also, explain the difference between negotiable and non-negotiable items and state that parents still retain their rightful authority with the latter. Give them two examples of non-negotiable items such as the following:

> Although it is the custom for high school seniors to stay out all night on graduation day, no one in the Smith family can do this until they graduate.

> Sixteen year old Susie cannot drive the family car without liability insurance. If she were to be responsible for an automobile accident, her family could be devastated financially by a lawsuit.

Then have the parents specify those items which are non-negotiable and explain to their children why these are non-negotiable items.

To teach the family listening and negotiating skills, give the members the Rules of Negotiating sheet, which is reproduced below, and review it with them. Make sure all family members agree to abide by each rule. You will note that most of these rules are ones we discussed in the chapter on emotional communication:

1. Everyone will have equal time to express his or her ideas and proposed solutions.

2. Everyone agrees to stay in the "here and now" and not drift into the past with example after example. Everyone agrees to stick to one issue at a time.

3. Everyone agrees to avoid name calling, badmouthing or zapping.

4. Everyone agrees to express requests in a positive manner, to let others know not what he or she doesn't want, but what he or she does want others to do.

5. Everyone agrees to cooperate by listening to each other. Everyone agrees, however, that listening does not necessarily signify agreement.

6. Everyone works with the idea of compromise—a give and take.

Now explain to the family members that they should write down the agreed solutions to their problems, assign responsibilities for each family member and specify what rewards and penalties, if any, will be used to insure that everyone carries out their responsibilities. Explain to them that sometimes agreeing to solutions in writing may not be enough to obtain cooperation. Often families need to back up their rules with positive and negative consequences. If you think the family members may have some difficulty understanding the use of contracts, you can show them a sample contract (see Figure 7) and explain it to them.

RESPONSIBILITIES	PRIVILEGES (meets responsibilities)	PENALTIES (NOT meeting responsibilities)
Sally to be home by 10 p.m. weeknights and 12 midnight Fridays and Saturdays.	Can go out until curfew with prior permission.	If 1/2 hour late, grounded for one night.
Clean room daily (make bed and pick up)	50 cents each day	Loss of allowance
Set table each night	25 cents each day	
Clean living room (vacuum, dust and pick up) by Saturday noon.	$1.25	Can't go out until living room cleaned.

I agree to the above conditions.

Signed: _____

Parents: We/I agree to grant the above listed privileges in exchange for the carrying out of the above listed responsibilities.

Signed: _____

_____

Witness: _____

Special Options:
Sally to call if to be late for any legitimate reason.

Figure 7. Sample family contract for hours and chores.

Next show them a blank copy of the same contract you will be using with them. Write down the proposed responsibilities, rewards and penalties for the family members as they agree to them. Add any special conditions the family members may want to include in the contract, have everyone sign it and sign it as a witness yourself. Then, if possible, make photocopies of the contract for all the family members and keep one copy yourself in their file.

At the Family Teaching Center, we usually list several problem areas about which families can negotiate and contract:

chores
hours
grades
use of the family car
use of the telephone
other _____

We then have the family members choose an easy item first so their initial success will engender a spirit of hope and cooperation. If they attempt to tackle their most difficult problem initially and fail, as well they might, they could easily become discouraged and give up on negotiating and contracting as a solution to their problems.

If the family members become stuck and are unable to come up with a solution to a problem acceptable to all, there are several things you can do:

—Keep encouraging compromises.

—Ask each member for the next best alternative—i.e., not what each would like but what each would settle for.

—Suggest they try a contract for a week. Tell the family members they're not setting anything in concrete. If the contract doesn't work, they can always modify it during the next session.

—Above all, keep the responsibility for a contract on them. It's their problem which must be solved by them, not you.

PUNISHMENTS

One thing you may have to help family members decide is what penalties to administer to the adolescent in case he doesn't follow the contract. Often, families present the extremes of either no consequences for misbehavior or very harsh consequences. If the parents want harsher punishments than the adolescent suggests, you may have them compromise by agreeing to the lesser punishments suggested by the adolescents for now. If the contract doesn't work, the punishments can be increased.

In the child program, we recommend time-out as the primary means of punishment, with loss of privileges as a back up if the child doesn't go into time-out or if a harsher punishment is needed. Usually, it is not. We believe adolescents are too old for time-out, however, so the family will have to find other ways to penalize unacceptable behavior.

Fleischman, Horne and Arthur (1983) propose a number of penalties which may work with adolescents. They are:

—Grandma's law. In her wisdom, Grandma would make us eat our carrots, which we disliked, before we could have our dessert. The same rule should apply to our own children and adolescents. Only after their chores and homework are done may they watch T.V., go out, or do whatever it is they've planned to do.

—Natural or logical consequences. These are consequences which flow naturally or logically from the misbehavior. They are "punishments which fit the crime." If a child loses his toy, for example, he does not receive a new one. If he breaks a window playing ball, he pays for its replacement. If an adolescent violates her curfew, she is grounded for a night. If she sleeps late and misses her ride to school, she walks, assuming school is not too far away.

—Extra chores. Extra chores can be given as a penalty. However, we would advise they not be daily or weekly routine chores since such chores are intrinsically unpleasant. To make them a punishment can increase their aversive properties and make adolescents even more unwilling to do them. Instead, we would recommend that the extra chores assigned as punishments be tasks adolescents don't do routinely such as cleaning the garage or painting the fence.

—Loss of privileges. This is probably the punishment parents of adolescents use most frequently. It can include loss of T.V., stereo and radio privileges, no friends over for the day, in the bedroom for the night, grounded for the weekend or loss of attendance at a game or show. Fleischman, Horne and Arthur (1983) argue—and we agree—that the loss of privileges should only be for twenty-four hours. Any grounding which is longer than a day is not only more difficult to enforce, it creates resentment in youths as they endure a punishment long after they've regretted their misbehavior or realized they've deserved a punishment.

In point of fact, at the Family Teaching Center, we believe in punishments which are aversive but relatively mild or of short duration—e.g., time-out for five minutes or grounding for twenty-four hours—because the milder the punishment, the more willing parents are to use it each and every time the misbehavior occurs. Hence, the greater its effectiveness.

Most parents are reluctant to administer harsh punishments— e.g., spankings or grounding for a week—but if these are the only disciplinary tools they have, they've restricted their capacity to discipline. What these parents typically do is not follow through with consequences for misbehavior because they don't want to be "mean," or they wait with mounting anger until their children's behavior is nearly out of control to punish them.

By contrast, parents should be willing to administer a mild punishment to their children after one warning each and every time the misbehavior occurs. In this manner, children and adolescents soon learn what is acceptable and unacceptable behavior. Thus, we can say to parents who believe punishment has to be harsh to be effective that milder or shorter punishments which are more frequently used constitute stricter discipline than harsher punishments which are less frequently used.

There are times when the loss of privileges should be used judiciously by parents. We would advise parents not to withdraw privileges when they have been earned as a reward or when a privilege is one which is important to the adolescent. If a daughter has been planning to attend a dance for weeks, she may become understandably furious if she couldn't go as a punishment. If she has misbehaved on Thursday and the dance is on a Friday night, perhaps she could be permitted to go but then grounded for the rest of the weekend.

In addition to the punishments described above, Norman and Harris (1981) suggest two other penalties which they claim adolescents prefer. These are:

—Creative punishments. Creative punishments are unique penalties which usually provide some learning experiences for adolescents. They may be required to do volunteer work, for example, attend a city government meeting to find out how the city is run or learn the correct definition and spelling of twenty new words.

—Self-imposed punishments. These are punishments which adolescents choose for themselves. Lest parents worry that such punishments would be too lenient, Norman and Harris (1981) found the opposite may be the case. Some of the adolescents in their study claimed they imposed a harsher punishment on themselves than their parents would have imposed on them for the same misbehavior.

FOLLOW UP

Once the family members have established contracts for what they consider to be their problem areas, your next function is to follow them up to insure the smooth implementation of their contracts. If the contracts are not working, you will have to use emotional communication to explore in greater depth the family dynamics and emotional pain. As we pointed out in the chapter on our child program—Chapter 6—we maintain telephone contacts with the family members in-between appointments to see how things are going and to be available to answer any questions or to resolve any crises. In the child program, we talk only with the parents. In the adolescent program, however, we believe it's a good idea to talk with all the family members so that no one either feels left out or solely responsible for the contract.

When we're confident things are going better with the family, we'll begin to see the members every other week or once a month until we all agree it's time to terminate. During these longer time periods between appointments, we may still stay in telephone contact with the family. After termination, we'll contact the family six months later for research purposes and to make ourselves available to the family members should they need further counseling.

There are some families, however, you'll have to carry for a long time, perhaps being available when crises arise and seeing them once a month for years. These are the chronic, multi-problem families who operate with limited resources under tremendous stress. Often, the family is headed by a single parent who operates from crisis to crisis, rarely following through with consequences or your instructions, because crises keep her from being depressed and provide her with a sense of being needed. Since you may be her major social contact, she may not want to lose you as a "friend" by acting more appropriately. Your approach to her must be firm and confrontive in that you expect her to carry out the homework assignments but also supportive in that you like her and are willing to see her on a long term basis.

Chapter 9

UNIQUE FAMILY PROBLEMS

M any of the problems we treat at the Family Teaching Center involve disobedience on the part of children and adolescents. However, we also encounter other problems which require special consideration and treatment. After outlining some steps you can take with all children's psychological problems, this chapter discusses these problems and gives suggestions on how to treat them.

GENERAL CONSIDERATIONS

With many youths, working to reduce their misbehavior through behavioral techniques may not be sufficient to bring about behavioral change. In addition to employing these techniques, there are several other things you can do to treat most behavioral and emotional problems displayed by children and adolescents:

—Gently challenge the family members' perceptions of the target child's behavior as individual and negative by relabeling it as interactional and positive. We have already discussed this strategy in Chapter 4 but it would be worthwhile to discuss it again here.

Most family members perceive the behavior problems displayed by the target child as his or her problems rather than their problems. If they do admit to any problems in the family, they may blame the target child for them. One way you can challenge these perceptions is by insisting that all family members come in for your diagnostic interviews and by exploring the problems in terms of family interactions. You want to bring the other family members to the point at which they realize they will have to change some of their own behaviors to change the target child's behavior.

The family members also perceive the target child's behavior as something negative or unpleasant. And in point of fact, it has been aversive to someone—school authorities, the neighbors, parents or siblings—else it would not have come to your attention.

If the target child already feels isolated in the family, if he is a blamed scapegoat, these perceptions will only serve to increase his sense of isolation. You may want to challenge these views by pointing out to the family members any positive consequences of his misbehavior. For example, it may have diverted them from other, more painful problems and brought them into counseling so they could work directly and effectively on these other problems.

—Another thing you can do to reduce the sense of isolation of the target child is to strengthen her family support system. Even if she is enmeshed with one parent, she is probably isolated from another. If there is a divorced parent who has not had much contact with her recently, you may want to contact him to see if you can re-establish that relationship. If it is not possible to strengthen the target child's relationships with her family members, or if this may not be enough support for her, you may want to provide additional support through individual counseling, a support group or a Big Sister.

—Express the hurt and unmet needs which often underlie the symptomatic behavior of the target child. Usually it is a cry of unhappiness, a sign a child feels his love and esteem needs are not being met. You can do this by using a doubling technique:

John, would it be O.K. if I tell your family what I think you're trying to say to them through your behavior?
Thanks.
I don't feel a part of this family. I wonder who really cares about me and that really hurts. But I express my hurt through my misbehavior. I want someone to pay attention to me rather than ignore me or punish me all the time.

How did I do talking for you?
Is there anything you want to add or change?

After you have expressed what you believe underlies the symptomatic behavior, have the parents agree to listen to him and then tell the target child he doesn't have to misbehave to be heard in the family. In other words, from now on he can go directly to his parents and tell them he's unhappy rather than send a message through misbehavior. In effect, you want to replace acting out with the verbal expression of emotions and frustrations.

—Do what you can to strengthen the self-esteem of the target child since it is usually quite low. This is not an easy task, but you can attempt to do this through your understanding and respect, cognitive restructuring and support for the target child from the family members.

—At the Family Teaching Center, we sometimes work on conscience development with acting out youths. You can do this by pointing out to the target child the harmful consequences of her anti-social behavior to herself, her parents and the victim. It hurt her because of the trouble it brought her, it hurt her parents who are worried about her and it hurt the victim by violating his rights. What you want to do is to develop some empathy for the victim by saying something such as the following:

> Sally, do you remember how sad you were when someone stole your bicycle and you never got it back? Well, the person you stole from must feel the same way.
>
> Since you don't want anyone to steal from you, you shouldn't steal from other people.

In effect, you want the youth to eventually take the position, "What I did was wrong because it hurt myself and other people. I am fully responsible for my misbehavior—no one forces me to do it—and only I can prevent it from occurring again."

—If these therapeutic maneuvers combined with behavioral techniques don't work to bring about behavior change, then, as we have said repeatedly throughout this book, you should provide more in-depth therapy to uncover and relieve whatever underlying family dynamics are interfering with your counseling efforts.

What follows is a discussion of specific problems you may encounter in your therapeutic work with families with behavior disordered children. The first group of problems—stealing, lying, vandalism, firesetting, temper tantrums and aggression—involves behaviors which are primarily directed towards other people or their property in angry, anti-social ways. The second group—bedtime problems, eating problems, enuresis, encopresis, school phobias, school problems and chemical dependency—are those behaviors which are more harmful to the self. Finally, the chapter concludes with a brief discussion of the diagnosis and treatment of sexual abuse in families.

STEALING

Most young children will steal or shoplift since they don't yet know it's wrong. When it occurs, however, it should be dealt with swiftly, firmly and with consequences.

If a young child steals something in the home, the parents should label the behavior as stealing, say that it is very bad and explain to the child that she should not steal because she wouldn't want someone to take something from her. Then, for the first offense, the child should be sent to time-out. Subsequent offenses could be punished by a loss of privileges.

If a child takes something from a store, the parents should take him back with the stolen merchandise and have a clerk or the store manager reprimand him.

If the stealing continues as the child grows older, we would urge the parents to consider calling the police the next time a theft occurs. We realize that this may seem like a harsh punishment but it is critical that stealing behavior be stopped early before it becomes habitual. A stern lecture by a police officer could be just what is needed to prevent further stealing by a child.

Before they call the police, however, have the parents tell the child what they'll do if he steals again. Do this in your office, perhaps by writing out a contract. Have the parents assure the child of their love for her which is why they're taking such an extreme measure. Also, if you're the one urging the parents to do this, perhaps the child will see you as the "bad guy" rather than them.

If the stealing continues, then you're dealing with a more serious problem which may require more law enforcement intervention. Encourage the parents not to intervene to protect their child from the consequences of his behavior. To intervene would only reinforce a behavior that has already become self-reinforcing. You might have to worry the parents by pointing out the probable consequences if their child keeps stealing and is not stopped at this time—i.e., that he will get into increasingly more serious trouble.

Encourage the parents to reduce the amount of unsupervised time allowed their child. Also, encourage them to assume that any suspicious item the child brings home, claiming he found it or was given it, is stolen. All such items should be returned or confiscated. If the child cannot recover a stolen item, he should be required to make restitution for it by work or payment.

It's difficult to reinforce not stealing since you can never be sure when it occurs. Parents could reinforce not stealing when the child is in fact stealing. Nevertheless, if the parents are convinced the stealing has not occurred for some time, have them reinforce their child primarily through praise and thanks.

If stealing is a function of emotional pain, obviously the pain has to be relieved at the same time the stealing is being punished. Often an acting out youth is a depressed youth with good reasons to be depressed. Her stealing may be a cry for help or attention because of emotional deprivation. If she's stealing from her parents, this may represent a hostile taking from them what she feels she can't get from them voluntarily—i.e., love and support. Obviously, you will need to strengthen the parent-child relationships in such a case.

Continued stealing, or any other chronic and serious anti-social behavior, despite all the above efforts may require a residential evaluation or treatment. Before deciding this, you need to determine whether you are dealing with an emotionally disordered youth or a personality disordered youth. We like to think of this distinction as involving a continuum with most youths falling between the extremes because they display a mixture of both disorders. In making the distinction between these two types of youths, we ask ourselves the following questions:

—What was the early history of this youth's upbringing? What kind of nurturing did he receive? Was he well cared for as an infant and so bonded with his caretaker, or did he suffer from abuse or neglect so was not able to bond to anyone?

—What was the history of this youth's discipline? Did he receive little or no discipline or very harsh discipline? Or was he effectively and caringly disciplined when he was younger?

—Does this youth have close relationships with peers and parents or is he a loner who does most of his acting out alone?

—What affect does this youth express? Does he display signs of depression or anxiety? Does he express guilt about his stealing? Or does he display mostly anger or emotional flatness? Is he primarily sorry or angry he was caught but displays no other remorse about his behavior?

In effect, we distinguish between youths whose stealing represents a budding sociopathy and those whose stealing represents an expression of emotional pain. We expect the personality disordered youth not to have bonded with a caretaker as an infant because of abuse or neglect, and to have been poorly or harshly disciplined as a child. We also find he has few, if any, close interpersonal relationships. In addition, he displays little affect, except anger, and little conscience development.

By contrast, the emotionally disordered youth has a normal history of nurturance and discipline. He has satisfactory interpersonal relationships, displays appropriate affect and expresses guilt about his behavior. Often, he is depressed for identifiable reasons. His anti-social behavior may be seen as an expression of his emotional pain as the following example shows:

> Even though she had been drinking before she killed a friend in an automobile accident, Janice was issued no driving ticket. She came from what was considered a "good family" and had never been in trouble before. But two months later Janice was arrested for shoplifting. The therapist hypothesized that her unexpected anti-social behavior was a demand that she be punished for accidentally killing her friend.

In making a recommendation for residential placement, you should bear in mind the distinction between a personality disordered youth and an emotionally disordered youth. The former would require a tightly controlled, structured, behavioral treatment regimen while the latter would respond better to an in-depth psychotherapeutic approach plus a behavioral approach. Obviously, the prognosis for the latter is more hopeful.

LYING

Lying and stealing often occur together as a child will lie to cover-up his stealing. However, you must distinguish between the lies told by an insecure child designed to impress others—e.g., "My Dad just made a million dollars!"—and the lies of a guilty child designed to cover-up her misbehavior—e.g., "Suzy did it." You have to treat the underlying insecurity if you are to be successful in eliminating the former type of lie.

Most, if not all, young children will lie because they don't know any better or because they are testing the limits of acceptable behavior. Lying can usually be stopped or reduced at this age if it is handled properly.

All lying should be labeled as wrong by the parents with an explanation of why it's wrong. The lie told to impress others should be challenged unless it's harmless fantasy—e.g., I've just talked to Santa Claus—but it's probably not a good idea to punish it. Similarly, punishing the cover-up lie could lead to problems. A child punished for lying might decide to continue lying to cover-up her lying! If the child is receiving more punishments than rewards from her parents, she is more likely to engage in cover-up lies. Accordingly, anything you can do to reverse the preponderance of punishments over rewards may reduce the incidence of cover-up lying.

If the offense which the child is trying to hide by lying is not too serious, the parents can tell the child, "I won't punish you if you tell the truth. It's really important to me that I can trust you." Then have them thank the child for his honesty.

If the offense is serious or repeated, the parents can reduce the punishment if the child tells the truth by saying, "Since you admitted to hitting your sister, you'll only have to go to time-out for half the normal time. Thanks for telling me the truth." What we want to avoid is punishment of the child for being honest— i.e., a child admits to a misdeed but is still severely punished and not reinforced for truthfulness. She may decide the best way to avoid punishment is to cover-up by lying.

In confronting a child about a lie, the parents should watch their own behavior. A shouted, angry "Did you do this?" is more likely to elicit a frightened and untruthful "No" than a calmer description of the facts ending with the statement, "I assume you did this."

VANDALISM

Like stealing, vandalism may be an expression of intense hostility because of emotional deprivation. Consequently, it must be punished but the strained parent-child relationship must also be improved if possible. Probably the most effective punishment for vandalism is restitution: either the child cleans up, repairs the damage or pays for the repairs.

If the vandalism involves firesetting, the child should be made aware of the extreme danger of playing with matches. Perhaps he should receive a stern lecture from someone in the fire department. If he's younger and curious about fires, a parent can teach him how to start a camp fire *but only under adult supervision*. In addition, the child should be required to make restitution for the damage caused by the fire and any strained parent-child relationship should be strengthened.

TEMPER TANTRUMS

The best approach to temper tantrums is prevention. We encourage parents to intervene in their child's behavior before it gets out of control by timing her out after one warning for not minding or immediately after aggressive behavior. The success of the child program should significantly reduce the incidence of temper tantrums.

There is little sense in trying to time-out a child in the midst of a temper tantrum so the best strategy is to ignore it if possible. When the child calms down, have the parents regive their command and time the child out if disobedience occurs again.

While temper tantrums are to be ignored, the controlled expression of legitimate feelings should be encouraged. If a child is hurt or angry, it's acceptable to talk about these feelings, draw an angry picture, punch a pillow, write a poison pen letter or go for a walk.

AGGRESSION

Aggression towards siblings or peers—kicking, hitting, slapping, teasing or biting—may be motivated by jealousy and insecurity and so will require a strengthening of parent-child relationships. It can usually be successfully treated by the child program using points or stars for playing nicely and time-out for aggression. However, the child should be allowed a controlled expression of his feelings so it's O.K. to feel like hitting his sister and O.K. to talk about those feelings, but it's not O.K. to actually hit her.

ELIMINATION CONTROL PROBLEMS

Bedwetting is a common problem which usually stops without treatment. If it persists past age 4, the parents can do several things to relieve it:

—No liquids several hours before bedtime.

—Make sure the child urinates before bedtime and perhaps have the parents awaken him to urinate before they retire.

—Provide a reward system for dry nights such as praise, stars or choice of breakfast to be used the next morning.

—Use an alarm system if all else fails.

An angry, punitive stance should be avoided. The only disciplinary action that should be taken is having the child change his sheets in the morning after wetting.

Daytime enuresis or encopresis—wetting or soiling—should be treated in the same way—i.e., with an enticing reward system and no punishment except to change and possibly wash wet or soiled underpants. Persistent elimination control problems should be referred to a physician for a medical examination. Also, these problems may reflect stress in the family—e.g., constant fighting between the parents or a recent, bitter divorce—which must be reduced if the control problems are to be relieved.

BEDTIME PROBLEMS

Bedtime problems are best handled with firmness and rewards. It's not appropriate to time-out the bedtime wanderer for that will only provide her with what she wants—i.e., to be able to stay up later.

Make sure the child has plenty of time to prepare for bed. Have her go to the bathroom, brush her teeth, get into her pajamas and take a drink of water. Then have the parents spend some time with the child while she's in bed.

Set up a reward system for staying in bed using praise, stars, points or choice of breakfast to be given in the morning. If a child gets out of bed, have the parents firmly but gently lead her back without lecturing or scolding.

EATING PROBLEMS

Eating problems should be treated using a reward system and a timer. If the child eats what he is supposed to eat in the time allotted by the parents, he can pick a special reward. If he fails to reach the goal in the allotted time, the parents should simply remove the food without lecturing, scolding or punishing. If the child is hungry later on, he can only have what he left on his plate *and nothing more* unless he finishes it.

Bear in mind that the child's body will tell him when he needs more of a certain type of food. If left to himself, he will eat the proper foods.

SCHOOL PROBLEMS

School problems—either poor grades or behavior problems—are best treated with cooperation between the home and the school. A daily or weekly home-school note program which specifies when a child has done well in school and when she has not done well should be set up. Then at home the parents can reward a positive home-school note and penalize a negative home-school note. The child's "forgetting" to bring home a note should be treated as a negative note and penalized.

After a home-school note program has been established, set up a contract with the parents and the child specifying the expected behaviors, rewards and penalties. The consequences—positive and negative—can be delivered daily or weekly and at the end of each marking period. For example, the child can earn a daily back-up reward for each daily positive home-school note. Or she can earn a special weekend treat for a weekly positive home-school note. Finally, she can earn a major reward for good grades or acceptable behavior displayed throughout a marking period.

Before setting up a behavioral program for poor grades, however, the reasons why the child's grades are poor or falling should be determined. By a process of elimination, you or the school should make a correct diagnosis of the problem. Specifically, the following questions should be asked and answered:

—Does this child have the intellectual capacity to function adequately in school?

—Is she learning disabled?

—Is there an auditory or visual impairment which is interfering with her ability to learn?

—Assuming the child is intact physiologically, are her poor or falling grades a sign of chemical abuse?

—Are there emotional factors which are interfering with her ability to perform academically? Is she depressed, for example, or angry at her parents for pressuring her to keep up her grades? Does she lack confidence in her intellectual abilities and so is not trying in school for fear of failing?

Needless to say, any one of these conditions should be corrected or treated before you attempt a behavioral program to improve her grades.

SCHOOL PHOBIA

The primary cause of a school phobia is usually an enmeshed parent-child relationship. The child is afraid to leave home or grow up—a fear covertly reinforced by the parent—and not necessarily fearful about anything in school. Consequently, treatment of a school phobia must be twofold:

—Have the child return to school as soon as possible. The longer he stays out, the poorer becomes the prognosis for him to return. You can attempt to do this using an in vivo desensitization of the child's reported fear of school. Have him return gradually and for longer periods of time as he becomes more comfortable at school. Perhaps the first day he can go for fifteen minutes or a half hour only. Then in conjunction with a reward system, gradually increase the amount of time he spends at school.

—Treat the enmeshed parent-child relationship which under-lies the school phobia by creating some distance—but not too much else you'll encounter tremendous resistance—between the parent and child. You can do this by insuring that both have sources of need satisfaction other than each other. If they are to separate somewhat, both need to have other friendships and sources of emotional support.

CHEMICAL DEPENDENCY

Although we encounter it frequently in our therapy, we don't treat chemical dependency at the Family Teaching Center since we're not chemical dependency counselors. We don't believe there is any sense in working therapeutically with a family member—parent or adolescent—who is chemically dependent because his behavior is so unpredictable. We usually refer that person for an evaluation or treatment.

Despite the fact that chemical dependency can be so debilitating to family functioning, you are still not helpless in the face of it.

There is much you can do to treat it. Specifically, you can correctly diagnose it, refer the dependent individual, provide primary care for the other family members and provide aftercare services for the entire family after the dependent has been in treatment.

To help you spot chemical dependency, we have already listed some questions you can ask the family member whom you suspect to be chemically dependent in the chapter on our intake interview (Chapter 5). To diagnose alcoholism in a parent, look for the following signs:

—A history of heavy drinking or alcoholism in the parent's family of origin. If one or both of his parents were alcoholic and if he drinks, his chances of becoming dependent are greater.

—A pattern of heavy use of alcohol. Even though he may claim he has no problem, the alcoholic may admit he drinks every day, or every weekend or that he becomes intoxicated once a month. We assume if a parent can't limit himself to two drinks whenever he drinks, he is flirting with chemical dependency.

—Loss of control. If the parent admits there are times when he drinks more than he intended to drink, or that he becomes intoxicated periodically, the chances are he is chemically dependent.

—Blackouts. Periods of time when the drinking person retained consciousness but still doesn't remember what he did are a serious sign of alcoholism.

—Denial. Since alcohol has become so important to him, the alcoholic will deny he has a drinking problem despite all the evidence he gives you to the contrary.

—Problems caused by drinking. Any problems due to excessive drinking—at home, at work, with friends or with the law—are another serious sign of alcoholism.

To diagnose chemical dependency in adolescents, look for the following signs. You can obtain most of this information from the parents and your own observations.

—A psychological predisposition. A troubled youth in emotional pain with low self-esteem is at risk for chemical dependency.

—Unexplained and unexpected personality changes. The parents describe the youth as recently and unusually irritable, hostile or depressed, for example.

—Behavioral changes. In contrast to past behavior, the youth has become irresponsible or anti-social. She stays out late, no longer does her chores, screams at her parents and has been arrested for several driving violations.

—Stealing. To maintain an expensive habit, the youth has to resort to stealing to obtain funds for her dependency.

—Lying. The dependent youth has to resort to lying to cover up her chemical dependency and associated anti-social behavior.

—Changes in academic performance. A sudden and unexpected drop in grades can be indicative of chemical dependency in a youth.

—Extremely secretive behavior. If the adolescent keeps to herself often, spends little time with the family, receives mysterious phone calls from unknown friends or behaves secretively and defensively in other ways, suspect chemical dependency.

—Friends who are known or suspected drug users. As she becomes more chemically dependent, the youth will tend to associate exclusively with friends who use chemicals also. You may be able to find out who her friends are by asking a school nurse or counselor.

—Hidden stashes of drugs, alcohol or drug paraphernalia such as pipes, plants, seeds, pills or spoons.

—Defensive avoidance when the subject of chemical dependency is brought up or strong, angry denial when questioned or confronted about drug use. Like the adult alcoholic, the adolescent is going to protect her habit as fiercely as she can.

—Physical signs of being under the influence of drugs such as poor coordination, slurred speech or the smell of alcohol on a youth's breath.

—Deterioration in family relationships. In addition to the strain caused by falling grades, lying, stealing, fighting and arrests, the chemically dependent youth will withdraw more from her family as drugs become more important to her and as her parents become increasingly suspicious of her behavior.

If you suspect an adolescent family member is chemically dependent, you can recommend a chemical dependency evaluation—either inpatient or outpatient—to the parents. They should be able to follow through on your recommendation even though the youth may protest. If you diagnose a parent as alcoholic, however, your task is more difficult. Unlike an adolescent, it is not always possible to force an adult into treatment. He must go willingly, although under pressure, if it is to be effective.

What you can do in cases of parental alcoholism is to provide primary care to the other family members because they are just as troubled by alcohol as is the alcoholic. If he is a dependent, they are co-dependents. If he is compulsive in his drinking behaviors, they are compulsive in their attempts to adjust to his drinking. If he is blind to the harm he is causing himself and others, they are equally deluded about the nature of the disease and its effects on them.

Following the work of Wegscheider (1981), your tasks in primary care are to break through the denial of the family members, help them to recognize and express their feelings and teach them the disease concept of alcoholism. In effect, you want to break their co-dependency, to help them shift their attention away from the dependent's drinking and refocus it on themselves. This may sound selfish—and perhaps it is—but paradoxically it creates the best chance they have to bring the alcoholic to sobriety.

No matter what their premorbid histories, alcoholism affects all members of the family in harmful ways. An alcoholic family is a troubled, pain-ridden family with constricted communication and a well developed delusional system. The drinking of the alcoholic has been a great source of pain to them but they have all learned to deny that pain. Communication is limited in such a family because they cannot talk openly about the source of their problems: the dependent's drinking. Their delusion system reassures them that the alcoholic is not alcoholic and that they have not been affected by his drinking. They contribute as much to the denial system of the alcoholic as he does, thus enabling him to continue drinking.

Your job—and it is not an easy one—is to gently but firmly challenge all of this. Using communication techniques, you should help the family members acknowledge and express their emotional pain. By teaching them about the course of alcoholism as a disease and how it affects family members, you need to challenge their delusions. If they are to regain health, they have to accept that the dependent is an alcoholic and that they are powerless to do anything about it. They must also realize the role each has assumed in the family—the enabler, hero, scapegoat, mascot and lost child, to use Wegscheider's (1981) classification—

as each attempted to adjust to the disease of alcoholism. Instead of focusing on the drinking of the alcoholic, the family members must free up energy for themselves.

As a result of your primary care, three things can happen to the family: the parents may divorce, the family members may learn to live with the disease but no longer as co-dependents or they may carry through with an intervention which brings the alcoholic into treatment. If the non-alcoholic spouse is considering a divorce—as many are—we may encourage her to do a formal intervention under the supervision of a drug and alcohol counselor instead. We advise her that the best way to force her spouse into treatment and thereby save her marriage is to be ready to divorce him. Having reached that decision, she is ready to tell him he will have to submit to treatment or else she will leave him.

A formal intervention is a planned, well rehearsed meeting of the family members, friends and possibly an employer with the alcoholic. During the meeting, the participants caringly confront the alcoholic with a factual description of how his drinking has affected them and then inform him of the consequences to him of his continued drinking. The non-alcoholic spouse, for example, may say she loves her husband but can't tolerate his drinking anymore. The employer may say that the dependent has been a good worker but will be fired if he doesn't stop drinking.

In the past, it was thought an alcoholic wouldn't stop drinking until he hit bottom. A planned intervention is designed to bring the bottom up to him sooner than he would descend to it.

We don't do these types of formal interventions at the Family Teaching Center but there are other types of interventions we can teach the family members to make to prepare them for a formal intervention. For example, we teach them to use "I" statements to tell the alcoholic how his behavior affects them but only when he is sober and will remember it. Specifically, the children can tell their father how hurt they are that he didn't take them to a movie last night as he had promised. Or the non-alcoholic spouse can say how hurt she was that he was intoxicated on their anniversary. We advise the family members to make these "I" statements without anger or nagging else they could backfire.

In an attempt to break their co-dependency, we also encourage the family members not to take any more responsibility for the drinking of the alcoholic. For example, we want the non-alcoholic spouse to say she will no longer call in sick for him when he's hung over, keep his dinner ready past six o'clock or clean up his vomit. In effect, we want her to stop being an enabler who allows her spouse to drink by protecting him from the harmful consequences of his behavior. Instead, we want her to begin to lavish some deserved care on herself. But we stress to her that without an enabler, he may stop drinking.

If the alcoholic eventually goes for treatment, you can be available for aftercare family counseling. In this type of counseling, again following the work of Wegscheider (1981), your tasks are to have the family members continue to share feelings, to promote forgiveness through an understanding of the disease of alcoholism, to help them break out of their roles and to encourage them to rebuild their family system.

SEXUAL ABUSE

As a family therapist, you are likely to uncover sexual abuse in some families you treat. If you suspect sexual abuse in a family, see the suspected victim alone and ask her the following questions:

Has anyone ever abused you either physically, emotionally or sexually?

Has anyone ever touched you in a way which made you feel uncomfortable or asked you to touch him or her in an uncomfortable way for you? Specifically, has anyone ever touched your breasts, buttocks or genital area?

Although there are always exceptions to patterns of behavior, there are certain signs you can look for when you suspect sexual abuse in a family. What follows is a discussion of signs which may occur in a family in which father is abusing his daughter:

—The daughter may be inexplicably depressed, guilty, angry, or withdrawn. She may be extremely uncomfortable talking about sex and/or behaving in sexually inappropriate ways.

—The relationship between the father and the daughter may be either very close or very distant. They may spend considerable time alone together, with father acting in an overprotective way with his daughter. Or the relationship may be very distant and hostile. She may be a runaway or extremely angry at her father for no apparent reason.

—In describing the child molester, Groth (1979) distinguishes between the fixated offender and the regressed offender. The fixated offender is so shy, insecure, inadequate and socially isolated that he feels too uncomfortable to function in a mature, heterosexual manner. In effect, he feels like a child and is primarily attracted to children. The regressed offender, by contrast, has been able to function adequately in the past but under stress regresses in his level of sexual functioning by exploiting a younger person.

—The mother in a family in which father is sexually abusive may be dependent, passive and submissive. She has, in effect, switched roles with her daughter. Often, she has a history of having been sexually abused herself as a child. Her daughter is usually extremely angry at her for not protecting her from the abuse.

—The marriage may be unfulfilling for both the husband and the wife whose dependency and sexual needs are not being met by each other. The family may be isolated and under considerable stress. The sexual atmosphere in the family may be either strict and controlled or too open and promiscuous.

The consequences of sexual abuse to the victim can be severe. If the disclosure is handled calmly and properly and if treatment is provided when necessary, the sexual abuse will not necessarily traumatize a victim. But without proper handling and treatment, the effects can include depression, guilt, self concept problems, unresolved anger, sexual dysfunctions or hypersexuality and difficulty trusting other people or forming close interpersonal relations.

If you suspect that sexual abuse is occurring, you must report it to your local child protective services regardless of the consequences to the family or your therapeutic relationship with the members. The abuse must be stopped as soon as possible, and the only way this can be guaranteed is by involving the proper authorities. Although it is true that disclosure may result in the break-up of the family, it may also result in the cessation of the abuse but maintenance of the family through therapy.

An extensive discussion of the treatment of sexually abusive families is beyond the scope of this book. To learn more about it, see Meiselman (1978), Burgess et al. (1978), Sgroi (1982) and Green and Stuart (1983).

Suffice it to say that the successful treatment of sex abuse should involve individual, group, marital and family therapy. Under the threat of prosecution or imprisonment, the offender must be kept in individual and/or group treatment which is designed to strengthen his inhibitions against sexual acting out and to give him the skills and confidence to function in a mature, healthy manner. If she has been traumatized, the victim should be in individual and group treatment also in which she learns that she is not responsible in any way for the sexual abuse, that she has not been soiled or damaged and that mature, heterosexual relations are not bad or dirty. Mother may also need individual treatment to handle her guilt, anger and confusion.

If the family is to remain intact, marital therapy should also be provided for the offender and his spouse to reorient their roles and to resolve any marital and sexual problems between them. Family therapy should also be provided to give the victim the opportunity to ventilate her feelings to the offender, to have him assume full responsibility for the abuse, to discuss ways to prevent it from ever occurring again and to promote the possibility of eventual forgiveness.

Chapter 10

MARITAL COUNSELING

P arents usually come to us at the Family Teaching Center because they're having behavioral problems with their children. However, some of them end up in marital counseling with us and a few of those parents eventually decide to divorce.

This is not a surprising state of affairs. Children's problems and marital problems are usually related. Framo (1965) claims that whenever there are problems with the children, there are marital problems, although the converse does not necessarily follow. In other words, although the existence of children's problems means there are marital problems, according to Framo (1965), the existence of marital problems does not automatically lead to pathology in the children. If the parents don't allow their marital conflicts to affect their parental relationships and obligations, their children will be stressed by the marital problems but not in a pathogenic way.

We don't find that Framo's (1965) assertion about the correlation between children's problems and marital problems is entirely true at the Family Teaching Center. As we pointed out in Chapter 6 on our child program, Thomas and Chess (1977) argue that temperament is an important factor to consider in diagnosing some behavioral problems. There are a few children whose behavioral problems are independent of parental functioning. Despite the parents' best efforts to discipline them, these children have been moodier, more intensely reactive and more resistive to discipline than other children since birth. It appears that a few children are

176

temperamentally more difficult to handle than others, and we should remind parents of this fact.

But we do find that Framo (1965) is right most of the time. The existence of marital problems usually does lead to problems with the children which can, in turn, stress an already stressed marriage.

Specifically, since healthy parental love consists of three abilities—to love, discipline and let go when appropriate—there are three ways marital pathology can contribute to children's pathology:

—Whenever marital problems, or any other debilitating condition such as alcoholism or depression, interfere with the parents' ability to love, support and nurture their offspring, the children will be adversely affected. If parents do not receive much love from each other, and did not receive much from their own parents, it is more difficult for them to give to their children what they themselves have not received. As a family therapist, your task is to strengthen parent-child relationships by reducing the problems which weaken those relationships.

Failing this, your task is to insure that children don't feel personally responsible for the limitations of their parents' love. In cases of poor parent-child relationships, children usually blame themselves rather than their parents because such blaming gives them a false sense of control in situations which are essentially beyond their control. By blaming themselves, inadequately loved children can maintain the fiction that if they changed, their parents would change. They can also continue to believe, again perhaps erroneously, that their parents are capable of meeting their emotional needs.

Obviously, you need to challenge this self-blaming. You don't want these children to blame their parents but you do want them to realize their parents have not been able to love them fully because of their own overwhelming adult problems, and not because they—the children—are not worthy of being loved. In effect, you don't want these children to blame themselves for problems to which they have not contributed and over which they have no control. You want them eventually to love themselves even though they have not been fully loved by their parents.

—Whenever marital problems interfere with the parents' ability to agree on rules and consequences and to support each other in their disciplinary efforts, the children will grow up without the consistent discipline of united parents. This is a major cause of the disciplinary problems we see at the Family Teaching Center. Through both our child and adolescent programs, we encourage the parents to support each other in providing consistent discipline to their children. When we succeed in doing this, we also succeed in strengthening the marriage even though we have not formally provided marital counseling services.

—Whenever the marital problems are so severe or chronic that one or both parents turn to the children for the satisfaction of their needs or for allies in their battles with each other, the children will be pathogenically triangulated in the marital pathology. As we saw in Chapter 4, this can occur in one of two ways. Not having her needs met by her spouse, one parent turns to a child to be her friend and confidant while the other becomes disengaged from that child creating what is called an odd-person-out triangle. Or both parents become enmeshed with a child either as an ally to help them solve their marital problems or as a scapegoat to distract them from those problems, creating what is called a double bind triangle. Either triangle puts pathogenic stress on the child which is your task to reduce.

If you are treating children's emotional and behavioral problems, you should be prepared to treat marital problems also. In describing successful marriages, the goals of marital therapy and the Family Teaching Center program of marital therapy, this chapter should give you some specific ideas about how to do this.

SUCCESSFUL MARRIAGES

What makes for a successful marriage? Before we can treat unhappy marriages and restore satisfaction to them, we should be able to answer this question.

Jacobson (1981) suggests three ways distressed couples differ from nondistressed couples and gives us some clues as to what makes marriages happy. First, both types of marriages have roughly the same number of problems. Distressed couples are not unhappy because they have more problems than satisfied spouses; rather they are unhappy because they are not as able to solve those problems as are the satisfied couples. And as we argued in Chapter

3 on healthy family functioning, they are not as able to solve their problems because they can't communicate as effectively with each other and compromise to solve their differences.

Second, distressed and satisfied couples differ in how they interact with each other. Stressed couples have more negative interactions with each other than positive interactions. They give each other more emotional pain than pleasure. Satisfied couples, by contrast, have more positive interactions than negative interactions. They have as many problems as the dissatisfied spouses, but they still give each other more pleasure than pain. And it is the pleasure they give each other that is a major part of the bond which holds them together.

Third, these two types of couples differ in how they relate to one another. Stressed couples relate more contingently while satisfied couples relate more non-contingently.

In effect, those who are dissatisfied with their marriages do what they believe is done to them. Receiving more pain than pleasure from their spouses, they retaliate in kind. Frustrated and hurt, each partner attempts to secure more love from the other by offering the opposite. Each attempts to control the other through punishments or the withholding of love. But, of course, such a strategy only hurts and frustrates the other who then retaliates by behaving the same way. The couples then become locked into the self-perpetuating cycle of hurt, anger and blaming which we described in Chapter 4 on unhealthy family functioning.

Satisfied couples relate to each other in an entirely different manner. They behave more non-contingently with one another. The behavior of the one does not influence the behavior of the other to the same painful degree as it does in stressed marriages.

This is due to two reasons. Having higher self-esteem, satisfied couples can be more independent of each other and therefore can be more intimate. They can be more open, honest, flexible and congruent in a close relationship because they are not as afraid of being rejected or smothered as are low self-esteem persons.

In addition, satisfied couples behave more non-contingently because they have a surplus of love to sustain their marriages through difficult times. Over the years, the preponderance of positive interactions over negative interactions has created a bank account which is full of love. They can give love fully and freely to each other, without demanding a return, because they know there is plenty of love in their bank account from which they can draw strength. They give pleasure to each other because they have received more pleasure from the other in the past, not because the other is forcing them to give through threats of punishment or the withholding of love.

But paradoxically, their non-contingent sharing of love appears to bring these satisfied couples more love in return. It works better in eliciting love from their spouses than does the punishment orientation of the unhappily married couples. Since love can never be forced, the non-demanding giving of love engenders more love for these satisfied couples.

GOALS OF MARITAL COUNSELING

The overall goal of marital counseling is to specify and implement those behavioral changes which will make the marriage more satisfactory for both partners. Since their marital interactions haven't been working for them, and since you are a change agent, your function is to help them change their unhappy relationship.

Following Jacobson (1981), the three sub-goals of marital counseling are to:

—Teach the couple to behave more non-contingently with each other and to discourage them from behaving contingently.

—Strengthen the spouses' problem-solving skills by teaching them to communicate and compromise more effectively with each other.

—Increase the number of their positive interactions by specific behavioral assignments.

When doing marital counseling at the Family Teaching Center, we first conduct a diagnostic overview of the marriage and then have the partners specify what positive thing each will do for the other during the next week. We make this a non-contingent agreement so that each is to do something positive for the other regardless of what the other does. We want to provide some immediate relief and encouragement for the couple by this maneuver but we also use it for diagnostic purposes. It can give us useful information to see how the spouses follow through with this assignment.

Next we work on the couple's communication and problem-solving skills by having them specify those behavioral changes which will improve their marital functioning. Then we give them more homework assignments to implement some of those changes. If this behavioral approach doesn't work, we may then take a historical approach to their marital interactions by working on any family of origin problems which the spouses may present to us. In this approach, we want to do two things: to strengthen the mental health of each partner by resolving any past problems and to uncover and modify any interactional patterns from their families of origin which may have been repeated in their present marriage.

Failing these behavioral and historical approaches, we may then switch to a paradoxical approach with the couple and encourage them not to change. The following clinical example demonstrates this process:

> Over a two year period, Jim and Mary had seen the therapist for marital problems. Twice they dropped out of therapy and twice they came back, but they still did little to resolve their marital disputes.
>
> Because of their lack of progress during a two year period, the therapist decided to use paradoxical techniques with this couple. He explained to them how difficult it is to change long-standing patterns of behavior and suggested that it might be too disruptive for them to do so.
>
> Mary looked puzzled by the therapist's remarks, but both she and Jim reported that immediately after they left his office, they had the best conversation about their marriage they had had in years.

If nothing works with the couple, we may then encourage the spouses to consider a divorce as a solution to their marital problems, especially if those problems have been unresolved for years with adverse affects for them and their children. Frankly, our hope is that by gently pushing two chronically unhappy and stressed spouses to the edge of divorce, each will look over, shrink back from that edge and decide they really do want to stay together by improving their marriage. We believe it takes less energy and fewer adjustments to improve a distressed marriage than to divorce. However, we're also convinced that living in a chronically distressed marriage uses up more energy than adjusting to a divorce. As a result, divorce must be considered as an option for some chronically unhappy marriages, especially those in which there is untreated alcoholism, emotional or physical abuse or serious and chronic depression due to the continuing marital problems. We don't believe people should stay in an unhappy marriage at the expense of their physical or mental health.

We don't believe that people should stay unhappily married for the sake of their children either. We take the position at the Family Teaching Center that while the best atmosphere in which to raise children is in a home with a mutually satisfying marriage, the second best atmosphere is in a divorced home which is relatively harmonious and conflict-free. Divorce stresses children but they can bounce back from that stress if both parents remain involved in their lives and can relate cooperatively with each other for the sake of the children. By contrast, children can't adjust as well to the years of stress to which they may be subjected by the chronically unhappy, conflict-ridden marriage of their parents.

We never tell people to divorce at the Family Teaching Center, however. We can't make that major decision for them. But we can help them to make it themselves by having them calmly and rationally consider all the problems and processes involved in divorce.

Marital counseling can then become a decision-making process. Its goal is not always to save marriages but to bring about behavioral change. Since there are only two ways a distressed couple can reduce their marital pain—by either improving their marriage or divorcing—we cannot always guarantee in which direction that change will go.

Of course, with some couples who come to marital counseling, one or both of the spouses have decided, consciously or unconsciously to divorce—a decision from which there usually is no turning back. When love dies, we assume it is almost impossible to revive it.

In such a case, your task is to make explicit what has been implicit or avoided. Even after one or both partners have decided to divorce, neither may be willing to put that decision into action for fear of being labeled as the one who wanted out of the marriage. When one finally contacts an attorney to sue for divorce, the other may be able to gain sympathy from family and friends by pointing the finger of blame. Since neither wants to be put into this difficult position, the spouses struggle to force each other to take that fateful step by escalating their outrageous behavior.

In effect, the couple can become locked into a destructive struggle in which each says to the other, "You go first," to which each replies, "No, you go first." Your function is to disrupt this interaction as it can become quite vicious and hurtful.

What happens more frequently in marital counseling, however, is that one spouse wants to save the marriage while the other is not sure what she wants to do. She is truly ambivalent. One advantage of defining marriage counseling as a process designed to help an unhappily married couple either to increase their marital satisfaction or to decide whether to divorce or not is that it gives you a better chance to keep the ambivalent spouse coming to your sessions. If she believes the purpose of marital therapy is to save marriages only, she may want no part in it.

THE TELEPHONE CONTACT

As is true of family therapy in general, the contest to gain control of the process of marital therapy begins with the first telephone contact. It is usually the wife who first calls, requesting an appointment. You should ask that both she and her husband come in together to see you, and then set up an appointment if she agrees to your request. If she balks at it, however, if she claims she wants to see you alone, you should do what you can to discourage this.

You might start out by asking if her husband knows she is calling you. If she says he does not, ask how he might react to this news and if he would be willing to come in for counseling. Explain to the caller that since marital problems are relationship problems, the best way to understand and treat those problems is by seeing both spouses together.

If the caller continues to insist she wants to see you alone, you may agree to her request as long as she agrees to meet with you once or twice alone and then have you meet with her spouse once or twice alone. If you are to see one spouse individually, you should also see the other individually to avoid the risk of being perceived as having taken sides. Remember, however, to accept no secrets during these individual sessions.

If the caller still insists she wants to see you alone for marital problems without involving or informing her spouse, then you are in a dilemma. If you agree to her request, you will have been triangulated in the marital conflicts on her side. If you refuse her request, you may lose her as a client.

At the Family Teaching Center, we would probably refuse to see the caller under her conditions. In effect, she is asking for individual therapy for what she describes as marital problems and we assume that such therapy would be ineffective at best and harmful at worst. As Gurman and Kniskern (1978) report, individual therapy for marital problems has resulted in almost twice the deterioration rate—11.6% vs. 5.6%—as has treatment for marital conflicts in which both spouses have been involved in therapy.

If you want to take the chance of being triangulated, you might agree to meet with the caller but we would suggest you continue to urge her to have the other spouse see you. We also believe you should explain to the caller the increased risk of deterioration if you see her alone for marital problems. She has the right to know of the risks of her chosen course of action. By agreeing to see the caller without informing her spouse, however, you may run the risk of a lawsuit by him, especially if the spouse you treat individually decides to dissolve her marriage during her sessions with you.

THE FIRST SESSION

Assuming that you succeed in persuading both spouses to come to the first marital counseling session, your tasks during this session are to conduct a diagnostic overview of the marriage, explain the process and risks involved in marital therapy, have the spouses informally contract with you for certain therapeutic goals and give them certain homework assignments. This is a lot to accomplish, so you should schedule more time for the first session.

In conducting a diagnostic overview of the marriage, explore both the problems and strengths in the relationship. The spouses will probably want to talk more about their problems but your task will be to note and reinforce their strengths as well.

We have already listed many of the diagnostic questions you can ask a couple about their marriage in Chapter 5. To uncover some of the strengths in the marriage, ask the spouses how they communicate and problem solve, how they express affection for each other and how they relate sexually. To uncover problem areas, ask them how they fight, if there have been any specific sexual problems or known affairs and if there have been any problems with money, their children or their in-laws.

You don't have to explore any of these problems in depth at this time since your task is only to conduct a brief diagnostic overview of the marriage. You can come back to discuss any major problems in later sessions.

Next ask the spouses what each would like to do about the marriage. Using this question, you want to find out if both want to save it, if one or both are not sure what they want to do or if both want to divorce. If they both express some hope for the marriage, ask next what changes each would like to make to improve the marriage. In receiving answers to this question, make sure each spouse does not talk exclusively about the other in an attempt to imply that only a change in the other will improve the marital relationship.

Now ask the spouses how each assumes marital counseling works and what each believes is its purpose. Using these questions, you want to understand their view of marital therapy and to clear up any misconceptions or unrealistic expectations they may have. For example, it is not your function to act as a judge by hearing each side and then pronouncing who is right or who is wrong. Nor is it your job to tell the couple what to do about their marriage—i.e., whether to divorce or stay together.

During the first session, you want to arrive at an informal agreement with the spouses about the goal of marital counseling and your role in it. Specifically, you want them to agree that they will meet with you to specify and implement those behavioral changes which will improve their marital functioning. Since what they have been doing in the past has not brought them marital satisfaction, their goal in meeting with you must be to change the ways they interact with each other.

Assuming that you and the spouses agree to continue to meet, you might explain to them what you plan to do during the next few sessions. We like to take a brief history of the marriage and then proceed to a fuller discussion of the marital problems and ways the couple can improve their relationship during the second and subsequent sessions. We then may explain to the couple that if change does not occur after several sessions, we may decide to take a more thorough history of each to determine if there are any family of origin problems which may be interfering with their marital satisfaction. Finally, we may warn the couple that if these approaches don't work, we may urge them to consider a divorce as a solution to their problems especially if those problems have been chronic and harmful.

To end the first session, give the spouses a homework assignment to non-contingently reinforce each other during the next week. Have each spouse specify what each would like the other to do but make sure the task is not too long or complicated. You want the couple to be encouraged by some initial positive changes and not discouraged by the failure of one or both of them to complete their homework assignment.

Finally, as we do at the Family Teaching Center, you can give the couple a list of questions to answer in writing and return by the second session. The questions are listed as follows:

> What hopes, expectations or dreams did you have for your marriage when you first married? What did you imagine married life with your spouse would be like? What did you hope to gain from your marriage?
>
> What needs of your's are being fulfilled in your marriage?
>
> What do you like, admire or respect about your spouse?
>
> What do you and your spouse have in common? What do you do together that you both enjoy? What pleasurable experiences do you share with each other?
>
> How do you and your spouse settle your differences? How do you arrive at a decision or compromise?
>
> To make your marriage more successful, what would you want from your spouse? What changes would you ask him/her to make?
>
> What changes in yourself do you think you should make?

Obviously, it is the last two sets of questions about changes which constitute the core of what you are trying to do in marital counseling.

THE SECOND SESSION

Taking a brief history of the courtship and marriage during the second session accomplishes two things: it gives you a better diagnostic picture and it puts the couple back in touch with happier times and emotions. Sometimes two angry, frustrated people can begin to smile at each other as they recall better moments in their married lives. Of course, if there are no such pleasant memories, if they can't recall any times when they were happy together, their bank account of love must be either very low or empty.

To take a history of the marriage, ask the following questions:

How did you two meet?

What attracted you to each other? Do you still find your spouse attractive in that way?

What was your courtship like?

How did you decide to get married?

What was your wedding day like? How did you feel or react on your wedding day?

What did your parents and in-laws think about you two marrying?

What was your honeymoon like? Where did you go?

What was the first year of your marriage like?

How did each of you react to the birth of your first child? What effect did his or her birth have on your marriage? Was he or she planned? (Ask these same questions about the second and subsequent children.)

When did you two begin to have serious marital problems? What was happening at that time?

After you've taken a history of the early marriage, you can review the list of questions you gave the spouses after the first session and asked them to answer in writing by the second session. Their answers can give you more diagnostic information, but more importantly, you can use the list to talk about the changes each believes are needed to improve their marital functioning.

You can also help the couple specify and implement those changes by employing many of the techniques described in the chapters on communications, negotiating and contracting: communication rules, homework assignments, doubling, "I" statements, Rogerian feedback, role reversals, compromising, negotiating and contracting. Having used these techniques with families, you can also use them with couples. The problems in marital counseling may be different than problems with adolescents but the underlying causes are partially the same: the inability to express love, to communicate and to problem-solve effectively.

After the couple has listed those changes which should benefit their marital functioning, your next task is to insure they begin to implement them. This can be done both in your office and at home. You can begin to implement the therapeutic changes in your office by employing the techniques which you should use in teaching clients any new skill: instruction, modeling and reinforced practice. In other words, teach the couple what to do, model your instructions and have them practice a new behavior in your office under your supervision and with your encouragement. You can also give them homework assignments, most of which should be non-contingent, to do at home. Some examples of such assignments based on agreed upon changes are:

The spouses agree to spend twenty minutes each evening talking about their day.

The spouses agree to give each other one hug, kiss or compliment each day.

The spouses agree to give each other three ten-minute backrubs during the next week.

The spouses agree to spend one night every other week out on a date without the children or friends.

The spouses agree to raise a miniature red flag which is located on the living room shelf whenever one of them feels hurt, frustrated, lonely or angry and wants to talk.

Even if one spouse doesn't want to talk about it immediately, the spouses agree to talk about a problem in their marriage within twenty-four hours after the problem is uncovered.

The husband agrees to call when he will be late and the wife agrees to check with her husband before accepting a social invitation for the two of them.

The wife agrees to cook dinner on week nights while the husband agrees to clean up and do the dishes.

Notice that not all of these assignments deal exclusively with problems. Some of them, such as the agreement to give each other a daily hug, kiss or compliment or to have a date every other week, are designed to strengthen the marriage in general without dealing with specific problems. This is because we are not necessarily in the business of solving specific problems but of teaching people the skills needed to solve the many problems which will arise in their families or marriages. If we only solved specific problems, our clients would have to return to us each time they encountered new problems. By teaching them how to communicate and solve problems more effectively, we can give them skills which could benefit them for a lifetime.

In addition, we concentrate on strengthening relationships because this may be the best way to solve or reduce many of the interpersonal problems which family members present to us. In marital counseling, for example, you will surely encounter some specific sexual dysfunctions. Since a discussion of them is beyond the scope of this book, you can learn more about the treatment of sexual problems by reading Kaplan (1974, 1979), Leiblum and Perirn (1980), and Humphrey (1984).

However, in treating any sexual problems presented by a distressed couple, one of the first things you should do is to strengthen the marital relationship by improving the communication between them. By increasing the emotional intimacy of the couple, you may be able to clear up the sexual difficulties without directly working on them. If a general improvement of the marriage doesn't reduce the sexual problems, you can then employ specific techniques to do so.

SUBSEQUENT SESSIONS

If a behavioral approach to marital distress is working, then obviously you want to continue with it and reinforce the couple for their progress. If it becomes obvious after several sessions that your approach is not working, however, then you should consider switching to another therapeutic strategy. Specifically, you can assume a historical approach to the marital problems by taking a detailed history on each spouse. What you should look for are family of origin problems which may be contributing to the marital problems.

In general, there are three ways in which problems from the past can contribute to present marital problems:

—When two people marry, each brings differing experiences, expectations and values to the marriage which must be integrated into a functional system if the marriage is to be satisfactory. As Sager (1976) argues, there are usually three sets of expectations, or contracts, in a marital relationship marriage: his, her's and their's. These expectations have been strongly influenced by the experiences each spouse has had in his or her family of origin. Each assumes, quite understandably, that the way things were done in his or her family of origin is the right way. The more similar their experiences and expectations, the easier it is to agree on a joint contract. By taking a history of each spouse, you may be able to uncover and make explicit some of these expectations as the following example shows:

Although it seemed like such a small matter, Bob and Mary would argue vehemently about who was responsible for splitting and bringing in the firewood. In Mary's family of origin, insuring an adequate supply of firewood was her mother's job, while in Bob's family, it was "man's work."

—Severe self concept problems which can interfere with marital functioning usually begin in the family of origin. By taking a history of each spouse, you can help the couple understand how their negative self concepts began and what they can do to change them.

—Unresolved emotional problems from the past do not mysteriously go away. They remain with the person for the rest of her life, flaring up occasionally under certain stimulus conditions. Often these problems are re-enacted in the present in an attempt to resolve them. Although partners are attracted to each other because of conscious factors—attractiveness, personality, traits, common interests and good times shared together—there are also strong unconscious factors which impel two people to choose each other over the many attractive, marriageable members of the opposite sex they meet during their single days. Typically, what is involved in these choices is the press of unresolved problems from the family of origin which the partners unconsciously hope to solve, if only vicariously, in the present.

Several clinical examples should illustrate this process:

A woman whose father was an alcoholic may marry an alcoholic because she is accustomed to compulsive drinking in a man. She felt responsible for her father's drinking and now feels responsible for her husband's drinking.

A man raised by a domineering mother may marry a submissive woman because of his fear of ever being dominated by another woman again.

A woman raised by an authoritarian father may marry an authoritarian husband and then rebel against him as she wished she had done with her father.

A man raised by a critical mother may marry a critical woman because he simultaneously feels he doesn't deserve a more loving wife and hopes he can gain from his wife what he never earned from his mother: acceptance.

You can uncover these repetitive family of origin problems by taking a history of each spouse and then point out to the couple how they affect their present marital functioning. Then either in individual sessions, conjoint sessions with the spouses or conjoint sessions with a spouse and her parents, you can work to reduce them.

To take a history of each spouse, ask first about one parent—the mother, for example—by getting her name, age and where living. If she has died, ask when, how and how your client reacted to her death. Then, to delve into the past, ask:

> What was your mother like when you were growing up?
> How did you two get along with each other?
> How did she discipline you?
> How did she show love to you?
> What message about yourself did you receive from your mother?
> How do you get along with her now (if she is living)?

Ask the same questions about the other parent, then ask about the parents' marriage:

> What was your parents' marriage like?
> How did they get along with each other?
> How did they show love for each other?

Then find out about any siblings in the family by asking their names, ages, where living and whether married or not. Again, to delve into the past, ask about each sibling:

> What was your relationship with your sibling like as you were growing up?
> How do you get along now?

Then ask about any other family members—grandparents, aunts, uncles or cousins—who may have had a significant impact on the spouse as she was growing up.

You can next ask about experiences in elementary school, high school and college:

> What was school like for you?
> What kind of grades did you receive?
> How did you get along with the other students?
> What activities were you involved in?

Then ask about the spouse's dating history, paying particular attention to any rejections or traumatic experiences with the members of the opposite sex:

> What was your social life like?
> Tell me about your first boyfriend. Your second. Your third.

Have you been married before? What happened?

Ask about the employment history and conclude with a general question about anything else in your client's past about which you should know.

Next ask the other spouse if there is anything in his spouse's history you may have missed. Then ask him about his impression of her family of origin:

What's your impression of your mother-in-law? Your father-in-law?

How do you see their marriage?

What kind of impact do you think your in-laws have had on your spouse?

What is your impression of your spouse's siblings?

What kind of impact have they had on her?

Having completed a history on one spouse, these same questions can be used to take a history of the other spouse.

DIVORCE COUNSELING

Let's assume that you have used both a behavioral approach and a historical approach to the couple's marital problems and yet they still show little evidence of change. You have met with them for many sessions without any appreciable improvement in their marital functioning or any movement towards a decision to divorce. What do you do next?

Frankly, this is a tragic interaction to witness. Whenever two people have been unhappily married for years, it is difficult to understand why they refuse to change or divorce, especially since they appear to be giving each other far more pain than pleasure. There are several possible explanations for this unusual phenomenon:

—Although the spouses experience more pain than pleasure in their marriage, to them the alternative—divorce—appears worse. They are afraid of the possible loneliness, adjustments, financial problems and emotional insecurity which accompany divorce. Both may be convinced that they could not find someone else and so decide that an unhappy relationship is better than none at all. Or they may feel they don't deserve anything more satisfying.

—An unhappy marriage in which there is much fighting can be an exciting marriage as long as the fighting does not get out of control. It can confirm the selfhood of each spouse, albeit in a negative way.

—Probably the major advantage to an unhappy marriage is that it provides a scapegoat for the spouses to blame for most of their problems. What typically happens is that both spouses blame each other for their unhappiness and thereby avoid taking full responsibility for their own emotional well-being.

If you arrive at such an impasse with a couple, there are four things you can do: keep trying to work with the spouses using non-paradoxical techniques, employ paradoxical techniques, encourage them to consider a divorce or terminate with them. In using paradoxical techniques, which will be discussed more fully in Chapter 13, you want to attempt to do two things: relabel their negative interactions as positive and induce them to change by resisting your suggestions not to change. The following clinical example should illustrate this process:

> Joe and Edna claimed they had been married for eighteen years but fighting with each other for twenty years. Although they had been to several marriage counselors in the last four years, they displayed little change in their marital functioning.
>
> To relabel their marital interactions, the therapist pointed out the advantages to them both of their continued fighting: it was exciting for them and it provided both with a scapegoat to blame for their problems. In addition, since neither would consider divorce as a solution to their marital problems, they both agreed with the therapist's interpretation that the alternative to fighting— no communication between them—was not acceptable.
>
> To induce change paradoxically, the therapist suggested that Joe and Edna try not to change because of the advantages to them of their continued fighting. He advised them to quit investing their energies in attempting to change and learn to live with their marital interactions.

To help the couple explore the possibility of divorce as a solution to their marital distress, there are several questions you can ask them:

> What you you think about divorce in general?
>
> Do you have any religious objections to divorce? If so, what are they?
>
> How do you think you would do if you were to divorce? What would you do to adjust?
>
> How do you imagine your children would react to a divorce? Your family? Your friends?

You then might ask the couple to list the advantages and disadvantages of each course of action.

If they do eventually decide to divorce, you should then switch roles and do divorce counseling. In an educational and supportive capacity, your function in this new role is to help the couple and their children adjust to the impending divorce as easily as possible. To do this, there are several things you can do:

—Teach the couple about the process and problems involved in the divorce adjustment process so each will know what to expect.

—Teach them how to tell their children about the divorce and to handle it in such a way their children will be able to adjust to it with a minimum of stress.

—If it is true, as it usually is, reassure them they did everything they could do to save their marriage before deciding to divorce.

—Be available to help the couple decide any custody issues about the children.

—After termination, be available to both spouses for supportive counseling during their divorce adjustment process.

By discussing in detail divorce, single parenthood, remarriage and custody issues, the next two chapters should give you more concrete suggestions about how to offer these services to a divorcing couple.

Chapter 11

THE CHANGING FAMILY

Many of the families who come to us at the Family Teaching Center—74% in our follow-up study—are what we call changing families: divorced, step, widowed or single parent (never married). Since you may also find a high percentage of changing families in your own practice, you should be prepared to deal with the unique problems these families present. In this chapter, we will discuss the processes and problems involved in divorce, single parenthood and remarriage.

Children of divorce are children at risk for behavioral and emotional problems. But it is not inevitable that they develop such problems if the divorce and remarriages of their parents are handled properly. In fact, with the passage of time, divorce and remarriage may bring advantages to the family members. It is our function as family therapists to attempt to insure that this happens. In considering the children, we want to help restructure the changing family in such a way that their psychological needs will continue to be met despite the adjustments they and their parents face in divorce and remarriage.

THE DIVORCE ADJUSTMENT PROCESS

In an intact, first marriage family, the psychological health of the children depends to a large extent on the psychological health of their parents and the degree of satisfaction provided by the marriage. In a divorced family, the psychological health of children may depend to an even larger extent on the psychological health of their parents since they live with only one parent at a time. Accordingly, one way you can help the children of divorce is to help their parents adjust satisfactorily to their divorce.

Divorce involves a transition from the married state to the single state, and like all transitions, it can be painful. In fact, adjusting to a divorce may be the second most difficult adjustment an adult has to make, second only to accepting the death of a child.

Krantzler (1973) describes three stages in the divorce adjustment process. The first involves the recognition that a relationship has died and no longer meets the needs of its partners. But this is not always easy to admit. No matter how painful or intolerable it may have become, the marriage may have provided a certain amount of security and certainty, even if only by the regularity of bitter fights or the dull ache of marital indifference. Given the time they have shared together, it is small wonder that some couples take years to decide their marriage has died and to marshall the courage to dissolve it.

A process of mourning occupies the second stage. Like the death of a loved one, the death of a relationship involves a painful loss, and must be mourned if the divorced persons are ever to let go of the past and build new lives for themselves. The mourning of a divorce involves the same emotional reactions which accompany mourning for a deceased person: grief, anger for having been abandoned, fear of an unknown and possibly lonely future, guilt for things said or done or not said and done and a temporary emotional withdrawal.

Because of the pain involved in mourning a divorce, recently divorced persons may find themselves longing for the old relationship, and tend to deny or forget its capacity to give pain. They may divorce in the hope of being happier but find themselves, at least initially, to be even less happy than they were when they were married. This is what Krantzler (1973) calls the "pull of the past." When experiencing it, recently divorced persons may think, "Being unhappily married was better than being this unhappy alone!"

The third state involves the gradual adjustment to the single life. In getting through the divorced adjustment process, the former spouses eventually come to the realization they can live contented, independent lives without each other. The "pull of the past" is over and the present is here to be lived to the full. The ex-spouses learn they are not half persons because they are single, and that they need not be involved in other relationships to be whole.

Two common mistakes which divorced people make are either to rush quickly into another marriage for fear of being alone, or to shun marriage altogether for fear of being hurt again. As a family therapist, you want divorced persons to take an intermediate, flexible position between these two extremes. Ideally, they should first establish themselves as independent, self-loving and self-sustaining persons. Secure in the knowledge they can make it on their own, each will then be in a better position to carefully and unhurriedly seek another relationship in which each may find more lasting love.

For people who have realized their marriages have been dead for years, the post-divorce adjustment process may be relatively short. Much of the divorce work—the working through of the anger, hurt and grief—has already been done during the marriage. But for the spouses who were left in the marriage, who opposed the divorce or were shocked by its announcement, the post-divorce adjustment process may take longer.

Divorce is not simply a piece of paper which says two people are no longer married. It's not a one time act that's over when the judge declares a marriage to be dissolved. Instead, it is a process which takes time. It is a pulling apart and a changing of well-established behavior patterns and feelings.

The ideal goal in the divorce adjustment process is that the ex-spouses will no longer react behaviorally or emotionally to each other as they once did. The hurt and anger—and love which underlies these emotions—are reduced to indifference or neutrality. What each could do to hurt or anger the other now only annoys each at worst.

In counseling a divorcing couple, there are several things you can do:

—Make them aware that the post-divorce adjustment process may take time. Although there are risks and probably inaccuracies in saying this, at the Family Teaching Center we tell people that adjusting to a divorce takes approximately two years. If two years after the divorce, one or both of the ex-spouses are still terribly hurt or angry, their divorce adjustment process is not proceeding as it should, probably because the spouses are still emotionally involved with each other even if only in bitter ways. The existence of intense anger long after it should have dissipated suggests that one or both of the divorced persons have not successfully completed the divorce adjustment process.

—Explain to a divorcing couple the course and nature of the divorce adjustment process. Give each permission to experience and express the strong emotions involved in divorce and tell them that each must go through a grief process, if they have not already done so, to recover from the divorce. Explain that a grief process which is denied is a grief process delayed.

—Reassure the ex-spouses they tried their best. Attempt to reduce their sense of guilt and failure. Make sure they realize neither of them is individually responsible for the demise of their marriage. Also, help them to understand why their marriage did not work and the part each played in its breakup. With greater insight into the causes of their divorce, each may be in a better position to make a future marriage more successful.

—Since the divorce adjustment process takes time, advise them to wait before remarrying. Explain to them that each must recover from the divorce before establishing another lasting relationship. To fail to do so may be to risk another divorce. If they are to consider remarriage someday, they should do so because they want to, not because they feel they have to to avoid loneliness.

—Above all, offer a divorcing couple hope. Reassure them there is life after divorce. To do this, I sometimes draw them a chart, shown in Figure 8, and explain to them that divorce may involve an initial period of greater emotional pain than that which they experienced during the marriage. But with the passage of time, their pain level should drop below the level they would have maintained by staying in an unchanging, chronically unhappy marriage.

THE CHILDREN OF DIVORCE

In perhaps what is one of the better studies of the effects of divorce on children, Wallerstein and Kelly (1980) studied 131 children from 58 divorced families over a five year period. To their surprise, they found that most of the children in their study did not want their parents to divorce no matter how unhappy, tense or

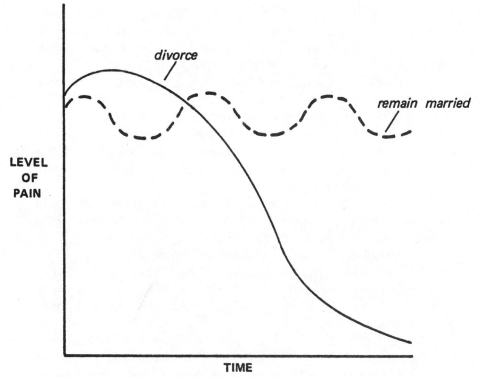

Figure 8. The expected course of emotional pain in the divorce adjustment process compared to the pain of an unchanging, chronically unhappy marriage. Initially, a divorce involves greater emotional pain which should diminish with time.

conflict-ridden family life had been for them. Less than 10% of them claimed they were relieved by their parents' divorce.

What this finding suggests is that divorce is initially stressful for children. At any upsetting time, children need love, support and reassurance from their parents. But since Wallerstein and Kelly (1980) found that two thirds of the mother-child relationships had deteriorated significantly at the time of the divorce, it would appear that divorcing parents are usually so upset themselves they are not able to fully respond to their children's needs. Happily, however, most of the mothers in this study eventually regained their former parenting skills.

Although the authors found children's initial reactions to their parents' divorce differed somewhat by age, they also found some common responses:

—Anxiety and fear. The major structure in the lives of these children had been rent asunder by the divorce, leaving them feeling vulnerable and insecure. Many of them expressed the fear they might be left by Mom as they had been by Dad.

—Sadness. Depression and grief were major reactions of these children to their parents' divorce.

—Yearning for the departed parent, usually the father. Fathers were missed intensely by their children, a longing that lasted no matter what their predivorce relationships with their children had been. And even if some rarely saw their children, they were still missed five years later.

—Worry. The children worried about how their mothers would adjust to the divorce, how their fathers would cope alone and how their own needs would be met by their distressed parents.

—Sense of rejection. The children felt rejected not only by their fathers who had left, but also by their mothers who tended to withdraw in response to their own anguish.

—Loneliness. Many of the children reported intense feelings of loneliness after the divorce.

—Conflicted loyalties. Many of them also felt torn between their parents, and did not want to take sides with either during the divorce struggle. Unfortunately, two thirds of the parents openly admitted to competing for their children's loyalty against the other parent, thereby further stressing their offspring.

—Anger. Anger was practically a universal reaction of these children. Nearly one quarter of them still clung to their anger five years after the divorce.

Wallerstein and Kelly (1980) found that these initial stress reactions, however intense, were not lasting but usually cleared up by their 18 month follow-up visit. If handled properly, divorce need not permanently scar children even though it is initially stressful for them. Unfortunately, in many cases, divorce does appear to have long term harmful consequences to children as these researchers found.

Five years after they divorce, 57% of the women and 50% of the men in this study were in good psychological health. Only 20% of them regretted the divorce or thought it had been ill advised.

By contrast, only 34% of the children were psychologically healthy five years later. 29% were having some emotional problems, while 37% were having serious emotional problems, primarily depression. 50% still thought their parents' divorce had been a mistake.

Of the children who were having serious problems, 17% felt rejected by their mothers and 39% felt rejected by their fathers. Their depression was manifested in a variety of ways: intense and chronic unhappiness, delinquency, poor learning, sexual promiscuity, anger, apathy, restlessness or a sense of emotional deprivation.

What is significant about this research is that it clearly shows that children can be negatively affected by divorce five years after it occurs. Divorce can hurt children. It doesn't have to, but it will if not handled properly.

Wallerstein and Kelly (1980) outlined several conditions which, if present, may better insure that children will not be damaged by divorce. As a family therapist, you should be aware of these conditions and work to insure they are present in the divorced family.

—Continued loving relationship with both parents. Because they have stopped loving each other does not mean that parents have to stop loving their children. Children of divorce need to be reassured their parents will continue to support and care for them.

It is especially important that the non-custodial parent— usually the father—continue to be involved with the children on a regular, frequent basis. He plays an important role in the development of self-esteem in his children, and his absence will bother them. It is more difficult for children to learn to like themselves if they feel their father doesn't care for them.

—Absence of conflict between the parents. Children will be negatively affected by a divorce if it does not solve or reduce the problems between their parents, or if it escalates the parents' hurt and anger. Parents who continue to battle each other after the divorce will inflict emotional damage on their offspring, especially if they use them as weapons or allies.

—Absence of severe economic stress and worries. Divorce is financially and emotionally stressful for all family members. Mothers' incomes usually drop after a divorce, while fathers may be burdened by the support of two households. If the economic stress in a divorce is severe, it will add to the already heavy emotional burden of the children.

—Good psychological stability of both parents. Whether married or divorced, emotionally disturbed parents tend to produce emotionally disturbed children. Parents in a divorce are subject to severe stress which usually, but temporarily, diminishes their parenting skills. If they can eventually recover those skills, their children will have a better chance of adjusting satisfactorily to the divorce.

In talking to divorcing parents about their children, there are several things you can do:

—Encourage them to tell the children together about their decision to divorce. Instruct them to be realistic about the reasons for the divorce although they don't have to go into details. They don't have to say, for example, that one of them has had an affair, but only that one of them doesn't love the other anymore or has found someone else to love.

—Have the parents make sure the children do not blame themselves in any way for the divorce. They should ask each child if he or she feels responsible and reassure each this is not the case. The parents should take full responsibility for the divorce and not blame it on the behavior of any other persons.

—Have the parents reassure the children they will still be loved and cared for by them even though mother and father have stopped loving each other. The children must be assured they won't be abandoned by either parent.

—Encourage the parents not to criticize or condemn each other in front of the children. If the children are to feel good about themselves, they must feel good about both of their parents from whom they issued. A child who is constantly told what a "rotten no good" his father is will have a difficult time developing a positive self concept.

—Encourage the parents not to ask their children which parent they want to live with. This is perhaps the worst double bind in which parents can place their offspring. To choose to live with one parent, no matter how diplomatically done, is to reject the other parent and to create a burden of guilt children could carry for the rest of their lives. The parents should decide on the custody and living arrangements, not the children.

—Teach the parents to expect some strong emotional reactions in their children which should abate with time if handled properly. Encourage them to keep the lines of communication open with their offspring. Ideally, they should be willing to listen to the expressed pain of their children and to admit that they too are hurt and saddened by the divorce.

—If it is possible, advise the parents to avoid further disruptions in their children's lives. The children of divorce have enough new adjustments to make so it is better for them if they can be kept in the same home, school and neighborhood.

In addition to working with their parents, there are also several things you can do in directly counseling the children of divorce:

—Give them the opportunity to express their feelings. Assure them it is O.K. to feel sad, scared, hurt and angry for they are in a painful situation.

—Ask each of them if he or she feels responsible for either causing the divorce or for getting mother and father back together again. You want to reassure them, as you have encouraged the parents to do, that the divorce is not their fault in any way. Nor is there anything they can do to reunite their parents. They may wish their parents hadn't divorced, but the reality is they have and don't plan to remarry.

—Assure the children also they are not responsible if one of their parents has been psychologically or physically absent since the divorce. It doesn't mean they are unlovable. Rather, it means their parent has been experiencing such overwhelming problems that he or she has been unable to respond fully to them.

—If the parents are still fighting, tell the children they don't have to take sides. Encourage them to say to their parents, "We want to love you both and not have to take sides," or deliver this message from the children to their parents yourself.

In effect, you want the children of divorce to reach the point at which they can say:

> Mom and Dad are not going to get back together again (or Dad's not coming back) and that makes me sad or angry. But it's not my fault; it was their problem. Despite their continued fighting, I can still love them both without having to choose sides.

THE SINGLE PARENT EXPERIENCE

If you think being a parent is difficult, try being a single parent. It's probably the most difficult job in the world.

Imagine rising early in the morning, getting small children ready for school or the day care center, putting in an eight hour work day, picking the children up after work, cooking dinner, getting them ready for bed and then collapsing in bed yourself. You also have to take care of medical emergencies, drive the children to doctor's appointments and ballet lessons, wipe runny noses, dry tears, listen to children's problems and dispense daily hugs. Weekends are spent cleaning the house, grocery shopping and doing laundry, leaving you with little time for a social or recreational life of your own.

There are three ways to become a single parent: through divorce, through the death of a spouse or by never marrying. Most single parents—about 70%—become single parents through divorce. What follows is a discussion of the problems faced by divorced single parents in which one, usually the mother, is a custodial parent and the other is a non-custodial parent. We will consider joint custody arrangements in the next chapter.

The problems of the custodial single parent are many and overwhelming. According to Weiss (1979), the single parent faces three types of overload:

—Responsibility overload. The single parent with custody has complete and total responsibility for the welfare of her children. All major decisions about them must be made alone, without the support and advice of another parent. Since she has to raise them by herself, she may feel how they turn out is entirely up to her, a heavy burden for anyone to carry.

—Task overload. In addition to responsibility overload, the single parent faces task overload. In any family with children, there are three sets of responsibilities—care and nurturance of the children, household tasks and financial support—which Weiss (1979) claims constitute two full-time jobs. In a two parent family, there are obviously two people to do these two jobs, while there is only one person to do them in a single parent family.

Finances are usually a problem for the single parent since most face a reduction in their income as a result of their divorce. Even if she receives child support payments—and only 50% of single, custodial parents do—they are rarely enough to meet the bills of the modern family. If she doesn't already have one, the single parent will probaby have to find a job. If she has helped put her ex-husband through school or hasn't worked in a number of years, she may have fewer skills, less education or limited experience with which to obtain a good paying job, or will face the lower salaries many women face.

—Emotional overload. The combination of responsibility overload and task overload may lead to emotional overload. As every parent knows, children can be very demanding. Emotionally, they take more than they give in return. While striving to meet the needs of her children, the single parent may have no other close, caring adult to give to her.

Loneliness can be an especially painful problem for the single parent. After her divorce, her married friends may tend to pull away from her because they may not be sure how to respond to her or include her socially, or they may be reluctant to take her side.

Dating may also be a problem for her. Her children may oppose her dating and she may feel guilty for leaving them. She may be afraid to date for fear of being rejected again or be so angry towards members of the opposite sex she may not want to date. Finding time to date in her already overloaded schedule may also be a problem for her.

As if these three types of overload are not enough, the single parent faces two other types of problems:

—Discipline. Discipline may be a difficult problem for the single parent for a number of reasons. She is alone in her efforts to discipline the children with no one to back her up or support her. She is often so upset by the divorce that her ability to be an effective disciplinarian may be diminished. In addition, her children may be more difficult to discipline because of their own emotional turmoil about the divorce. At a time when she needs them to be more cooperative may be precisely the time when they present more discipline problems.

—Visitation problems. One especially annoying problem for the custodial parent is that she has to be more of the disciplinarian with the children while the non-custodial parent can have more fun with them. During his visits, he can take them to ballgames, the zoo or shopping, even though he has not been paying his child support payments on a regular basis. As a result, he may be viewed as the "good guy" by the children, while she is perceived as more "mean."

This contrast can be especially apparent immediately after a visit of the non-custodial parent. Since they have had such fun with him and don't want to return yet to the custodial parent, she may find them especially restless, unhappy or obstinate at this time.

Lest it sound as if single parenting is a completely overwhelming negative experience, there are some advantages to being in a single parent family. Although there is a danger of her becoming pathologically enmeshed with her children, the single parent does have an opportunity to develop a close relationship with them. She is also able to provide them with more consistent discipline than would have been possible with two warring parents who constantly undermined each other's authority. And since there is one less parent to operate and support the family, the children in a single parent family usually have to pitch in more and become more responsible than children in a two parent family.

Our description of the custodial parents is not meant to imply that the non-custodial parent doesn't have his share of problems also. All is not fun with the children for him. Instead, the problems which he faces are often the opposite of what the custodial parent faces. If she feels overloaded, he may feel bored and useless. If she is burdened with too much responsibility for the children, he may feel he has lost influence in the lives of his children. One frequent complaint non-custodial parents make is that they are expected to financially support their children but have no say in how they are raised.

Whether or not the non-custodial parent maintains regular contact with his children depends upon four factors: the custodial mother's responses to his visits, his children's reactions to him, his second wife's reactions to his children and his own adjustment to the divorce.

No matter how she may feel about him, it is important that the custodial parent encourage visits by her ex-spouse and not make him feel uncomfortable when he does see the children. His visits can provide an opportunity to reawaken old fights and wounds, but these will only hurt the children and discourage him from seeing them.

The children's reactions to the non-custodial parent can also influence his visitation patterns. If they are angry at him for the divorce, or cool toward him for fear of being hurt again, this will make it painful for him to see them, especially if he is already feeling guilty about the divorce.

If the non-custodial parent remarries, his second spouse's feelings about his children can also influence the frequency and regularity of his visits. Rivalries and jealousy are normal in any family but are naturally more intense in stepfamilies. If the stepparent is excessively jealous of her spouse's attention to his children, or threatened by his contacts with his ex-wife about them, she can make it more difficult for him to be a loving, involved parent.

But perhaps the most important factor in the non-custodial parent's visitation patterns is his own adjustment to the divorce. If he is depressed because of the divorce or feeling excessively guilty because he initiated it, contact with his children may reawaken those painful feelings. If he doesn't visit his children often, it may be because it is too painful for him to do so.

In counseling the custodial parent, your main function should be to provide her with support. Emphasize to her that she can't do all that might be done. Perhaps the house can't be as clean as she would like it to be, or her meals as fancy and varied. Since her needs must be met if she is to meet the needs of her children, tell her she will need other sources of support and time for herself.

You can help her with discipline by teaching her the skills described in our child and adolescent programs. You should also be aware of the tendency for the single parent to become enmeshed with her children and do what you can to reduce that enmeshment.

In counseling the non-custodial parent, do what you can to keep him involved in the lives of his children. Because of the influence they may have on his visitation patterns, you may have to see his present spouse, if he has remarried, and his ex-spouse to successfully do this. Often, a non-custodial parent may wonder if he still counts in the lives of his offspring, especially if his children have acted defensively distant or angry during his visits. You should reassure this parent that this is, in fact, the case and that he will be missed by his children if he does not see them often.

REMARRIAGE

In Chapter 2, we described the conflict between intimacy and isolation which we all face. It is a classic double approach-avoidance conflict in which the advantages of intimacy are the disadvantages of isolation, and vice versa.

In few situations can this conflict be more acute than for those who have divorced and are considering remarriage. As is shown in Figure 9, divorced persons probably do not experience this conflict immediately after their divorce because they have decided to stay uninvolved for fear of being hurt again. They avoid this conflict because their fear of intimacy is high while their desire for intimacy is low. With the passage of time, however, their fear of intimacy may decrease while their desire to be intimate increases. They may become romantically involved with someone but at the same time be afraid to be hurt again. It is probably at the intersection of these two conflicting reactions that their greatest conflict is experienced.

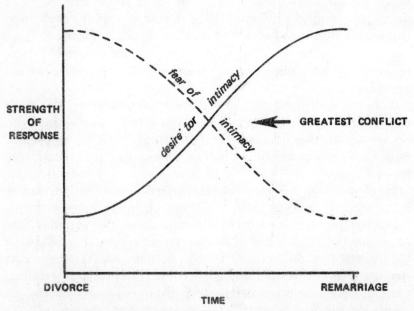

Figure 9. The change in a desire for intimacy versus a fear of intimacy for divorced persons. With the passage of time, their desire may increase while their fear may decrease. It is at the intersection of these competing responses that divorced persons may experience the greatest conflict regarding remarriage.

But many divorced persons eventually work through this conflict. Their desire for intimacy becomes stronger than their fear of intimacy and so they decide to take a chance and remarry. 80% of them do so, but unfortunately 50% of them divorce again. As family therapists, it is our function to prepare divorced persons for remarriage so they don't have to face the stress of a divorce again.

Carter and McGoldrick (1980) have listed a number of conditions which they believe make remarriages more difficult. Some of these are as follows:

—Denial of the loss which occurs in divorce and/or a short time between marriages. Either of these conditions prevent the divorced persons from fully working through the divorce adjustment process. At the Family Teaching Center, we advise people to wait two years after the divorce before remarriage unless they did most of their divorce work while married.

—Intense bitterness towards the ex-spouse. To us, this is a sign the divorced spouses are still emotionally involved with each other. To remarry at such a time would be to create a triangle of involvement which few new marriages could stand. Just as children must emancipate themselves emotionally from their parents before they can successfully marry, so ex-spouses must emancipate themselves emotionally from each other before they can successfully remarry.

—The erroneous belief that the remarriage will present no difficulties for the children. In the glow of their love for each other, persons considering a remarriage may assume their children will love their new spouse and vice versa. Alas, if love between stepchildren and stepparents ever does develop—and often it does not—it takes several years to occur.

—The erroneous belief that the stepfamily will be just like a happy, intact, first marriage family. Born of loss, the stepfamily faces not only the usual problems of the intact, first marriage family, but also problems which are unique to it. We will discuss these problems in the next section.

—An insistence on loyalty to the new family unit, combined with an attempt to exclude natural parents or grandparents from it. If firm boundaries are drawn around the new stepfamily by the parent and stepparent, with the message that all within those boundaries should love one another, and all without them are not welcome, they will present themselves with a difficult, if not impossible, task. Love can never be forced; it can only be allowed to grow gradually and spontaneously. In addition, the children of divorce want to love and be loved by both their parents and all of their living grandparents. Any attempts to interfere with that love may generate resentment in them.

—A change in custody near the time of remarriage. If father unexpectedly obtains custody of the children, for example, just as he is about to remarry, this will complicate his plans for marriage. The unplanned arrival of his children may interfere with the development of a closer relationship between the newly-weds. She may feel she married more than she contracted for, while he may feel caught in the middle between his new wife and children.

In counseling those who plan to remarry, your task is twofold: to insure they have completed the divorce adjustment process and to help them prepare for the normal problems expected in a stepfamily. What you want to help people avoid is their going from marriage to divorce to marriage again, too soon after their divorce. Instead, you want them to go from marriage to divorce to the single state and then to a remarriage. Having accepted the single state, they can carefully choose to remarry, not because they feel they must to avoid loneliness, but because they want to remarry a particular person with whom they believe they can make a successful second marriage.

THE STEPFAMILY

If being a single parent is the toughest job in the world, being in a stepfamily can be second in stress to single parenthood. In addition to the normal problems which any family faces, the stepfamily faces problems which are unique to it:

—A history of trauma or loss. Unlike the intact, first marriage family, the stepfamily has a history of hurt, loss or trauma which may put a burden on the stepfamily members to succeed because they feel they have failed before. This may or may not work to their advantage.

—The existence of two homes for the children. In the case of a divorce, the stepfamily members must contend with a biological parent outside its structure whose presence can cause problems. Ideally, the children in a stepfamily should feel loved and accepted in two homes. But all too infrequently, this does not happen. If there is continued conflict between the biological parents, the children may feel a severe conflict of loyalties. Not wanting to, they may feel they have to take sides in their parents' battles. But to be loyal to mother may be to be disloyal to father, and vice versa, a terrible, no-win double bind for children to be in. They would rather love and be loved by both their parents without having to choose sides.

In addition, the presence of a biological parent outside the stepfamily, whether remarried or not, can cause jealousy in the stepparent. And if the emotional relationship between the natural parents, which can include feelings of hurt and anger, has not been resolved, that jealousy can be realistic.

Also, the stepparent may resent her stepchildren as a symbol of her spouse's former marriage. She may have been given the responsibility to raise someone else's children, a role with its limitations and drawbacks. However good a job she does, she may not receive any credit for it. In fact, her stepchildren may resent her for her efforts at discipline, a resentment they may express by claiming, "My real Mom would have let me do it," whenever they want to question her disciplinary decisions.

Secretly, stepchildren may want the stepmarriage to fail so their biological parents can reunite or they can have their parent to themselves without having to compete for his time and attention with the stepparent. Their disruptive behavior—should some occur—may be an attempt to drive a wedge between their parent and stepparent.

Displaced anger may be especially common in a stepfamily. The stepchildren may be hostile to the stepparent because they have been hurt by the separation from their natural parent but don't know how to express that pain except by angrily blaming the stepparent.

—Forced relationships between people. The stepfamily also entails forced relationships between the family members. The two adults in the stepfamily have decided to join together voluntarily but this is not true of the children. Stepparents, stepchildren and stepsiblings may live together because they have to, not because they chose to, and their joining in a stepfamily unit can cause tremendous jealousies, conflicts and resentments. The happy wedding of the parent and stepparent may not be viewed as a happy event by the children. Positive, caring relationships can grow out of these forced relationships, but not without time, patience, understanding, communication, and compromise.

One of the pitfalls which stepfamily members must avoid is what Roosevelt and Lovas (1976) call the myth of instant love. Remarried newly-weds may hope to create a close-knit, caring family like the intact family they never had or had once but lost. They may dream their new family will abound in love and closeness. They may assume, usually unrealistically, that because they love each other, there will automatically be love between step-children and stepparents. They may think, "I love you; therefore, I'll love your children. You love me; therefore, your children will love me."

Unfortunately, it doesn't always happen this way, at least not quickly or easily. For a number of reasons, the stepfamily may never be as close or cohesive as the intact, first marriage family. It can never be a family which has not suffered the trauma of a divorce or death. The marriage of one parent may be viewed by the children, not as the gain of another parent, but as the loss of a close relationship with the first parent. The stepparent may be resented as a intruder who is trying to take the place of the other parent. Or his marriage to the first parent may be correctly perceived as a sign that the biological parents are never going to get back together again, something the children secretly wish for.

Children may also be afraid to become too close to a stepparent because they have already been hurt by the loss of one parent and may not want to risk another possible loss. Or they may feel that affection for a stepparent may represent disloyalty to a natural parent now living outside the home.

—Discipline. Another common problem in the stepfamily is discipline. Having raised the children by herself for a number of years, the custodial parent in a divorce—often the mother—usually feels overburdened by the care and discipline of her offspring, and welcomes a new spouse to relieve her of that burden.

But the person who marries into a family with children may be placed in a precarious position. As a newcomer to the family, he can't effectively discipline his stepchildren until he has formed an affectionate relationship with them. But that takes time—usually one or two years—or is not always possible to achieve. On the one hand, if he is aloof with his stepchildren, he may never develop a close relationship with them. On the other hand, if he engages the children too quickly, they may rebuff him, or if he is too harsh with them, mother may become overprotective even though earlier she said she wanted his help in disciplining them. To compound these disciplinary problems, the children may rebel against any stepparent authority by saying, in effect, to him, "Why should we obey you? You're not our father."

parent and the caught-in-the-middle biological parent. Since the stepparent is joining an already established unit, he often feels like an outsider trying to join a tight-knit clique. On her part, the biological parent often is caught in the middle between her children and her spouse, all of whom she loves. They may complain to her about the stepparent while he may complain to her about them.

In counseling the members of a stepfamily, the first thing you want to do is to strengthen the marital relationship. As is true in the intact, first marriage family, it is the key to the success or the failure of the stepfamily.

You should also make the members aware of the problems expected in the stepfamily and do what you can to help them cope with those problems. Three problems you may have to work on directly are discipline, the stepparent-stepchildren relationships and the existence of two homes for the children. To work on the discipline problems, you can teach the family members the principles involved in our child and adolescent programs. It is especially important that the parent and stepparent discuss disciplinary matters thoroughly and be in agreement about rules and consequences. With a new stepfamily, we advise the biological parent to be the primary disciplinarian since the stepparent does not have the affectionate parent-child relationship which makes discipline more effective. Since his first task should be to work on that relationship, his being the disciplinarian in the stepfamily will interfere with its development.

To work on the stepparent-stepchildren relationships, give each permission not to like each other, although they do have to be civil to one another. Suggest that perhaps someday they may come to like or love each other, but establish as a realistic goal that they learn to get along together. In doing this, you want to emphasize the point that caring in these involuntary relationships can never be forced.

To work on the problem of two homes for the children in a stepfamily, you may have to contact the biological parent. The rarely achieved ideal you want to promote is that the children will come to feel accepted in two homes by three to four caring parents who can cooperate with each other for the sake of the children. How to do this will be discussed in the next chapter on custody counseling.

Chapter 12

CUSTODY COUNSELING

As a family therapist, you will inevitably encounter problems with custody issues in divorced families. Even if you don't do custody counseling, you should still be aware of these problems to be able to advise your clients about them. And if one of your functions as a family therapist is to restructure the changing family in such a way that the children's psychological needs continue to be met, you must have a knowledge of custody issues to do so.

However, once you've gained some experience teaching families communication, negotiation and contracting skills, you should be able to do custody counseling since it simply involves the application of these skills to custody disagreements. In saying this, I'm making a distinction between divorce mediation, which does require special training and expertise, and custody counseling which most experienced family therapists should be able to do.

Divorce mediation involves the entire package of issues which a divorcing couple must settle: property settlements, custody issues, child support and alimony payments. To do divorce mediation, you need a knowledge of legal and financial matters which most family therapists don't have.

By contrast, custody counseling only involves those issues which directly affect the children: custody, living arrangements, visitation schedules, holidays and vacations. Helping divorcing parents to negotiate and contract about these issues does not require a knowledge of legal and financial matters on your part.

THE ADVANTAGES OF CUSTODY COUNSELING

To be honest, custody counseling can be very stressful for you. Your task is to encourage two hurt, hostile people to agree about certain issues when they sometimes don't even want to be in the same room together. But it also presents you with the opportunity to prevent serious psychological problems in children. If you can enable divorcing parents to avoid litigation by deciding upon a workable custody arrangement themselves, you can help them avoid a great amount of emotional turmoil.

Since a court battle is usually so expensive, stressful and ineffective as a solution to a custody dispute, the goal of custody counseling is to avoid litigation which Irving (1980) found was accomplished in 70% of the 100 families he studied. And even though you may never interview them, the concern in custody counseling should always be focused on the children. It is primarily their welfare you are working to insure.

To the parents, the advantages of custody counseling are many. You may want to list these advantages as you attempt to convince them to agree to some custody counseling sessions with you:

—It is less expensive than litigation. Parents can usually arrive at an agreement in four to eight sessions and avoid most of the legal fees involved in a court battle.

—It is a self-determining process. The parents decide what's best for their children, not a stranger in a black robe who knows far less about the children than they do.

—It is a process which can increase the level of trust and communication between the parents which will benefit all members of a divorced family.

—It arrives at a plan for the children which has a better chance of being successfully implemented since both parents have voluntarily agreed to it. A custody arrangement decided by litigation may not work since the "losing" parent may sabotage it or challenge it year after year in court in an attempt to reverse it.

—It avoids the mudslinging which is usually involved in litigation. Since the legal system is essentially adversarial and involves the declaration of winners and losers, in a custody dispute each parent's attorney will attempt to prove his or her client is a better parent for the children by proving the other is an unfit parent. Mother's attorney will suggest that father has a drinking problem, for example, or that he once slapped one of the children in an abusive way. Father's attorney will counter that mother is an unstable person because she was recently hospitalized for stress.

Obviously, what this process of mutual mudslinging does is to increase the hurt, bitterness and mistrust between the divorcing parents. Before litigation, they could sit down and talk with each other; after litigation, they may refuse to be in the same room together. What may have started out as a "friendly divorce" may be turned into a bitter, hurtful dissolution of the marriage.

A THREE STEP PROCESS

Custody counseling may consist of a three step process: facilitation, arbitration and litigation. As a custody counselor, your first function is to act as a facilitator to encourage the divorcing parents to decide upon a custody arrangement for their children themselves. In this capacity, you have no decision-making authority. If your facilitation doesn't work, you may then proceed to the next step, arbitration.

In arbitration, you are given the legal authority by the parents, and their attorneys, to decide upon the custody issues they have been unable to settle. This may occur late in the custody counseling process when the parents have reached the limits of their tolerance to compromise with each other. Perhaps they have come very close to an agreement but are too uncomfortable to push on to reach a final agreement. Perhaps each feels unable to compromise further and still maintain face.

Since it would be a shame to resort to litigation at this point, you can offer to arbitrate the dispute for the parents. The advantages to them of accepting your offer are that it avoids the stress and expense of litigation, enables them to save face by not having to give in at an impasse and provides them with what would probably be a better agreement. With your expertise in family dynamics and your knowledge of this particular divorcing family, it is reasonable to assume that you can arrive at a better custody decision in less time than can a judge.

In arbitration, your decision can be either advisory or binding. If it is binding, both parties agree beforehand to accept your custody plan. This may not pose a problem if they are very close to an agreement and you simply declare a compromise both can live with. For example, if father wants the children for eight weeks during the summer, while the mother insists on four, you can split the difference by granting father six weeks of summer time with his children.

If your arbitration is advisory, and the parties do not both agree to it, your decisions may then be used in the next and final step in custody counseling, litigation. At this point, you should be prepared to be called as a witness in court to explain and perhaps defend what you have decided.

At the Family Teaching Center, we avoid being called as witnesses in custody disputes. Frankly, we feel it involves us in stressful, no-win situations, especially if both parents are equally capable, or incapable, of taking care of their children. During our first custody counseling session, we usually have both parents sign an agreement which states that neither will subpoena us to testify in court if they're unable to arrive at an agreement during their custody counseling sessions with us. By cutting ourselves off from any possible involvement in the legal system, we believe we protect ourselves from attempted triangulation by the parents. Since we won't be available to testify or make specific recommendations, there is no sense in either parent inducing us to take his or her side. Each can then be freer to relate to us and each other in a more honest and open manner in our counseling sessions.

THE FIRST SESSION

Custody counseling proceeds under the assumption that the marriage between the parents is ended, and that there is no chance of reconciliation between them. The parents are in your office to decide on certain custody issues and not to reconsider their decision to divorce. Accordingly, the atmosphere provided by you should be very businesslike. You should work on instrumental communication between them but not emotional communication. The parents need to settle their dispute as calmly and rationally as possible, and not express their mutual hurt and anger.

As is true of marital and family therapy, you should attempt to see both parents together for their first session. If one or both of them insist on seeing you individually at first, you can agree to their request as long as you give each the same number of individual sessions—preferably one apiece—accept no secrets during these sessions and insist that both eventually meet with you together.

In mediating custody disputes, it is not necessary that you meet with the children since your function will not be to make recommendations about them. You may do so, however, if the parents insist on it, but don't ask the children what types of custody and living arrangements they would prefer. These matters should be decided by their parents, not by them. For any of the children to say they would prefer to live with one parent can be to subject themselves to years of guilt for having, in effect, rejected the other parent.

We usually don't take a formal history of the marriage and its decline when doing custody counseling. To do so may be to stir up some bitter feelings that would interfere with the spirit of compromise and cooperation which is a necessary ingredient in successful custody counseling. Besides, a history of the marriage usually emerges informally in our sessions with the parents.

Start your custody counseling sessions by asking the parents how they were referred to you, what they expect and how they see custody counseling working. As you do in family and marital counseling, you want to clear up any misconceptions the parents may have about custody counseling. Specifically, you want them both to understand that initially you are available to help them decide what to do about their children, and not to decide these issues for them.

After you've heard their views on custody counseling, carefully explain its process to them. Specifically, stress that your job is to act as a facilitator by encouraging them to arrive at a decision about the custody and living arrangements for their children themselves. Stress that the best decision is one to which they agree, and not one decided by a judge.

Then explain to the parents that they should be able to arrive at an agreement in four to eight weeks to give them a sense that custody counseling will be a time limited process. Tell them if they can't agree on the custody issues affecting their children in eight sessions, they'll probably never be able to reach an agreement and so will have to go to court to resolve their dispute. At this time, we don't tell them we may make ourselves available as arbitrators at a later date because we don't want either of them to begin to attempt to triangulate us. Arbitration is something we offer only as a last resort when our efforts at facilitation have failed.

In difficult cases, there are several things you can do before you begin your sessions to motivate the parents to arrive at a custody agreement:

—Ask the parents if they want the best for their children. When each answers "Yes," explain to them that what is best for their children is that they arrive at a custody agreement and avoid a court battle.

—Describe the consequences of their failure to arrive at an agreement. Explain that they will have to go to court, and then describe the results of litigation: the stress, the expense, the mudslinging, the increased hostility and mistrust, and the formulation of a custody arrangement which could never be as satisfactory as one they determine themselves.

—In especially difficult cases, you might predict that the parents won't be able to arrive at an agreement, and so will have to admit their failure by going to court. Using this maneuver, you may be able to induce them to prove you wrong by coming to an agreement.

Then explain to the parents the issues they have to decide in their sessions with you: custody, living arrangements, visitation schedules, holidays and vacations. At the Family Teaching Center, we give the parents a list of these issues and ask them to write down what each wants in their custody agreement. By comparing their responses, we can determine how close, or apart, they are to an agreement. If they are quite far apart, we may ask them what each would settle for rather than what each wants.

After our first custody counseling session, we contact each parent's attorney to make sure he or she supports our efforts. If one or both of the attorneys is not in agreement with our goals and methods, the chances of custody counseling working are greatly diminished. We also like to ask the attorneys to cease all legal activities during the custody counseling sessions since the exchange of threatening letters or appearances in court about other divorce issues at that time will only make our job more difficult.

THE SECOND AND SUBSEQUENT SESSIONS

Once you've secured the parents' agreement about the goals and course of custody counseling, you can proceed to negotiating and contracting about specific custody issues. To establish a spirit of hope and cooperation, start with the easiest issues first. Most parents should be able to agree to rotate holidays, for example, and then go on to agree on summer vacation schedules.

If the parents become stuck on any issues, there are several things you can do to encourage them to reach an agreement:

—Keep stressing the importance of compromising with each other for the sake of the children. Keep them aware also of the negative consequences to them and their offspring of their not being able to arrive at an agreement.

—Go on to another issue if the parents become stuck on one particular issue. If they can't agree on a visitation schedule, for example, have them negotiate about a summer vacation schedule. Once they've agreed to it, they may be in a better frame of mind to agree on weekly visits.

—Encourage the parents to consider some trade-offs. If the mother agrees to the father having the children for four weeks during the summer, for example, even though she would prefer only two weeks, he'll agree to having them in two two-week periods rather than for a full four weeks. That way, the children will not be away from mother for so long a time.

—Ask the parents to carefully consider a still disputed issue for a week rather than press for a decision in one session. In effect, give them a chance to get away from each other for a while to more clearly think about their positions.

—Separate the parents, either in two offices or by seeing one first and then the other, and ask each alone about specific proposals or compromises. It may make it easier for them to compromise or agree to a proposal when the other is not present. To ask for a significant compromise or agreement when both parents are in your office may be to increase the reluctance of them both to be the first one to concede.

At the Family Teaching Center, we remain as neutral as we can regarding the specifics of a custody agreement. Although Luepnitz (1982) found that joint custody is reported to be a more satisfactory custody arrangement for the parents she interviewed and for their children, we know of no studies which support certain living arrangements or visitation schedules over others. We are aware of no research evidence, for example, that a month-to-month rotation of the children in a joint custody arrangement is superior to a week-to-week rotation schedule.

But based on the research of Wallerstein and Kelly (1980), we do know that the continued fighting of the parents or the absence of one parent in a divorce will harm the children. Our goal in custody counseling, then, is to prevent either of these conditions from occurring. And helping the parents to arrive at a custody agreement is the best way we can promote this goal.

In other words—and we frequently say this to the parents—the specifics of a custody agreement are not as important as the spirit of cooperation between them which it engenders. What is best for the children is that they—the parents—stop their fighting and remain involved in the lives of their offspring in loving, supportive ways. The best custody arrangement is not one we advise for them but one to which they both agree. If each supports a particular custody arrangement, it will work for them and their children. If they don't support it, it will not work, and no amount of advice from us will make it work.

Once the parents reach an agreement, we type it up for them, have each sign it and ask them to take it back to their respective attorneys for approval. The attorneys then usually take it to court for incorporation in the final divorce decree.

With most of our custody counseling cases, we follow up the parents once a month for several months to insure the smooth implementation of their custody agreement. We have found that without this follow-up, some agreements break down shortly after they are signed by the parents.

THE CUSTODY ISSUES

There are usually five custody issues the parents must settle in their custody counseling sessions with you. What follows is a discussion of each of these issues.

Sole or Joint Custody

The only two possible custody arrangements for children of divorce are for one parent to have sole custody or for both parents to share custody. If both state they want joint custody, or one does while the other doesn't, your tasks in custody counseling may not be too formidable. But if both parents claim they want sole custody, you may have difficulty getting them to agree on a custody arrangement. One of them would have to make a major concession which neither may be willing to do.

Contrary to the expectations of some divorcing parents, joint custody does not necessarily involve a fifty-fifty split of the children's living arrangement. Rather it is a legal decree which simply states that both parents legally remain parents to their children. Both retain the legal rights and responsibilities they had as parents before their divorce. Neither parent is declared not to be a parent in the eyes of the law.

If certain conditions are met, we favor joint custody arrangements at the Family Teaching Center for the following reasons:

—It better insures that both parents will remain involved in the lives of their children since both are legally responsible for them. No parent is denied his or her legal responsibilities and duties to the children.

—It can provide a better financial arrangement for the divorced family. Both parents can contribute to the financial support of the children or if one parent is not working, the other may be more willing to keep up his support payments since he is still legally a parent to his children.

—It usually avoids the overload involved in single parenting as the children live with both parents at different times. Each parent can have some time away from his or her children, knowing they are being cared for by someone who loves them.

But joint custody will not work as effectively, and probably should not be implemented, if certain conditions are not present in the divorced family. These conditions are as follows:

—Both parents accept that the marriage is over so that one parent is not using a joint custody arrangement to maintain contact with the other parent in the hope of winning him or her back.

—Both parents favor joint custody. It is not being forced on one parent by the courts or agreed to because of guilt or under pressure to be cooperative.

—Neither parent wants to restrict the access of the other parent to the children. Each realizes it is in the best interests of their offspring that they have frequent contact with both their parents.

—The parents are willing and able to cooperate and communicate with each other for the sake of their children. They may still be angry at each other, and not yet fully trust each other, but they can temporarily set aside these feelings and work cooperatively to raise the children in two separate homes.

Although it is not an absolute requirement that the parents with joint custody live in the same town, it makes things easier if they do. If they don't live in the same town, one of them has to make a major concession about living arrangements when the children are old enough to attend school. Specifically, one of them must agree to the children living with the other during the school year and living with him or her only during school and summer vacations. Otherwise the children would have to switch schools as they moved back and forth between the parents, something we would strongly caution the parents against. The children of divorce have enough adjustments to make without having to adjust to being in a different school each year.

If the parents live in the same town but different school districts, the children can switch their residences during the school year as long as they attend the same school. In this case, the parents would have to make arrangements to provide transportation to the school from the home of the parent who lives outside of the children's school district. Obviously, the ideal situation would be one in which the parents live in the same school district, so we often advise the parent who is moving out of the home to find an apartment or another house in that district if possible.

Living Arrangements

Living arrangements are usually not a problem if one parent has sole custody. In such a case, the children live with the custodial parent and are with the non-custodial parent only during certain holidays, vacations and scheduled visitation periods.

But when the parents have joint custody, they can disagree about living arrangements as each struggles for as much time with the children as he or she can get. As stated above, we usually do not take a position about what are the best living arrangements in joint custody since there is as yet no research on the matter, although we wouldn't favor any living arrangements in which the children have to switch schools. But what we do repeatedly stress to the parents is the importance of their both staying involved in the lives of their children without constantly fighting with each other over their offspring.

Visitation Schedules

For the non-custodial parent or the joint custody parent during her time when the children are living with the other parent, the visitation privileges are usually every other weekend and one night per week. Since we want the children of divorce to spend as much time with both their parents as is possible, we wouldn't want visitation schedules to be any less than this. The ideal situation in a divorced family is one in which the children have free and easy access to both their parents. But unfortunately, the greater the hostility and mistrust between divorcing parents, the more the custody arrangements must be clearly and firmly structured to avoid continued conflict between the parents.

Vacations and Holidays

Deciding on vacation times for their children is usually not a difficult task for divorcing parents. Summer vacations can last from one week to the entire summer. If a scheduled summer vacation with one parent is longer than two weeks, you may want to encourage the parents to decide on a visitation schedule for the other parent during that time.

Deciding on holiday visitations should be even less of a problem since most parents agree that the fairest thing to do is to rotate them annually. Accordingly, in your negotiations with the parents you may want to start with this issue first so as to engender a spirit of cooperation through the successful resolution of one custody issue.

To rotate holidays on an annual basis, the parents must choose an odd number of holidays which may include each child's birthday. An odd number of holidays makes an annual rotation of holidays possible. For example, if the parents decide to rotate Easter, Thanksgiving and Christmas, one parent would have the children on Easter and Christmas of the first year while the other parent would have them on Thanksgiving. The following year, the second parent would have the children on Easter and Christmas, while the first would have them on Thanksgiving.

Chapter 13

PARADOXICAL TECHNIQUES

I f you think that psychotherapy does not involve the manipulation of your clients, you may be in the wrong profession. Whatever their focus or theoretical underpinnings, all psychotherapists are manipulative.

As therapists, we are not in the business of being warm, understanding and supportive only. Certainly, caring and empathy are important ingredients in therapy, but they are usually not sufficient to bring about therapeutic change. To encourage people to change, we must use all our powers of influence, persuasion and manipulation. And there are times when we must be deliberately deceptive.

In no other type of psychotherapy is this fact more apparent than in the use of paradoxical techniques. In using many of them, we deliberately attempt to manipulate people in deceptive ways. Obviously, we do this because people come to us with a need to change but a reluctance to do so. Although paradoxical techniques can be used in all types of therapies, they are especially useful for the family therapist who may find herself confronted with greater homeostatic pressures against change than the individual therapist. Based on the categories compiled by Weeks and L'Abate (1982), what follows are descriptions and examples of several paradoxical techniques you can use in your work with couples and families.

RELABELING

The way we perceive internal and external events can influence our cognitions, emotions and behavior. We can see the glass as half full or half empty, for example, or the weather as partly cloudy or partly sunny, and react to these things according to our perceptions of them.

Relabeling is a technique you can use to change family members' views of certain events in such a way that they may behave more constructively with each other. With many families, we do this routinely at the Family Teaching Center. For example, we attempt to relabel the target child's problem as interactional—the result of family processes—rather than individual—the responsibility of the target child only. We also attempt to show that by his misbehavior, the target child may have done the other family members a favor by bringing them into therapy and providing them with the opportunity to work on their own problems.

Other examples of relabeling we frequently use are the following:

—We define emotional pain or confusion as a prelude to change, crisis as an opportunity to grow or a marital problem as a chance for a couple to strengthen their marriage by resolving it.

—We define hatred as a poison which hurts the person who hates more than the person who is hated.

—We define forgiveness not as an admission that the hurtful things another person did were not wrong, but as an act which benefits the forgiver more than the forgiven by enabling her to let go of her bitterness. In other words, forgiveness frees the forgiver from the past but does not necessarily relieve the forgiven of the burden of his wrongdoing.

—We define anger as anguish, a sign that the person who is angry is in emotional pain. We also define anger as a sign of caring even though it is difficult for most people to see the connection.

—To a parent who is having difficulty applying consequences to her children because she doesn't want to be "mean," we define a good parent as one who is a firm, strict disciplinarian. We also stress that she can enjoy her children more if they are better behaved than if they are out of control.

—We define a family as strong, rather than weak, for having come to family therapy even though they were initially embarrassed to do so.

CONTINGENT ENACTMENT

Contingent enactment is a technique you can use to help the family members gain insight about their behavior. You simply instruct them to do what you believe they are already doing. For example, you may tell mother to pick a fight with her husband whenever she feels ignored by him. Or you may tell the target child to misbehave when he wants to communicate with his parents about something important but can't get their attention.

By laying bare what you believe may be occurring in the family, your goal in using contingent enactment is to produce insight but you may be able to change the behavior of the family members also. If father knows that mother has been fighting with him because she feels ignored, for example, he may be more willing to respond to her before a fight breaks out. Similarly, if the parents realize their son's misbehavior may be a cry for attention, they may be willing to positively respond to him before he misbehaves.

COMPLIANCE BASED TECHNIQUES

Compliance based techniques can be used with compliant, cooperative family members whom you expect will follow your instructions. You can use them in two general types of cases: with those clients whom you want to accept their symptoms and with those whom you want to give up their symptoms.

In the first case, compliance based techniques may be used to treat anxiety states, obsessions or other symptoms which the client makes worse by fighting. For example, a student is very anxious about having to give a talk in class. But the sources of his anxiety are twofold: he is afraid to give the speech and he is afraid he will be afraid. By instructing him to be as anxious as he can when he gives his presentation, you may help him to reduce one source of his anxiety, his fear of being anxious.

Another example of a compliance based technique is the following:

Maria experienced periodic visual hallucinations which frightened her. Rather than fight against them as she had been doing, the therapist instructed her to relax and enjoy them as much as she could. Whenever she began to experience them, she was to stop whatever she was doing, turn on some good music, lie down in a comfortable position and enjoy the visual show. He also relabeled her hallucinations as a "free acid trip" which she experienced without the risks and expense involved in taking drugs.

Having learned to accept them, Maria later reported that her hallucinations decreased in both frequency and intensity.

In the second case, compliance based techniques may be used to treat symptoms by making them more aversive. By doing so, you can induce family members to give them up by making them too uncomfortable. For example, you can attempt to loosen an enmeshed parent-child relationship by encouraging the enmeshed parent to become even more enmeshed. Instruct her to spend even more time with her child, and more energy worrying about him, because she wants to be the best parent she can be. If she follows your instruction, she should find her maternal duties so burdensome she may decide to spend more time on herself and less with her child.

DEFIANCE BASED TECHNIQUES

The goal of psychotherapy is to help people change the ways they behave with each other but, as we have pointed out often in this book, change can be frightening. Family members may want to make changes in their lives but resist them at the same time. If their resistance to change is too strong, you may have to resort to defiance based, paradoxical techniques to induce change by paradoxically encouraging them not to change.

At the Family Teaching Center, we use defiance based techniques only with resistant families when all else we have tried has failed, and with chronic families who have been to many therapists over the years with no apparent changes in their patterns of behavior. Before using defiance based techniques with resistant families, we would first attempt to bring about therapeutic change using non-paradoxical techniques. If these techniques did not succeed, we then might reverse ourselves with the family members and begin to talk about the advantages of their not changing in the hope they would resist our ideas and begin to change. With therapy wise, chronic families, we might begin to employ defiance based, paradoxical techniques from the very beginning of our sessions since we assume that our other colleagues who treated them without success already used non-paradoxical techniques.

As outlined by Weeks and L'Abate (1982), there are several families with whom we would recommend that you not use defiance based techniques. These are as follows:

—With families who are in crisis. These families are probably ripe for therapeutic change because they are in such emotional pain. In addition, what they need to hear from you is an expression of hope, not some advice to accept their crises.

—With suicidal or homicidal family members. As is true of families in crisis, you don't want to encourage the suicidal or homicidal member not to change. Both need to be restrained from what they plan to do and to be given hope that there are better ways for them to solve their problems. Obviously, you should never tell the suicidal client to become even more depressed, for example, or advise the homicidal client to intensify his angry feelings in order to study them.

—With sociopathic family members. The sociopath needs firm, structured limits, not the freedom to continue doing what he is already doing. Since his behavior is socially unacceptable, he must be made to change, if possible, through external rewards and punishments.

—With paranoid family members. Since the paranoid is already suspicious of you, using techniques which are based on deception and manipulation will only increase his suspiciousness, and rightfully so. You want to gain the trust of the paranoid, not increase it by not being fully honest with him.

—With family members who are not involved in therapy. The use of defiance based techniques with uninvolved persons is not so much contraindicated as a waste of time. In response to your instructions not to change, these clients will neither resist your suggestions nor cooperate with you.

What follows is a list and description of several defiance based, paradoxical techniques. What is common to all of them is that you use them to encourage family members not to change in the hope they will resist your suggestions and begin to make changes in their lives. It is best to give these instructions as homework assignments at the end of each session so the members can't comment on them or argue with you about them.

Prescribing the Symptom

To prescribe the symptomatic behavior, instruct the family members to continue doing what they are already doing, although you may add a variation to their behavior patterns to change them however slightly. For example, you may tell an argumentative couple to continue to fight but to change the time or place of their fights. Or you may instruct a depressed person to schedule her periods of depression between ten and eleven o'clock each morning.

Since most clients realize that psychotherapy is designed to bring about change, they may be puzzled at first by your instructions to do the same things. To relieve their bewilderment and to encourage them to follow your paradoxical instructions, explain to your clients that you want them to study their symptomatic behaviors by performing them voluntarily. As an example, you may say to an argumentative couple something such as the following:

> You two are here because you're tired of fighting with each other, but in order to stop it, we first have to understand it. I know this may sound crazy, but I want you two to keep on fighting with each other. While you're fighting, however, I want you to do something different: study what you are doing. Note how the fight started, how it was maintained and how it ended. Afterwards, write down what you observed and bring your notes to our next session so we can figure out what's going on.
>
> Plan to have two to three fights next week, and then let's see what they'll tell us about how you two interact with each other.

Another way you can present paradoxical instructions so your clients will accept them is in terms of control. Explain to the same argumentative couple, for example, that you want them to gain some control over their fighting by having an argument only in the evenings between seven and eight o'clock. Again, instruct them to have two to three fights that week but only during the times specified by you or agreed to by them as good times for arguing.

Restraining Change

There are three ways you can restrain change in family members to induce them to change:

—If they are already changing, encourage the family members to slow down their pace of change. Explain to them that too much change which is brought about too quickly can lead to a major relapse, leaving them disappointed and less willing to attempt to make further changes.

—Forbid the family members to change by giving them specific instructions to avoid certain behaviors. In the treatment of some sexual dysfunctions, for example, couples are instructed to engage in certain sensate exercises but are forbidden to have sexual intercourse. The purpose of these instructions is to enable the couple to give each other physical and sexual pleasure without any pressure to perform sexually. However, it is expected that in this pressure-free atmosphere, the couple will successfully have intercourse in violation of their instructions not to do so.

—Discourage the family members from changing by pointing out the advantages of not changing and the disadvantages of changing. Since many symptoms are maintained because they benefit family members, you should be able to easily find reasons why they should not give up certain symptomatic behaviors. A married couple should continue to fight, for example, because their arguing provides them with excitement in what would otherwise be a dull marriage, gives each a scapegoat to blame for his or her problems and prevents them from achieving an intimacy which both fear.

Discouraging family members from changing puts you in a no-lose situation since only two things can happen: either they will resist your advice and change, or they will agree with you and accept their situation. Whichever course of action they choose will benefit them, although they probably won't give you any credit for the improvement in their psychological health.

Predicting a Relapse

After the family members have made some changes in the way they function, you can better insure they'll maintain those changes by predicting a relapse. In effect, suggest to the family members that long-standing patterns of behavior are not easy to change, so it would be perfectly understandable if the symptomatic behavior reoccurred as a result of their returning to their old behavior patterns. If it does reoccur, they can simply reapply what they learned in their sessions with you. You might even relabel a relapse as a favor to them since it reminds them to keep working to maintain the gains they've made in therapy.

The nice thing about predicting a relapse is that it again puts you in a no-lose situation. Either the family members will not experience a relapse, and so maintain the gains they made with you, or they will revert to their habitual ways of relating. If they do relapse, your creditability will be enhanced because you predicted it. However, because of your warning, the family members will not be too disappointed by the relapse and will know what to do to reverse it.

Prescribing a Relapse

You can also prescribe a relapse in successful cases to better insure the family members will maintain their therapeutic gains. If they have found some relief in their counseling with you, the last thing they'll want to do is to revert to the emotional pain of the past. Again, you can present your instructions for a deliberate relapse as a way for the family members to study what they would have to do to completely relapse. In effect, tell them you want them to have a relapse so they fully understand what they must do to prevent further relapses.

A variant of this technique which we use with successful cases at the Family Teaching Center is to have the family members remember at termination how stressful things were when they first came to see us and then to note how much better things are now. Then we engage them in a discussion about what they would have to do to return to that earlier style of family functioning. We may get them to agree, for example, that the parents would have to stop backing up their rules with consequences, or the target child would have to act out rather than verbalize her feelings, or the spouses would have to ignore each other rather than talk about their conflicts.

Declared Therapist Helplessness

Declared therapist helplessness is a technique you should use only as an absolute last resort when you have nothing else to offer the family members. In employing it, say to the family members what is, in fact, a reality: there is nothing more you can do to help them. In saying this, however, blame yourself for the therapeutic failure, not them, and apologize for your inability to help them.

Again, declared therapist helplessness will put you in a no-lose situation since there are three ways the family members may respond to your declaration of helplessness. One, they may accept your apology and depart. Two, they may feel sorry for you and begin to make some changes to help you feel better. Or three, they may begin to make some changes because they will have realized they've come to the end of the line and have no one else to help them but themselves. If the family members respond in the first way, you can terminate on good terms with each other. If they respond in the second or third ways, you will have induced them to change by paradoxically declaring your inability to help them change.

Declared therapist helplessness is based upon the premise that a show of strength elicits strength and pressure produces resistance. By contrast, a soft word does turn away wrath and an apology does elicit sympathy and forgiveness. To continue to pressure resistant family members, to attempt to force them to change by overwhelming them with your expertise or personality, is to strengthen their resolve not to change. But to back off in an apologetic display of failure, to admit that they have won, is to create the only opportunity you have to regain the influence you claim you have lost.

POSITIONING

The judo master never meets his opponent head-on. Rather, he uses the momentum of his opponent to flip him. Similarly, as a family therapist, you should not always meet the family head-on. If you do, if you get into an argument with any family member, you will probably lose. Instead, what you can do is to use the family member's positions to gain influence over her.

To use positioning as a paradoxical technique, never argue with a client or try to force your views on her. Instead, assume her position, agree with it and then carry it even further than she would carry it herself. In this manner, you may be able to induce her to modify or abandon her position.

Several examples of positioning should illustrate this process:

Father claimed that family therapy was a "bunch of B.S." which wouldn't work. Rather than argue with him, the therapist simply responded by saying, "We have a program which works for many families but if you don't think it will work for your family, it won't." This maneuver put the responsibility for the success of family therapy squarely where it belonged: with the family members.

The Jones family members were not sure they wanted to commit themselves to the effort and expense involved in family therapy. Rather than pressure them to commit, the therapist agreed that perhaps the family members were not ready for family therapy at this time since it would take so much strength and courage. She added that perhaps they would be ready later on if their problems became worse, but asked them not to wait until things were nearly out of control to come back for therapy.

In a custody counseling case, father threatened to break off the sessions with his ex-wife and to take his custody dispute to court. Rather than pressure him to eschew this course of action, the therapist sided with him. She advised him that if he felt so strongly about it, he would have to proceed to litigation despite the stress, expense and negative consequences to the children which would surely be involved in a courtroom battle.

In the family diagnostic sessions, the youngest adolescent was passive-aggressively silent. Every question the therapist asked her was met with a shrug of the shoulders, a barely audible "I dunno" or a hostile stare. Finally, the therapist told the adolescent that her best strategy was to keep silent. That way, she could protect her parents from the stress of exploring what was wrong in the family.

In an individual session with the therapist, mother kept criticizing her child, and could think of nothing positive to say about him. Since the therapist was unable to deflect mother from her constant criticism, he began to attack the child himself by saying that he doubted counseling would work with a child who was so ill-behaved.

Immediately after he said this, mother switched to the defense of her child by claiming he wasn't that badly behaved. It was fine for her to criticize her offspring but she certainly wasn't going to let anyone else do it!

In addition to attempting to reverse her behavior, verbally attacking a child yourself in response to unremitting criticism from a parent can give you diagnostic information. Most parents will defend their children against criticism from you. If a parent doesn't, if she agrees with you, you can suspect she is either an ambivalent or rejecting parent.

Chapter 14

THE GOALS OF FAMILY THERAPY

I n case you have not yet noticed it, I am a good compulsive. I am comfortable with things that are structured and orderly, and I have written this book in an orderly, step-by-step, this-is-how-you-do-it fashion. I have also included practical suggestions for specific programs and exercises in this book.

But compulsivity may not be your way of relating to the world and your clients. You may be more comfortable with a less compulsive, more spontaneous and free-flowing type of therapy. If this is so, it doesn't mean you are right and I am wrong, or vice versa. Each of us must conduct therapy in the ways in which we are most comfortable. Each can be successful with certain clients with our unique styles of relating. You may be better equipped by personality to treat certain types of persons than I, but I may be better able to treat certain other clients than you.

If you are a beginning family therapist, however, the more structure you bring to your therapeutic sessions, the more comfortable you may feel. This is one of the primary reasons why I have written this book. But as you become more experienced and comfortable in family therapy, you may require less structure and can become more spontaneous and use more of yourself. Specific programs and exercises have their place in therapy, but to be effective, we must move beyond them at times and be creative and innovative. The ultimate therapeutic tool we have—that which can have the greatest impact on those we treat—is ourselves—our personalities, our feelings and the common humanity we share with our clients.

To be consistent, however, I would like to conclude this book in the manner in which I wrote it: compulsively. By way of a review, what follows is a discussion of the goals of family therapy as outlined in our intake interview, with specific suggestions about how to reach them. Since there are more people, more interactions, more dynamics and more information involved in family therapy than in individual therapy, it might help you in dealing with the complexities of family therapy to concentrate on these goals.

One thing you should keep in mind in considering the goals of family therapy, however, is the limits of what you and the family members can accomplish. The most you can expect of family members is to make those changes which they can tolerate. If you push them too far to change, they may rebel against your efforts. With many families, you cannot expect the family members to make the transition from pathology to health in one grand leap. Rather, as Haley (1976) points out, your goal should be to encourage a process of gradual, step-by-step change which you hope will continue after the family members stop seeing you. And if they terminate therapy only after they have gained symptomatic relief, even though you may feel they could make some more changes in the ways they function as a family, that's all right. You must respect the emotional and financial limits of the capacity of the family members to change. If you've done a good job with them, they'll be back to see you should another problem arise.

THE PRESENTING PROBLEMS

The overall goal of family therapy as practiced at the Family Teaching Center is to maintain the family without symptoms. Although we recognize that divorce or an out-of-home placement of youths must be considered in certain cases, we do all we can to prevent a breakdown in family relationships.

But we certainly do not want to maintain the family at the expense of one or more of its members. If the price of family togetherness is the development and maintenance of symptomatic behavior in one or more family members, we would not be a party to solidifying that kind of arrangement. Our primary goal is to teach the family members new ways of relating to each other so they can stay together without symptomatic behavior. In effect, we want to substitute more effective behaviors for symptomatic behaviors in such a way that the family members can relate more satisfactorily with each other.

In working with any family, the first thing you should focus on is the presenting problem as described by the family members. They have come to you for symptomatic relief, and it is this they expect to receive from you. If instead of concentrating on the presenting problem, you head off in another direction to another problem you think the family members really need to work on, you will probably lose them as clients. On the other hand, if you concentrate all your energies on the presenting problem and never confront the family members about other problems which may be contributing to the presenting problem, you may not be able to provide them with the symptomatic relief they seek.

In working on a behavior disorder in a youth, there are three things you can do:

—Relabel the misbehavior as interactional rather than as individual, and as positive for the family rather than as negative.

—After having established family emotional support for the target youth, work directly on the presenting problem using behavioral techniques.

—In cases involving anti-social behavior, work on conscience development by pointing out the negative consequences of the youth's behavior to himself, his family and the victim.

OTHER FAMILY PROBLEMS

If there are other problems in the family in addition to the presenting problem—as there usually are—note these problems and in most cases confront them only after your other efforts to relieve the presenting problem have failed. The most common problems you may encounter in your family counseling are chemical dependency, psychiatric problems, marital problems and self-esteem problems.

Chemical Dependency

At the Family Teaching Center, we do not work with family members who are chemically dependent because we believe that family therapy for other problems with a chemically dependent family member will not be effective. We are convinced that the chemical abuse must be stopped before other family problems can be tackled. Accordingly, if the dependent is an adolescent, we refer him or her for a chemical dependency evaluation or treatment. If the dependent is a parent, we work with the other family members to break their co-dependency. To do this in the case of an alcoholic parent, you can:

—Break through the denial of the other family members that the alcoholic is not dependent and that they have not been affected by the disease of alcoholism.

—Help them to recognize and express their feelings about the parent's drinking.

—Teach them about the disease concept of alcoholism and about the various roles which usually develop in the alcoholic family.

—Encourage the family members to shift their energies away from the parent's drinking, which they could never control despite their most determined efforts, and to refocus it on themselves. Suggest that the non-alcoholic spouse go out with some of her friends without her husband, for example, and not worry about whether or not he stays home alone and drinks too much.

—Encourage the family members not to protect the dependent from the negative consequences of his drinking. He will have to call in sick himself when he is hung over, for example, or will have to make his own dinner when he doesn't arrive home after work until 10 P.M.

Psychiatric Problems

If we uncover significant psychiatric problems in our intake sessions—depression or anxiety, as examples—in one or both of the parents, or one or more of the children, we would either treat these problems within the context of family therapy or refer the troubled family member for individual therapy and/or psychotropic medication. In other words, at the Family Teaching Center, we don't believe it is possible for the same therapist to effectively combine individual therapy with family therapy. What we prefer to do instead is to have someone else work with the individual family member while we continue to meet with the entire family, including the member in individual therapy, about the family's collective problems. Of course, in doing this, we obtain written permission to consult with the individual therapist, and stay in frequent contact with her to insure we are both working towards the same therapeutic goals.

Marital Problems

Unless one of the spouses calls asking specifically for marital counseling, we do not work directly on marital problems at the Family Teaching Center when first working on a behavior problem in a youth. It is only after our direct approach to the presenting problem has not succeeded because of the interference of marital problems do we confront the parents directly and suggest marital counseling for them. However, there are many things you can do to work on marital problems without specifically offering marital counseling to a distressed couple:

—Force them to agree on discipline and provide them with a positive experience together by teaching them our child program.

—Teach them the skills needed for a satisfactory marriage by teaching all the family members the communications, negotiating and contracting skills involved in our adolescent program. By helping the parents solve their problems with their teenager, you may help them solve some of their marital problems.

—Challenge any parental or spousal hierarchy you may encounter in a troubled family. Both our child and adolescent programs are designed to do this by having the parents agree on discipline rather than one parent dictating what shall be the family rules and consequences.

—Strengthen the boundary between the spousal and parental subsystems so that a disagreement about child rearing, for example, does not influence the parents' marital satisfaction.

—Strengthen the generational boundaries in the family in such a way that the parents' primary sources of need satisfaction and support are provided by each other and not by either the grandparents or the children. One way you can do this is to encourage the parents to spend more time alone together.

Self-Esteem Problems

Since it is probably safe to assume that most persons in therapy are struggling with self-esteem problems, all therapies should have as a secondary goal the enhancement of self-esteem in clients. There are several ways you can do this, again without directly letting the family members know what you are doing:

—With all family members, reduce their sense of blame and guilt. Reassure them that they have all tried to do their best.

—Find the strengths in the family members, point them out and reinforce them. Perhaps the most therapeutic attitude you can develop towards your clients is admiration for their having struggled so long with such overwhelming problems without outside help or support.

—Encourage the family members to praise, support and reinforce each other. They can be far more powerful and longer lasting sources of positive self-esteem for each other than you can ever be. One way you can do this is through the use of a technique called the hot seat which is described in Chapter 7 on communication skills. Using this technique, have all the family members tell the person on the hot seat what each likes or admires about him or her.

—Consider referring a family member for individual therapy for a self-esteem problem, or provide that therapy yourself after you have terminated the family therapy sessions.

—Whatever successes the family members can experience in therapy will increase each member's sense of accomplishment and self-esteem. The truth of the matter is that self-esteem consists of two separate components: a sense of belonging which says a person is lovable and a sense of accomplishment which says a person is capable. Although you can, and should, give your clients the sense of being accepted unconditionally, people have to earn a sense of accomplishment by the successes which only come through hard work.

THE FAMILY MEMBERS' RELATIONS WITH THE TARGET CHILD

There are five relationships between the family members and the target child which we would consider to be detrimental to her psychological health. Each of these relationships is listed below with suggestions about how to modify them.

The Blamed Scapegoat

Directly pointing out how the family members may be blaming the target child for their problems will probably do little to move her from her scapegoated position. Nevertheless, there are several things you can do to relieve the blamed scapegoat of some of the blame she is receiving from the other family members:

—Gently uncover other problems in the family and suggest that perhaps these need to be worked on also.

—Suggest, with empathy, that all the family members are in pain, not just the blamed scapegoat.

—Relabel the symptomatic behavior of the blamed scapegoat as interactional and positive for the family rather than as individual and negative for the family.

—Develop as much expression of emotional support by the family members for the blamed scapegoat as you can. Discover what they like about him and emphasize those traits.

—If the family members can find nothing positive to say about the blamed scapegoat, criticize her yourself in a last resort attempt to force them to defend her.

The Enmeshed Parent-Child Relationship

It is not easy to loosen an enmeshed parent-child relationship because it usually satisfies strong needs in both parties. Usually, the enmeshed parent has a poor relationship with her spouse or is a single parent. And although it may prevent him from becoming fully independent, enmeshment can provide short term benefits to the enmeshed child in the form of excessive parental attention.

Rarely will it prove effective to confront the enmeshment head-on, although you may have to attempt this when everything else you have tried has failed. Many enmeshed parents will not accept your expressions of concern about their relationships with their children. Instead, they will assume you don't fully understand or appreciate their love for their children, and may seek elsewhere for a therapist who will support them. To loosen an enmeshed parent-child relationship, then, you may have to approach it indirectly using the following suggested techniques:

—The key to weakening an enmeshed parent-child relationship is to help both parties, but especially the parent, meet their psychological needs in other ways. You must help the enmeshed parent find need satisfaction in her marriage, her work, her friendships or in alternative support systems. Similarly, you should encourage the enmeshed child to develop contacts and interests outside of his relationship with his parent.

—Use homework assignments to encourage separation between the enmeshed parent and her child. Encourage the parent to take a course at the local college, for example, join a church group, invite a friend over for dinner or go dancing with her spouse.

—Subtly maintain a separation between the parent and child in their sessions with you. Do not allow the parent to speak for the child, for example. Or ask the child to sit next to you instead of next to her parent when you are discussing what the parent can do to find more enjoyment in her life.

—See the parent and child individually for some sessions rather than together all the time. In especially difficult cases, see each in individual therapy or refer them for individual therapy but make yourself available for conjoint sessions.

—In a two parent family, if one parent is enmeshed while the other is distant, work to strengthen the relationship between the child and the distant parent.

—As a last resort or in cases of chronic enmeshment which has not responded to the efforts of other therapists, work paradoxically to reduce the enmeshment by encouraging the parent to become more enmeshed to the point at which it becomes aversive for her.

The Distant Parent-Child Relationship

Just as you cannot expect to loosen an enmeshed parent-child relationship too quickly or too radically, so you cannot expect to greatly decrease the emotional distance between a distant parent and his child. As was pointed out in the beginning of this chapter, your goal in working with the family is to encourage those changes the family members can tolerate. Although you want to encourage a distant parent to become more involved with his children, you must also respect his desire to have some distance at times.

To decrease the emotional distance in a distant parent-child relationship, some of the things you can do are to:

—Use seating arrangements to have the distant parent sit closer to his child as he talks with him.

—See the parent alone with the child.

—Give homework assignments to have the parent and child spend some time together doing things they both enjoy.

—Take a history of the parent in front of the child so she may realize that her parent has been limited in his ability to be a close parent because of his own upbringing. You don't want her to blame herself for the lack of a close parent-child relationship.

If, as often happens, one parent is distant with a child while the other is enmeshed, you must keep in mind the reaction of the enmeshed parent to your efforts to involve the distant parent with his child. You must insure she doesn't feel too threatened by your maneuvers. If she has to lose some of the closeness she has had with her child, you must help her to find something else to replace that loss.

The Ambivalent Parent-Child Relationship

The ambivalent parent-child relationship is probably the most stressful for the child of all pathological parent-child relationships. It sends a double message to him which says, simultaneously, "I love you; go away." Not knowing which is the correct message, but fearing the worst, the child who receives this message may act out to obtain more attention from his parent. But of course, his acting out behavior may only drive her further from him, increasing his anxieties and consequent misbehavior.

In working with an ambivalent parent-child relationship, it is a good idea to have some individual sessions with the parent rather than see the entire family together all the time. There are some issues you may want to discuss with the parent which you would not want the child to hear at least initially. Specifically, in working with an ambivalent parent individually, you should do the following:

—Empathize completely with her ambivalence. Inform her that all parents feel the way she feels at times, and that you are not going to condemn her for her feelings.

—Give her permission to admit that part of her doesn't want her child and wishes he had never been born. By doing so, two things may happen. The first is that she may face and accept her ambivalence and decide she does want to be a parent to her child. In effect, by giving her permission to reject her child, the ambivalent parent may choose to love him instead. By contrast, to insist she must be a loving parent may be to increase the guilt and ambivalence she already feels.

The second thing that may happen when you encourage an ambivalent parent to accept her ambivalence is that she may decide she really doesn't want to be a parent any more. Although this will be a stressful message for the child, it may be better for him to hear it in the long run. As long as his parent remains ambivalent, he will remain confused and anxious about his status with her. Once he knows she no longer wants to be his parent, he will be hurt, depressed and probably in need of residential treatment, especially if he has been rejected by both his parents, but at least he will know where he stands. After he recovers from the shock of his parents' rejection, he can get on with his life by reinvesting all the energy he used to please his parents in himself. This process may take years but at least the child is headed in the direction of health.

In working in conjoint sessions with the ambivalent parent and her child, there are two things you can do:

—If the child is misbehaving to gain his parent's attention, whatever you can do to reduce that misbehavior using behavioral techniques may improve the parent-child relationship. If she can bring her child's behavior under better control, she may develop better feelings about him and about herself as a parent.

—Take a history of the parent in the presence of the child to give her some insight into her ambivalence and to give the child a sense that he is not responsible for his parent's attitude towards him.

The Rejecting Parent-Child Relationship

Thankfully, few parents are completely rejecting of their children. Most would like to be good parents to their children but are unable to do so because of their own upbringing and/or because of the overwhelming problems with which they are struggling in their present lives.

The impact of rejection on children is usually devastating. To be rejected by one's parents must be the ultimate rejection. Children rejected by both parents usually require intensive residential care, not only to protect them from the risks of suicide, but also to provide them with the tremendous support which is required to work through the pain of parental rejection.

Specifically, intensive treatment of these children should strive to:

—Enable them to quit blaming themselves for their parents' rejection of them. Although such self-blaming usually provides rejected children with the comforting illusion that if they changed their behavior, their parents would love them again, it contributes to feelings of self-hatred.

—Enable them to give up the fantasy that their parents will care for them again someday so as to get on with their lives. What these children must learn to do is to stop wasting their energies trying to gain their parents' attention through misbehavior or win them back through good behavior, and learn to care for themselves.

They must come to the realization, which obviously is not easy to achieve, that because their parents don't love them doesn't mean they are unworthy of being loved.

EMOTIONAL COMMUNICATION

If emotional communication needs to be improved in the family you are treating, there are several things you can do:

—Give the members homework assignments to do fun things together as a family. Discuss what each can do individually and collectively to get more pleasure out of life.

—Teach the family members some of the communication techniques discussed in Chapter 7 to enable them to express more love and support for each other. The techniques of doubling, "I" messages and the hot seat can be used specifically to do this.

—Relabel anger as a sign of caring.

—Relabel hate as that which hurts the one who hates more than the one who is hated, and forgiveness as an act which benefits the forgiver far more than the forgiven.

—If all else fails, gently, caringly but directly confront the family members about the negative emotional ambience in their family and their lack of support for one another. Then provide more in-depth counseling to uncover the causes of their mutual emotional pain and to discuss ways to reduce it.

CONFLICT RESOLUTION

If conflict resolution is a problem in the family you are treating, there are several things you can do to help the members improve their abilities to resolve conflicts:

—The first thing any group of people must do to resolve their conflicts is to communicate accurately about them, so the first thing you must do to help a family better resolve their conflicts is to teach the members instrumental communication skills. Specifically, review the Rules of Negotiating sheet discussed in Chapter 8 with them.

—Eliminate all communication switchboards in the family. In other words, through direct instructions, seating arrangements, homework assignments and appointments, have the family members who are in conflict communicate directly with each other and not through another person.

—Teach the family members the negotiating and contracting skills discussed in Chapter 8. Stress to them the importance of compromise for the sake of family harmony.

—Challenge any hierarchies in the family which may be causing resentment and the breakdown of cooperation. This suggestion may especially apply to parental hierarchies in which one parent covertly sabotages the rules or decisions handed down from above by the other parent.

—Stress to the family members the relativity of viewpoints. Teach them that everyone in the family has their points of view, which may or may not agree with their own, but which are, nevertheless, legitimate to the family members who hold them.

DISCIPLINE ENFORCEMENT

To help a family provide more effective discipline, there are several things you can do:

—Strengthen the parents' resolve to effectively discipline their children. With parents who are reluctant to discipline their offspring for whatever reasons—because they do not want to be "mean" parents, or want to be friends with their children, or are still rebelling against their own upbringing—stress that good parents are strict, consistent parents. Emphasize to them the negative consequences of their failure to be effective disciplinarians.

—Teach the parents of children, ages three through ten, effective discipline skills using our child program.

—Have the parents of adolescents set up rules and consequences for negotiable items using negotiating and contracting.

—Make sure that the family rules are clearly stated, reasonable and enforceable.

—Make sure the parents follow through with both positive and negative consequences for the keeping and breaking of the family rules.

—Encourage the parents to use more rewards than punishments in disciplining their children. Make sure the punishments used are not excessively long or harsh.

—Make sure the parents support each other in their disciplinary efforts.

RELATIONSHIPS WITH EXTENDED
FAMILY MEMBERS

In working on extended family relationships, there are generally two types of problems you may encounter: those involving the grandparents and those involving a divorced, biological parent living outside the home. What you would do with a problem involving the grandparents would depend upon the nature of the problem:

—If the grandparents are collusively involved with their grandchildren and undermining the disciplinary authority of the parents, do what you can to reinforce the parents' authority against the grandparents.

—If the grandparents are enmeshed with their adult offspring to the point at which it interferes with the marriage of the parents, again do what you can to strengthen the marriage and weaken the enmeshment of the grandparents.

—If the relationship between the grandparents, the parents and the children is strained or broken, do what you can to reestablish those relationships. Encourage the parents to contact the grandparents, or contact them yourself, and offer to see the grandparents and parents together for some reconciliation counseling.

Similarly, what you would do with a problem involving a divorced, biological parent would depend upon the nature of the problem:

—If the parent is not involved with the children on a regular, caring basis, contact him in an attempt to reestablish a relationship with his children. If he is willing to come to your office, offer to see him and his children in some sessions together.

—If both biological parents are still fighting about the children, do what you can to reduce the conflict between them. Point out as caringly but strongly as you can the negative consequences of continued fighting for their children, and offer custody counseling to them if they are in conflict over custody issues.

FAMILY STRESSES

There are two general types of family stresses you will encounter in your therapeutic work: those caused by unexpected crises and those caused by delays at a family developmental stage. Whatever the cause of the stress, there are several things you can do to help the family members cope with it or reduce it:

—Educate the family members about the nature of their stress. Give them permission to feel tense, hurt or frustrated, and encourage them to share their feelings with you and with each other.

—Engage the family members in a constructive dialogue about what they can do to reduce their stress.

—If appropriate, relabel the stress as providing the family members with an opportunity to grow closer together to solve a common problem.

—If appropriate, refer the family members to other helping professionals—a member of the clergy, a credit counselor, an employment counselor or an alcohol counselor, as examples—for services to reduce the cause of their stress.

FAMILY STRENGTHS

Perhaps the most constructive thing you can do for any family you treat is to strengthen their coping and problem solving resources. Certainly, you should do what you can to reduce the stress that a particular family is under, but you should also work to strengthen the family as a functioning unit by strengthening the members' capacities to cope and their abilities to solve problems. To accomplish this, there are several things you can do:

—Teach them the discipline, communication, negotiating and contracting skills which will enable them to handle any problems which they may encounter and not just the particular problem they are presenting to you. This is what family therapy as practiced at the Family Teaching Center is all about, and this book was written to give you the tools to do this.

—Encourage the family members to strengthen their own support and coping systems. Advise them to develop some hobbies and interests which will give them more pleasure in life. Encourage them to become more involved in church or social activities. Suggest regular exercise for those family members who are in need of it.

—Be a source of support and information for the family members yourself. If you come to care for them or admire them for their ability to hold up under such tremendous stress, tell them so.

—Uncover, point out and reinforce the family members' own sources of strength. Encourage them to support and care for one another, especially in times of crisis. If you do little else for the family members, do this as much as you can. If you can start a process which will enable them to better meet each other's love and esteem needs, you will have given them the greatest gift you have to offer. They can thereby continue growing and enjoying each other without further sessions with you by putting into practice what you have taught them. Then you can part with them, perhaps with some sadness but with the assurance that the family members will be able to handle whatever problems life brings them.

BIBLIOGRAPHY

Barton, Cole, and Alexander, James F.: Functional family therapy. In Gurman, Alan S., and Kniskern, David P. (Eds.): *Handbook of Family Therapy*. New York, Brunner/Mazel, 1981.

Burgess, Ann W., Groth, A. Nicholas, Holmstrom, Lynda L., and Sgroi, Suzanne M.: *Sexual Assault of Children and Adolescents*. Lexington, Lexington Books, 1978.

Carter, Elizabeth A., and McGoldrick, Monica (Eds.): *The Family Life Cycle: A Framework for Family Therapy*. New York, Gardner, 1980.

Coopersmith, Stanley: *The Antecedents of Self-Esteem*, 2nd ed. Palo Alto, Consulting Psychologist, 1981.

Epstein, Nathan B., and Bishop, Duane S.: Problem-center systems therapy of the family. In Gurman, Alan S., and Kniskern, David P. (Eds.): *Handbook of Family Therapy*. New York, Brunner/Mazel, 1981.

Fisch, Richard, Weakland, John H., and Segal, Lynn: *The Tactics of Change: Doing Therapy Briefly*. San Francisco, Jossey-Bass, 1982.

Fleischman, Matthew, Horne, Arthur M., and Arthur, Judy L.: *Troubled Families: A Treatment Program*. Champaign, Research Press, 1983.

Fleischman, Matthew, and Szukula, Steven A.: A community setting replication of a social learning treatment for aggressive children. *Behavior Therapy, 12:* 115-122, 1981.

Framo, James L.: Rationale and techniques of intensive family therapy. In Boszormenyi-Nagy, Ivan, and Framo, James L.: *Intensive Family Therapy*. New York, Harper and Row, 1965.

Goldenberg, Irene, and Goldenberg, Herbert: *Family Therapy: An Overview*. Monterey, Brooks/Cole, 1980.

Gordon, Thomas: *Parent Effectiveness Training*. New York, New American, 1970.

Green, Joanne G., and Stuart, Irving R. (Eds.): *The Sexual Aggressor: Current Perspectives on Treatment*. New York, Van Nostrand-Reinhold, 1983.

Groth, A. Nicholas: *Men Who Rape: The Psychology of the Offender*. New York, Plenum, 1979.

Gurman, Alan S., and Kniskern, David P.: Deterioration in marital and family therapy: Empirical, clinical and conceptual issues. *Family Process, 17:* 3-20, 1978.

251

Gurman, Alan S., and Kniskern, David P. (Eds.): *Handbook of Family Therapy.* New York, Brunner/Mazel, 1981.

Haley, Jay: *Leaving Home: The Therapy of Disturbed Young People.* New York, McGraw-Hill, 1980.

Haley, Jay: *Problem Solving Therapy.* San Francisco, Jossey-Bass, 1976.

Hoffman, Lynn: *Foundations of Family Therapy: A Conceptual Framework for Systems Change.* New York, Basic, 1981.

Humphrey, Frederick, G.: *Marital Therapy.* Englewood Cliffs, Prentice-Hall, 1984.

Irving, Howard H.: *Divorce Mediation: A Rational Alternative to the Adversary System.* New York, Universe, 1980.

Jacobson, Neil: Behavioral marital therapy. In Gurman, Alan S., and Kniskern, David P. (Eds.): *Handbook of Family Therapy.* New York, Brunner/Mazel, 1981.

Kaplan, Helen S.: *Disorders of Sexual Desire.* New York, Brunner/Mazel, 1979.

Kaplan, Helen S.: *The New Sex Therapy: Active Treatment of Sexual Dysfunctions.* New York, Brunner/Mazel, 1974.

Karpel, Mark A., and Strauss, Eric S.: *Family Evaluation.* New York, Gardner, 1983.

Krantzler, Mel: *Creative Divorce.* New York, New American, 1973.

Leiblum, Sandra R., and Pervin, Lawrence A. (Eds): *Principles and Practice of Sex Therapy.* New York, Guilford, 1980.

Levant, Ronald· F.: *Family Therapy: A Comprehensive Overview.* Englewood Cliffs, Prentice-Hall, 1984.

Luepnitz, Deborah Anna: *Child Custody: A Study of Families after Divorce.* Lexington, Lexington Books, 1982.

Madanes, Cloes: *Strategic Family Therapy.* San Francisco, Jossey-Bass, 1981.

Maslow, Abraham H.: *Motivation and Personality.* New York, Harper, 1954.

Maslow, Abraham H.: *Toward a Psychology of Being,* 2nd ed. Princeton, Van Nostrand, 1968.

Meiselman, Karin C.: *Incest: A Psychological Study of Causes and Effects with Treatment Recommendations.* San Francisco, Jossey-Bass, 1978.

Napier, Augustus, and Whitaker, Carl: *The Family Crucible.* New York, Harper Row, 1978.

Norman, Jane, and Harris, Myron: *The Private Life of the American Teenager.* New York, Rawson, Wade, 1981.

Patterson, Gerald R.: Interventions for boys with conduct problems: Multiple settings, treatments and criteria. *Journal of Consulting and Clinical Psychology, 42:* 471-481, 1974.

Roosevelt, Ruth, and Lovas, Jeannette: *Living in Step.* New York, McGraw, 1976.

Sager, Clifford J.: *Marriage Contracts and Couples Therapy.* New York, Brunner/Mazel, 1976.

Satir, Virginia: *Peoplemaking.* Palo Alto, Science and Behavior, 1972.

Sgroi, Suzanne: *Handbook of Clinical Intervention in Child Sexual Abuse.* Lexington, Lexington Books, 1982.

Skynner, A.C. Robin: An open-systems, group analytic approach to family therapy. In Gurman, Alan S., and Kniskern, David P. (Eds.): *Handbook of Family Therapy*. New York, Brunner/Mazel, 1981.

Tarvis, Carol: *Anger: The Misunderstood Emotion*. New York, Simon, 1982.

Thomas, Alexander, and Chess, Stella: *Temperament and Development*. New York, Brunner/Mazel, 1977.

Wallerstein, Judith S., and Kelly, Joan Berlin: *Surviving the Breakup: How Parents and Children Cope with Divorce*. New York, Basic, 1980.

Walsh, William M.: *A Primer in Family Therapy*. Springfield, Thomas, 1980.

Watzlawick, Paul, Beavin, Janet, and Jackson, Don: *Pragmatics of Human Communication*. New York, Norton, 1967.

Watzlawick, Paul, Weakland, John H., and Fisch, Richard: *Change: Principles of Problem Formation and Problem Resolution*. New York, Norton, 1974.

Weeks, Gerald R., and L'Abate, Luciano: *Paradoxical Psychotherapy: Theory and Practice with Individuals, Couples and Families*. New York, Brunner/Mazel, 1982.

Wegscheider, Sharon: *Another Chance: Hope and Health for the Alcoholic Family*. Palo Alto, Science and Behavior, 1981.

Weiss, Robert S.: *Going It Alone: The Family Life and Social Situation of the Single Parent*. New York, Basic, 1979.

INDEX